In this season...

may the full moon and approaching spring
rain on you blessings;
may the spirit of Death passover your door
and the spirit of Life dwell with you;
may your slavery be ended and your liberation
from מצרים, your stuck narrow places, be at hand;
may you resist the Temptation of the golden calf
and ascend the Mountain of the Lord;
may you be led in time across the desert
and the Great Water,
and into your own Promised Land

that you may enter + eat of the fruits
which are rightfully yours —
reaping them with songs of peace
and thanksgiving

From Amy to Rabbi Joseph and Tzipi Heckelman after Passover seder 1974.

HAM

BY ALL MEANS, RESUSCITATE

A Memoir

David L. Chamovitz, M.D.

Library of Congress Number:		2001118258
ISBN #:	Hardcover	1-4010-2590-0
	Softcover	1-4010-2589-7

Published by OhSheBubbeeDoo Press, 2000

This book was printed in the United States of America.

To order additional copies of this book, contact:
Xlibris Corporation
1-888-7-XLIBRIS
www.Xlibris.com
Orders@Xlibris.com

CONTENTS

AM

POTPOURRI

ALIYAH

AM

ACKNOWLEDGEMENTS

"Begin with autobiography. Most first-time writers do." This was the answer of Doreen Stock when I asked, "But what would I write about?" And thus, in preparation for retirement, I started this memoir, a three-year enterprise. Doreen was also the first to suggest that my writing showed promise.

Uncle Harry Jackson is no longer around to hear my praise for his voluminous and tender autobiography taking me back to his Russian village of Karinyetz. But fortunately his son Daniel is. He, a retired lung specialist, became my first editor, teaching me the importance of maintaining flow in my writing as he mercilessly rearranged sentences and paragraphs. Our relationship as cousins graduated to that of brothers.

From Marcia's writer-cousin Zelda Kessner I learned to break out of the case-history reporting mode. Zelda gets credit also for encouraging dramatic touches. And another cousin, Bernice Eger Miller, spent numerous of her jet-lagged-hours here pointing out unclear passages.

It was only after I worked with a professional editor, Alex Auswaks, that my book began to take shape. He promised that I would have a better book if I accepted at least ten percent of his suggestions; he had it all wrong as it was only ten percent that I rejected. Our major problem was trying to decide whether I should adopt the language of this native Brit or keep my own.

It was a fortuitous decision to ask Laura Popenoe to proofread what I thought was a finished product. How wrong I was.

An unexpected spin off of my writing has been the joy of wordplay with my wife Marcia. She has been my personal interactive thesaurus. Discussing the nuances of similar words provided hours of entertainment. How often I interrupted her activities to seek her discerning ear. Both Marcia and our children elaborated when memory faltered.

This book could not have left the hand-written page if not for the instruction on the use of the word processor that I received from my son, Danny, and my son-in-law, Zvika. And additional thanks to Danny for the many hours he spent beautifying the book's layout.

There is yet another important friend who doesn't know me and yet when Tristine Rainer wrote *Your Life as Story*, I had the feeling that she was writing to me personally. Her encouragement that I had stories to tell had a profound effect.

Blessings on you all from Israel.

Tel Aviv, 2000

PREFACE

A gnawing in the pit of my stomach wouldn't let me rest. I recognized the symptom from Dad's description of his pain before he bled massively from an ulcer. But there I was, in the third month of my freshman year at Harvard Medical School, struggling with each of my courses: anatomy, histology, and biochemistry. I was terrified and certain that I would be the exception to their rule that "We get everybody through." Fearing that a label of medical disease on my record would further decrease my chances of "getting through," I delayed seeking medical help.

Turning to medical textbooks and reading about ulcers, my anxiety level soared as I even sweated out the possibility of cancer. Finally I made the decision to "turn myself in" to the students' physician. I was no less anxious and despondent as I stood in the dark behind a fluoroscopic screen swallowing barium, when I heard the austere radiology professor say, "Hmm" and "Oh, yes." Nor did a renowned Harvard gastroenterologist offer me respite, when, after confirming that I had an ulcer, he said something like, "You know you're too young to be in medical school."

"That's it," I thought. "My life is over. I'll never realize my dream to be a doctor. I'll never follow in the footsteps of my oldest brother, already a doctor, or my two other medical-student brothers. I'll never be able to face my parents."

I asked myself: Why didn't I kiss Harvard good-bye and head home to the warm nest of a prosperous family shoe business? Was selling shoes so contemptible? And didn't Dad say I would make a good lawyer? Why did I dare to risk recurrent ulcer disease and its dire complications by continuing the grind of medical school? Was I a masochist to persevere or was I an irrepressible optimist?

An answer came fifty-five years later as I pondered a title for this memoir. "By all means, resuscitate!" hardly speaks of cynicism. Rather, the opposite. It implies a splendid life, one not always delightful, but clearly fascinating and fulfilling. A life that, given the essential ingredient of an alert mind, I would want prolonged even at the expense of broken ribs from external cardiac massage and skin burns from electric shocks administered during heroic resuscitation.

In the process of writing my memoir, I found myself prying stories out of family, friends, and even casual acquaintances. Almost everyone modestly claimed dull lives but all eventually related vignettes that would make interesting chapters in their own books had they written them. Obviously, here in Israel, the stories of lives bound up with life and death struggles and the Holocaust are apt to be more spellbinding than those of us middle-class American-Israelis who progress through life without encountering monumental upheavals. In response to my probing, one particular Holocaust survivor, in the five minutes of dressing after a swim, related the names of the three concentration camps he had endured, his transportation to and his escape from them, and his eventual fighting alongside the partisans. Hearing that I was writing a memoir, he challenged me, "Tell me, what do you have to write about?"

Stung by this put-down, I was nevertheless motivated to contemplate answers, not for him, but for myself. True, all Holocaust stories must be recorded and published, but life also has many lighter sides. These too merit study by historians, and placement in context alongside our pain and suffering.

It is evident as I review all that I've written, that I, too, have interesting stories to tell. I am amazed at the wealth of experience that has seasoned my life.

A divorced relative once expressed disappoinment that he hadn't known that I had once broken an engagement to be married. The implication was, "It may have given me the courage to do likewise." I hope that my readers, especially the young ones, will profit from my stories and their challenges; even more than entertaining, I would like to be instructive.

FOREWORD: SERENDIPITY WAS THE KEY

"How would you like a fellowship in radioactive iodine?", asked the most esteemed Harvard Medical School professor, Herrman Blumgart.

"I'd love it. What is it?" And with this flip, *chutzpadick* (shameless) retort, I embarked on the path that led me to the inestimable joy of doctoring, to Marcia who would become my wife, and to Israel.

I had known a few setbacks in my life. The first, a painful memory for several years, was my being passed over for the eighth-grade American Legion Award "because we gave it to his brother last year." Does that seem too trivial?

Then consider this. I wrote for an application to Temple Medical School in 1943, and was informed that all places for the class beginning in 1944 were filled. Three weeks later my Geneva College roommate not only received an application from Temple but was promptly accepted; his name was Lyons, unquestionably Anglo-Saxon.

When my English professor, Dr. Allen Morrill, suggested that I apply to Harvard Medical School, I replied, "Who you kiddin'?" and therewith risked flunking English. Well, I did apply and ultimately was accepted. On that same glorious day, I received a "We are sorry..."

reply from St. Louis University School of Medicine. To the four medical schools from whom no reply had yet been received, I wrote, "Please withdraw my application. I've been accepted at another medical school." To St. Louis I wrote, "Please withdraw my application. I've been accepted at Harvard!"

Four years later an encouraging critique by the dean's office made me confident that I would receive a much-coveted Boston internship. Not so; I achieved the disappointing placement of fourth alternate at the Beth Israel Hospital (B.I.). Not one of the alternates moved up the list.

The Pennsylvania Hospital invited me for an interview. The first question from the panel of haughty interviewers was, "Whom do you know in Philadelphia?"

Knowing my fate, I answered defiantly with the truth, "I have a cousin who owns a candy store on Spruce Street." Humbled I hastily retreated to home territory for an internship in Pittsburgh.

A year later I fought my way back to Boston – for me, it was "Mecca" – with an application to the B.I. for a residency in internal medicine. Undaunted by another rejection, I applied to Monroe Schlesinger, Professor of Pathology at the B.I. (During that era a year's training in pathology provided a solid basis for the study and practice of internal medicine.) Thus, it was on my timorous walk in a corridor of Yamin's Research Institute at the B.I. that I encountered Professor Blumgart. HE (for he came close to being a deity in my world) stopped and greeted me with, "What are you doing here, Ch*aa*movitz?" (a Cambridge upgrade of the name's pronunciation and, note well, Dr. Blumgart was seven inches taller in height than I, and even more so in stature).

The encounter continued as follows: "Well, you turned me down for an internship and then for a residency; so, I'm on my way to see Dr. Schlesinger for a job with him."

Then came the pivotal invitation – or was it a summons? "How would you like a fellowship in radioactive iodine?" What I was soon to learn was that I^{131} (radioactive iodine) was the first radioactive isotope to be used in clinical medicine and that, if I consented, I would be the

AM

fifth yearly "fellow" in that subject. As indicated at the outset, I accepted without hesitation. At last, I was "home!"

Follow me a bit farther. During that fellowship year not only did I work with Dr. Blumgart but even more intimately with his assistant, Professor A. Stone Freedberg – may he continue to 120 years! Because of A. Stone (Al), that was the happiest year of my unmarried life. Not only was I steeped in scientific methodology but also, Al introduced me to chamber music; I was hooked by the first hearing of Dvorak's *Dumky Trio*.

As a reward for arduous labors with Al, I did obtain that coveted residency in internal medicine. More important to my story line, Al subsequently facilitated my getting a post-army residency appointment in internal medicine at the Veterans Administration (V.A.) Hospital in New Haven, Connecticut.

My sister-in-law Helen, Irv's wife, let me know that she had a friend, Rosebud Frankel, who lived in Bridgeport thirty miles from New Haven. They had met years before in the Poconos where Helen was recovering after her fiancé, my brother Allen, was killed in the Air Corps in 1943.

Ever the matchmaker, Rosebud invited me to a party at her home. Little did I know that had I responded in time with a definite "Yes," a young woman would also have been invited. Unaware of any plot, I was introduced to Elaine, sister of the "young woman." During the evening I found myself attracted to her and to her husband. Flirting, I asked Elaine if she had a sister. Having earned her approval, I was told, "As a matter of fact, it just so happens that I do."

When I returned to West Haven, I immediately wrote a letter to this sister; her name was Marcia. Before the letter arrived, Marcia had heard from her gushy sister about "this marvelous young doctor, who went to Harvard and who plays the cello." In spite of the saccharine description, Marcia, tired of "playing the field," told a friend, "I'm going to marry this doctor." After an exchange of three letters, I called Marcia; it was my birthday. Marcia claims she has ESP (which I claim is a combination of coincidence and intuition) but she did answer the phone, "Hello, David."

Three days later – it was November, Friday the thirteenth – I drove to her parents' home in Brooklyn. Marcia met me at the door wearing a gray high-necked dress with pink polkadots. The chemistry was instantaneous. We were married four months later.

We honeymooned in New Haven the last few months of my V.A. Hospital residency and for two years in Boston while I completed my medical training at Lahey Clinic. Thereupon, we dug deep roots in Aliquippa, my hometown in Pennsylvania, where my career paralleled the rapid growth of the Aliquippa Hospital.

Three years after the hospital received its first patient, a department of nuclear medicine opened with me as its director. It was so successful that when nineteen years later I had to choose between my subspecialties, cardiology and nuclear medicine, for a volunteer position in Israel, I chose the latter. Between 1979 and 1983 I spent five months in the Nuclear Medicine Department at Hadassah Hospital in Jerusalem, noting on visits to other hospitals that there was a need for nuclear medicine specialists throughout Israel.

This brings me to the end of my saga. Five years later, in 1984, when we moved to Israel, a number of job opportunities were still available in nuclear medicine. And as is well-known, meaningful work is crucial to a successful move to Israel.

Thus, my story line extends from that fateful, serendipitous encounter with Herrman Blumgart in 1949, to a contented life in Israel fifty years later. Some days I ask myself, "What if I had arrived at the B.I. one minute later or had chosen to walk in a different corridor?"

FAMILY

FROM THE MOLDAVIAN MOUNTAINS TO THE OHIO VALLEY

My mother, Malka Eger, the oldest child of her father's second marriage was born on Feb. 4, 1887 in the village of Dorahoi in the Moldavian Mountains of Romania. Uncle Harry Jackson, in a biography prepared in honor of my parents' sixtieth wedding anniversary wrote, that she later moved to a village called Milynkee. When Mom developed typhoid fever, she was sent to another village, Saven, to recover in the home of her half sister Dora and her husband Berish Chaimovitz. Berish had a younger half brother, Moshe Yonah (my father), born July 18, 1888. Uncle Harry relates that Dad was told that if he would run to the drug store for medicine for Mom, he would be allowed to marry her – Dad was eleven, Mom twelve.

As the nineteenth century came to a close and the twentieth got underway, Romania witnessed the emigration to the United States, the *goldina medina* (the golden land), of 10% of its Jews. My parents' families were among those fleeing wave after wave of anti-Semitic fury. It was not uncommon for them to be forced out of their villages in the middle of the night, returning a day or two later only after paying heavy bribes to the local authorities. A further inducement to leave was the government's policy of restricting trades and professions which Jews could enter.

Emigrating with Berish, Dora was the first Eger to arrive in Pittsburgh, Pennsylvania. Mom's father Harry Eger was the next to come. Then, in 1899, Mom, traveling in steerage, came alone but was chaperoned by another family. Mollie, Malka's Americanized name, preceded six younger siblings, two older half brothers, and her mother Rebecca (Bobie). All of them headed for Pittsburgh because of Berish who was working for the Hebrew Immigrant Aid Society (HIAS) or its predecessor. HIAS, maintained by Jewish philanthropies, supported Jews in transit to the United States of America and also during the early period of adjustment. It was a time of a booming economy and a massive influx of immigrants from Europe. I can imagine her wistfulness as she contrasted industrial, smoggy Pittsburgh with the forested hillsides enveloping her village in Romania. But neither she nor Dad ever expressed a wish to make a return visit. One of her earliest American memories was the assassination of President William McKinley in 1901.

At an Eger family reunion in Pittsburgh in 1998 there was a flurry of excitement that we Egers might be descended from the dynasty of the revered Torah scholar, Rabbi Akiva Ben Simhah Bunim Eger, the Elder, which started in Hungary in the mid-1700s. Certainly had we been, the older generation would have touted this lineage and requested larger dowries from prospective spouses. Shortly after this reunion I met with a descendent, Akiva Eger, a member of Kibbutz Netzer Serini. We exchanged family trees. His was his life's work; it offered no hint that we might be cousins. Subsequently, I reviewed Uncle Harry's biography of my parents. In it, he placed my mother docking at Ellis Island, and imagined her concern, "What's going to happen to our old name, Bunimovich (son of Bunim)?"; there are no documents attesting to this name. But note that Bunim was one of the given names of three of the revered Akiva Egers. Doesn't this suggest a possible relationship between us? Was the switch to the name Eger made to further cement that relationship while at the same time arranging a more acceptable

American sounding name? If on the other hand, an Akiva Eger connection is pure fantasy, how then did the family name get to be Eger, especially since Eger is the name of a town and river in Hungary with no connection to Romania?

Like so many greenhorns Mom got a job in Shafler's Toby Factory. Tobies were long, slender cigars made from inferior-grade tobacco. The factory was owned by a pious Jew; *Shabbat* (Sabbath) ordinances, important in my mother's youth, were observed; that is, the factory was closed on Saturday. Evenings she studied English and attended Americanization classes, presumably in the Irene Kaufman Settlement. Over the years she lost her Yiddish (language combining Hebrew and German) accent. I wonder if she was as fastidious about her fingernails in her early years as she was in the last twenty-five. Even in her 80s she would take the bus to Pittsburgh, an hour away, just for a manicure. She once intimated that she was trying to shift people's attention away from her thick ankles. She checked both, nails and ankles, when she first met Marcia.

At a railroad station in Dorahoi, Romania, three years after Mom's departure, my father, a *yeshiva bocher (*a Talmud student) who had been studying to be a *shochet* (a ritual slaughterer), the youngest son of Eliyahu Chaim, kissed his father good-bye for the last time and traveled westward. His father, my *Zeyda* (grandfather in Yiddish), soon headed eastward to die in Palestine, as was the wish of pious Jews of his day.

The story has it that as soon as Dad, newly named Morris, arrived in Pittsburgh, he went looking for Mom, finding her when he heard her singing. Imagine her surprise after a three-year separation to see her full-grown, tall Moishala with his military posture, and also her shock upon seeing him without *peyas* (earlocks). Dad chose not to resume his studies to be a shochet like his father though I remember his pride as he described tuberculosis in a cow's lung at the time I was dealing with this subject in medical school. Instead, he too, worked in the toby factory and soon after in a grocery store. In order to see Mom, he taught the Eger children to read and write Hebrew and to *daven* (pray) but got fired when Bobie Eger found his love notes to Mom. He too, studied English and soon little remained of his Yiddish accent. Nor did it take long before observance of *Shabbat* fell by the wayside despite an excellent *yeshiva* background and a continuing commitment to the daily donning of *tefillin* (phylacteries).

Mom's mother, and presumably her father Harry, fought the betrothal of Mom and Dad. My father's potential for siring children was considered suspect since Mom's sister Dora had been in a childless marriage with Uncle Berish. Why Bobie acceded to her daughter's wishes was finally unearthed many years later in a conversation between Mom and Marcia's mother, Madge. "Tell me, Mollie. Your boys always wondered what happened in Wheeling, West Virginia." Mom had always evaded answering us and did so in such a manner as only to whet our appetite for the story.

"Well, Madge, one day after six years of wanting to marry Morris, I was sent to Wheeling for a visit with my aunt. Morris followed me there and sent a telegram threatening my parents that if they didn't relent, I, a *maidel*, would return a *veibel*," that is to say, her chastity would have been compromised. Bobie caved in.

On *Purim,* 1910 Dad gave Mom an engagement ring and soon after on May 26 – it was *Lag B'omer*, the holiday between *Pesach* (Passover) and *Shavuot* when weddings are permitted – Mom and Dad were married. Dad's half brother Aaron Hirsch David, a pious layman, performed the ceremony, which took plae in Uncle Jake Eger's home in Carnegie. Dad liked recalling that this was also the year of the founding of the Boy Scouts of America.

They set up housekeeping in Carnegie, a mill-town suburb of Pittsburgh. For a while Dad was in business with Uncle Jake but moved to Ingram and back again to Carnegie in relation to work stoppages in the coal mines. Mostly, Dad worked as a peddler, walking many miles each day with a pack on his back. He sold linen, chenille bedspreads, and clothing to immigrant coal miners in Moon Run. Life became easier after he could afford a horse and buggy, and in 1924, a car. He would drive his customers to clothing stores in Pittsburgh to arrange their purchases for which Dad was paid a commission. *Moritz*, as he was affectionately known, was a welcome guest in the homes of scores

My grandmother, Bobie Eger at age 80

of his customers. Cousin Dan Jackson recalled for me, "When I accompanied your father on the road, I remember that, in addition to dispensing merchandise like linoleum for a kitchen floor, he gave advice regarding medicine, illnesses, politics, and the raising of children – always the *maven* (expert)." From time to time, many years after the stock-market crash of 1929 and during the subsequent depression, Dad would receive a letter of apology with a dollar bill, payment on a long-forgotten debt.

After two years of marriage, Jerry (Jerome, Yakov) was born. Dad's father wrote requesting that a boy be named Daniel after Dad's younger brother who had died at age three. I assume that Bobie Eger, a strong-willed, superstitious woman, vetoed this bidding and successfully lobbied for her father's name. Years later Dad was pleased when, without any direction from him, Marcia and I quite mystically fulfilled his responsibility by naming our son Daniel.

When Jerry was six, Mom was hospitalized with a recurrence of typhoid fever. The story goes that Mom feared that she had tuberculosis. Dad kissed her on the lips, saying, "Now, would I do that if I thought you had TB?"

Mom and Dad in front of their house, 1959.

After Jerry there was a hiatus of eight years. However, between 1920 and 1925 Allen, Irvin, Robert, and I issued forth. Marcia deduced and revealed to Mom that she was pregnant with me at Jerry's *bar mitzvah* (boy achieving religious maturity at age thirteen). "I don't know," she said. "In those days I was always pregnant." When Mom appeared in the labor room of Pittsburgh's Magee Hospital for Bob's birthing three-and-a-half years after Allen's birth and two-and-a-half years after Irv's, the head nurse met her with, "What! You here again?" Mom was so insulted to be made to feel like a greenhorn that she prevailed on her doctor to admit her to West Penn Hospital when my turn came fourteen months later.

Dad would contrast himself with the comedian, Eddie Cantor, who had five girls. He and Mom had longed for a girl, which may explain my girlish, pageboy hairstyle until I entered first grade. When our first child was born, Dad took a box of cigars to his fire-station cronies with a note, "My son is a better man than I am; he had a girl."

Mom and Dad spoke primarily Yiddish during the early years of their marriage. Of us five boys, only Jerry could speak the language. If a subject involved curses and profanities, Dad switched to Romanian.

Brothers Irv, Jerry, Bob, and me. Chanukah, 1983.

Even throughout the Depression, Dad remained cheerful and optimistic. Many a time in my life did he reassure me, "God will help you." (In the chapter about Jerry I discuss his belief in God.) I was in awe of Dad as he refused to press charges against robbers, who one wintry evening, stole blankets from our house. "Obviously," Dad figured, "these people had to be pretty bad off." I was covered with a sheepskin coat that night.

Our income was augmented significantly by renting out the attic, at first to two steelworkers until they were laid off, and later to a Greek family of four. I mention "Greek" because the cooking odors were repugnant to me.

Dad played the dominant role in our household. True, Mom could write checks, but Dad balanced her check book. She wasn't privy to their financial status. I believe she envied her friends who had a stronger voice. It was a painful moment for all of us sons in 1968 when we met in Dad's house to lay down the law, that because of Mom's cardiac limitations, he had to move from his four-storied home – they had lived there for forty years – to a one-storied bungalow. It was like a scene from *King Lear* as Dad bellowed, "I'm still your father. This is the home where I have all my memories. I'm not leaving." When moving day came, he went passively.

Only once did I ever see my Dad drunk. It was the night of *Simchat Torah* (holiday celebrating the completion of a Torah reading cycle) when it is a custom to have a drink after being called to the Torah. As Dad drove us terrified boys home, it was obvious that he had had many "calls." I still see him trying to prove his sobriety to Mom as he failed the heel-to-toe test.

Back to 1926. In Carnegie, Dad became president of the Orthodox synagogue but being a freethinker, he attended lectures by a liberal rabbi in Pittsburgh.

In 1927, the year that Charles Lindbergh flew the first solo airplane flight across the Atlantic, Dad went into business in Woodlawn on the Ohio River; a mine strike in Moon Run forced this move. Because of steady employment of thousands of workers at the Jones and Laughlin Steel Mill (J&L) located in Woodlawn, this was a wise move. The town was renamed Aliquippa around 1930.

Two years before the 1929 stock market crash, we moved into a new, red brick house in Woodlawn. Our steep hillside lawns were a challenge to the lawn mower and sickle. We enjoyed the friendship of our neighbors, an Irish mill foreman, an Italian dentist, a Scotch-Irish chief of police, and Irish and German steelworkers. Whatever may have been preached about Jews in their churches – the oft-heard expression Christ-killer did not originate from nowhere – there was rarely any overt manifestation of anti-Semitism.

When Dad opened his first store, it was to sell household linens. It wasn't long before he joined Uncle Harry Jackson, Aunt Rose's husband, in a variety store. I remember that we sold firecrackers before Independence Day – when they were still legal. More than once I burned my fingers exploding these firecrackers. Soon after, the two brothers-in-law went into the shoe business together. This partnership continued until approximately 1971 when Dad sold out to Uncle Harry. (Dad had begun to show signs of aging in 1969 when he was eighty-two years old.) In all those nearly forty years they operated on a handshake, and at times, not even that. Uncle Harry built up the business to eight stores, reducing the number as he switched to shopping mall locations. In all his ventures my uncle had the support of Aunt Rose and my mother while Dad's standard reaction was a negative, "What do we need it for?" Uncle Harry reassured me that Dad's role was an important one. Among other reasons, Dad was on good terms with the banks; the business had no problem borrowing large sums of money to get the maximum discount for early payment of shoe shipments.

What a secure view of the world I must have had. Within a span of one city block was our shoe store, Young's 5&10 owned by Mom's sister Jenny and her husband Uncle Lou, and Uncle Herman and Aunt Sarah Eger's jewelry store. This must certainly have given me a sense of belonging, of importance. When I didn't have the nickel for a ticket to the movies, the owner, a family friend, would occasionally let me in free. Aunt Jenny lived in an apartment above her store. I used to spend hours there looking from her window at the pedestrians and the passing cars and streetcars below. It was consistent with Aunt Jenny's artistic talent that she had an Italian, black-and-purple porcelain bathroom; the sink and toilet were black. I found it spooky and, therefore, exited quickly after using it.

Bobie lived with Aunt Jenny in the early thirties. I remember well when Bobie returned from a trip to Romania; she brought back presents for us all. I can see them heaped on the dining-room table. I knew nothing else about the trip. Years later we heard a story from my Israeli cousin, Nachman Leibovitz, who recalled Bobie's visit to his family in 1933. Bobie, who hadn't seen her sister in thirty years (another had died), had intended to stay for six months. However, at the end of one month she hastily departed. Why? "I'm not staying here another minute now that this madman, Hitler, has become chancellor of Germany" – that was Jan. 30, 1933.

Aliquippa had once been featured in an article in the *Philadelphia Inquirer* titled, "Aliquippa, the Siberia of the USA." It described the ownership of the land of Aliquippa and the control of everything and everybody within it by the Jones and Laughlin Steel Corporation (J&L). Before and after World War I workers were recruited from Italy, Yugoslavia, Greece, Ireland, and Poland. Thousands responded, flocking to guaranteed employment. They were provided cheap housing, with each ethnic group clustered together but separated on the many hills, called "Plans," leading down to the Mill along the Ohio River. Blacks (then called Negroes), who had made their way north in search of jobs, were segregated in Plan 11 Extension bordering the garbage dump.

The Mill owned the Company Store where the workers could charge all their purchases of food, clothing, and furniture. Prompt payment was assured by deductions from the worker's next paycheck. Small businesses tried to compete by offering extended charge accounts and personalized service. The Mill also owned the water and electric companies. It gave exclusivity for the vastly lucrative cement contracts for building homes, roads, and sidewalks to one company, P. M. Moore.

As a syndicalist, advocating a government under the control of trade unions, Dad was devoted to John L. Lewis, president of the United Mine Workers. He voted for Norman Thomas, the Socialist candidate for president, probably even against Franklin Delano Roosevelt (F.D.R.) in 1932. Once it was obvious that F.D.R. was pulling us out of the Depression, he became the object of hero worship. "We have nothing to fear but fear itself," he declared during his first inaugural address. How we gathered around our Atwater-Kent radio to hear his comforting *Fireside Chats.* These chats were in stark contrast to the anti-Semitic diatribes delivered nationwide on Sundays by the Catholic priest, Father Charles Coughlin. Our only newspaper was the *Forward,* Yiddish and politically socialist; its cost and use were shared with Uncle Harry. Also, during the Depression it was symbolic that we shared a lawn mower. When good times returned, we couldn't be sure whose mower it had been.

The reality of public life in Aliquippa was that politicians – only Republicans need apply – served at the pleasure of the Mill's owners. In 1936 Dad marched dutifully in a parade touting Alfred Landon, the Republican candidate for president against "that communist" F.D.R. Like many of the marchers, Dad wore a sunflower, Landon's state flower, in his lapel, but pinned on the underside was "I'm for Roosevelt."

The Mill also dominated the Woodlawn Bank. The latter stood by as a smaller bank in Woodlawn failed and, possibly not unlike other banks during the Great Depression, it foreclosed unmercifully on mortgaged homes. One law office Ruffner and (again) Moore was given control of all the bank's legal transactions, continuing even after

Woodlawn Bank was bought by Mellon Bank, one of Pennsylvania's largest banking firms.

Permit me to jump ahead in time as I relate my travails with Mellon Bank. Planning to build a home-office combination in 1958, I needed a mortgage for $55,000. Where the bank and I locked horns was over their requiring all supplicants to work with the bank's lawyers. I knew that John Atkinson, an insurance agent from a prominent Catholic family, was the first to buck the system by trying to hire his own lawyer; he failed.

So, along I came, self-confident, already a prominent internist, son of the highly respected Morris Chaimovitz, he a longtime customer of the bank, asking that my mortgage be handled by John Stern. John, an old family friend, would have been the ideal choice. He had a reputation for intelligent, honest dealings and, despite being Jewish (at that time an almost insurmountable obstacle), he had been President of the Beaver County Bar Association. Further to John's credit from the bank's point of view, he was a Republican.

I made my proposal to a bank officer. His answer came a few days later delivered orally to me at the bank: "The bank's policy is that we deal only with Ruffner and Moore." He added in a whisper, "If you make trouble, it will go against you when you try to join the Masons."

"The Masons! Who in the hell cares about the Masons?" I thought. Well, Dad did. He had been a member for decades and assumed that I would likewise seek membership. Even my brother Jerry had acquiesced to Dad's wishes and became a Mason. Dad excused his membership by explaining that the connections he made were a potential source of protection against threats to the Jewish community. Surely this thinking was a product of the European Jewish experience. And yet I can't believe that he was so naïve to think his acceptance was wholehearted. I wanted no part of a secret organization where one anonymous negative vote could veto a membership application and where anyone wishing to rise to the highest ranks (at that time) had to profess faith in Jesus Christ. Dad was disappointed when I expressed these negative feelings.

In regard to the mortgage, Dad's advice was, "You need the money.

Don't make a fuss." Accordingly I accepted Mellon's precondition. Subsequently and despite my ambivalence, I enjoyed working with Jim Ruffner, a junior member of the law firm and became good friends with James Rowley, son of another law partner.

Of course, I didn't let it go at that. As soon as the money was delivered to my account, I reported the offensive bank officer to Dr. John Miller, one of my referring physicians and a high official in the Masonic Lodge. He said that he, in turn, reported the misuse of Lodge influence. I never knew its result. I hope it galled the culprit to see me make early redemption of the mortgage, advance in prominence in the Aliquippa Hospital, become his wife's physician, and years later, switch my accounts to Citizens National Bank, the first competing bank in Aliquippa in a generation.

What a monumental occasion it was when Dad, as treasurer (an honored but working Council appointment) of the newly formed Aliquippa Water Authority, handed an official of the Mill a check for $1,000,000. I have a photo of this moment in 1960 when Aliquippa became free of one of the Mill's tentacles. Control of the Company Store and transportation system, as well as the anachronistic monopoly of other services, was also soon to cease.

Scattered among the various neighborhoods were about 100 Jewish families. By "gentlemen's agreement" none lived in Plan 6 (where the Mill executives lived), Sheffield Terrace (Scotch-Irish), or later, Hillcrest. Our Orthodox synagogue was a mile from our home. Bob and I walked to after-school *cheder* (Hebrew school) four days a week. When the time came for us to be *bar mitzvah*, we had more intensive training from short, aged, toothless Rabbi Adolph Klein at the one room *shul* (synagogue) in West Aliquippa. On *Shabbat* mornings his small congregation made a fuss over us, especially when we attended services after *bar mitzvah* when our presence could be counted toward completing the *minyan* (quorum of ten people) necessary to read the Torah.

In those days Americanization classes were a serious activity. The teacher, herself an Italian immigrant, was the beloved Mrs. Lucy Docchio. I recall the tearful, swearing-in ceremonies as her students became full citizens. Which of us second-generation Americans knows the Bill of Rights as well as did those new citizens?

During my childhood Mom had the help of Vicki, a Polish farm girl who, for room and board and six dollars a week, tended the house and all of us. This included giving me my Saturday-night bath. Mom did most of the cooking.

Vicki's parents lived on a run-down farm in Independence, ten miles from Aliquippa. Living with us was a step-up for her. Vicki's relaxed manner complemented Mom's demeanor and provided us with an orderly household. In her thirties she was married and had two sons. We got to know one another as adults only when she became my patient. She had settled for a less than happy marriage.

At age six I started elementary school at Spaulding, a five-minute walk from home. There were two great teachers that I remember at Spaulding. One was Betty Sheehan who years later became director of the Sewickley Child Guidance Center – she tested both our daughters before they started school. The other was Mr. Herbert Gregg, a gentle poet, who taught us to enjoy poetry, how to open a dictionary efficiently, and proper table etiquette.

My first awareness of the sex act occurred at Spaulding. A tall, heavy girl showed me a palm-sized booklet of pictures, which when flipped, showed a penis in advancing stages of erection. I grabbed it from her, tore it up, and gave her a nickel, fearful that she might strike me. Several years later my sex education began and ended with Uncle Harry telling me, "It's okay to put your hand inside a girl's blouse;" I was appalled.

How magnificent was our town library! Deserving a classical European setting, it nevertheless was situated on Aliquippa's main street half a block from the business district. It was a tall one-story concrete building with Corinthian embellishments. Inside, it was palatial with thirty-five-foot ceilings. The architect had brought entire walls and cornices from Europe. The floors and pillars were of Italian marble. There was little need to request, "Quiet;" the atmosphere spoke of Vespers. And every Saturday morning was story time in a little room off the main reading room. There, Mrs. Davies would transport us into the world of fairy tales. The library was a gift of Elizabeth Horne, daughter of one of the owners of J&L, B.F. Jones. Unlike the Mill's co-owner Laughlin, who gave a library with an endowment fund to sustain it to the town of Ambridge across the Ohio River, Mrs. Horne gave no maintenance funds. Coming in 1929 at the time of the Great Depression, this gift placed an onerous burden on the town's budget.

I remember Franklin Junior High primarily because of my homeroom teacher. Each morning she would read from Corinthians, "When I was a child, I spoke as a child . . ." There followed a classroom recitation of The Lord's Prayer, as was the custom those days, "Our Father which art in heaven, hallowed be thy name." Its Christian nature was unclear to me. This lady, I was told, was the key figure in my not receiving the prestigious American Legion Award. Noting that brother Bob had received it the year before, she asserted that it would be unfair that the same family should receive it two years in a row. I still remember the sinking feeling at the assembly when the Most Deserving Student's name was announced, "Ed Grey," and not mine.

On the lighter side I have a photograph of my teammates and me to remind me that we were the championship junior high school volleyball team. I am shown in knickers – long pants came in high school – with a Black, George Pitts, who became a sports writer for a Negro newspaper, the Pittsburgh Courier, and with Joe Pukach. Joe, though five inches shorter than I, beat me in the finals of a ping pong tournament in high school and even though so short, he went on to be an All-State basketball player. I saw Joe at our class's fifty-fifth reunion; George had died. The best part of my Junior High days were Boy Scout Troop No. 412 and private piano lessons with Margery Selkovits. (More about Margery in other chapters.)

High school was a world apart. I had outstanding teachers. Marcia explains that had the job market been more open even after the depression, many would have had college appointments. Certainly among these would have been Mr. Ralph Edeburn, an inspiring science teacher. The music department I will describe in the coming chapter, "My life's refrain": Dr. Arthur Davenport who taught every instrument but strings was a musical giant and Grace Mansell, an enthusiastic choral director.

Her form-fitting, blue-angora sweaters gained our unfaltering attention, especially when, shoulders back and placing her hands on her waist, she exhorted, "Sing from your diaphragm." And Miss Catherine Sowell, the stately, white-haired Latin teacher, made a dull subject enjoyable. We sewed our own togas, and wore them.

The most exciting of them all, barring only the music teachers, was Mr. Eric Garing who taught "Problems of Democracy" and, I do believe, how to think. As a liberal in his formative teaching years, he clashed with the school board and had to fight to keep his job. It was he who sponsored a debate in assembly. Given: Aliquippa is a Fine Place to Live. I eagerly accepted the affirmative while Marvin Simmons, a Black, took the negative. I, full of rose-colored platitudes, was humbled as Marv recited a litany of indignities suffered by the Black community. I remember thinking "How unfriendly" when a Black student chose to sit in the theater balcony rather than sit with the rest of us on a class outing, never realizing that Blacks were prohibited from sitting downstairs. Marv was ahead of his time in discussing unfair hiring practices. I was ashamed of my naiveté.

Mrs. Alpharetta Martin, probably typical of her generation of guidance teachers, was limited by her class consciousness. Visiting our lovely house and knowing my brothers, she declared me to be college material. But, for brilliant Jesse Steinfeld, who lived in an apartment over his parents' hardware store in West Aliquippa bordering the Mill, it was a different matter. Mrs. Martin tried to direct him to the shop course to prepare for a mill job. Fortunately Jesse was able to circumvent her and went on to become dean of several medical schools, Surgeon General under Richard Nixon, and responsible for the cigarette package warning, "Smoking may be dangerous to your health."

It was a time of awkward dating and clumsy necking. Puritanical values wrestled with glandular surges. I remember a date with Pauline Cochran only because I drove to her home in Sheffield Terrace where no Jews lived. Watching tennis players' bouncing breasts was about as far as I would get. Friday-night socials were painful as I struggled to muster the courage to ask someone to dance. It was a successful night if I would be on the dance floor for the final number, "Moonlight Serenade" recorded by Glenn Miller.

In dreamy moods I used to take solo walks in wooded areas never expressing my thoughts to anyone in words or in writing. How restricted were my communication skills! My diary had shallow descriptions, as after hearing Sergei Rachmaninoff play with the Pittsburgh Symphony Orchestra, "Swell pianist."

It was teacher Allan Chotiner who informed our class that those male students planning to be doctors, could leave high school a semester early and still receive a diploma at graduation time. This was late 1942. America had already been at war one year; the army presumed it would be a long war and feared a shortage of doctors. With accelerated programming I would have my M.D. by 1947 instead of 1951.

I remember having no misgivings about leaving school or friends or the coeditorship of our high school yearbook. I was anxious to get on with my medical career. Avoiding the draft wasn't a thought as my eighteenth birthday was another nine months off. Thus it was February 1943 that I left Aliquippa for Geneva College, and sixteen months later, for Harvard Medical School.

Analyzing my Aliquippa experience, I conclude that it provided me with a psychologically healthy milieu. First and foremost I grew up as the youngest child in a loving family. And among the youngest of my generation, I was surrounded by dozens of cousins and by many uncles and aunts who doted on me. I was proud to be the son of everyone's friend, Morris Chaimovitz. The incomparable Margery Selkovits was my piano teacher. The schools provided a rich curriculum and superb teachers. The broad ethnicity of my school friends and our neighbors gave me the ease to deal with people. Leaving this extended womb, I was cheerful, optimistic, and self-confident that I would find my place in the world beyond.

It's interesting and a bit frightening to speculate what might have been, had circumstances not forced my parents out of Romania. Would my mother have delivered five healthy sons? Would I have become a *shochet* rather than a doctor? How many of us would have survived the Holocaust? Under the same scenario Marcia's family would have been in Russia with no common meeting place for her and me unless we met as dedicated Zionists involved with illegal immigration to Israel. I can think of only one plus; were I a multilingual Romanian, Hebrew, just another language, would not have tormented me so.

ZEYDA WAS A CHASSID

From early childhood I knew that my father's father, "Zeyda," had spent the last years of his life in the venerable town of Safed in northern Palestine. It is known that he left Romania soon after sending Dad to America in 1903. From Dad's description I can see my Zeyda crying as he kissed my father, his *"mazinik"* (the youngest child), good-bye at the railroad station in Dorahoi. Watching as Dad boarded the train, Zeyda knew full well that he would never again see his son.

Their comments to one another were probably brief: "Stay well, Tateh."

"You know, Moishele, many of our people stop being religious in America. Do your best to hold on to tradition. Promise me, at least, to keep kosher (according to Jewish dietary laws)."

"You don't have to worry about me, Tateh."

"And write me and your mother a word or two from time to time."

It is highly improbable that he ended with, "I'll soon be sailing to Palestine to die in the Holy Land." He may have thought, "Why should I depress my son."

Only one son of Zeyda's four children and two stepchildren remained behind. This was cousin Bernard Haimovitz's father, called Zaida from infancy in hope of his recovering from an illness to live to

My Zeyda in Palestine, 1903.

an old age. Of Zaida's family only Bernard eventually immigrated to the United States departing by ship from Calais on Aug. 31, 1939, the day before World War II broke out. (That was also the same date of the year forty-five years later that Marcia and I arrived in Israel.) Three of Bernard's sisters survived the war and moved to Israel with their families in 1948 – 1950; a fourth, Clara, along with her husband, a son, and a daughter, perished in the Holocaust. It was a mournful, bonding experience for me to subsequently fill out their four forms for Yad Vashem.

Evidence that my Zeyda was a learned man is derived from two sources. First, by profession he was a *shochet* for which scholarship and piety are prerequisites. Surely my Zeyda, deriving no pleasure from killing animals, would perform his task quickly and deftly.

Second, his postcards and letters from Safed always began with the title of that week's Torah portion. Several Pittsburgh rabbis whom brother Jerry consulted, confirmed these prerequisites. Why he chose Safed over Jerusalem can only be conjectured. Many *Chassidim* (a sect of Jewish mystics) like my Zeyda settled in Safed over a century ago. Especially if he were interested in Cabala, in mysticism, this city would have attracted him. Maybe he joined a specific rabbi.

Zeyda's second wife Rissel had borne him my Dad and later Daniel who died at age three. My grandmother was an educated woman. She read in Yiddish to the women of her village and led them in prayer in her home. There is considerable mystery as to the whereabouts of Rissel. Bernie Haimovitz stated that she was depressed and remained with relatives in Romania. This was later confirmed from translations of Yiddish and Hebrew postcards that Dad received from his mother in Botajan, Romania, 1909 and 1910. And yet strangely, Zeyda's postcards and letters from Safed from 1910 to 1913 included regards from "your mother Raisal" or Risa or Rissil depending on the translators of his Yiddish. If writing to Uncle Berish, Dad's half brother, he would refer to Raisal appropriately as "your stepmother." Is it possible that she did eventually join him? I doubt it.

Dad seldom spoke of his mother, and Uncle Harry Jackson, the family chronicler, never once mentioned her in his detailed biography of Mom and Dad. Could it be that Dad thought that she was genetically depressed and did not want us to carry that concern for our families?

Were they poorly mated? We only know that Zeyda was a *Chassid*, a very pious man. A picture reveals him, long bearded, in a *strimmel* (a fur cap) and wearing a caftan, a long sleeved robe with a broad waistband. His resemblance to me and even more so to brother Bob is striking. But was she proud to be a *Chassid's* wife or was she uncomfortable with his life style? Did she refuse to leave her family? Did she refuse to move to Palestine where life would be arduous? Would she risk divorce by refusing to accompany her husband to Israel? The mystery is unresolved.

Zeyda's letters and postcards gave blessings to Mom that she should have a healthy son, and later acknowledged Jerry's birth in 1912. These communications addressed to both Dad and to Uncle Berish Chaimovitz, thanked them for money needed for food and medicine. One postcard thanked my mother's father for the one dollar he had sent while another thanked Dad for the one dollar that he sent. "I was surprised for you usually send me more every *Pesach* for the expenses of the holiday and the rent." Mostly the letters consisted of blessings for Mom, Dad, and Yankele (Jerry) and prayers that Uncle Berish would also have a son; he and Aunt Dora remained childless.

By design Zeyda went to Palestine wishing to die there as did so many pious souls. He lived in Safed approximately fifteen years, dying probably in 1918 but definitely before 1920. This is certain since brother Allen, born in 1920, was named Eliyahu Chaim for him.

We have always assumed that Zeyda was buried in the immense hillside cemetery in Safed. Of this we have no proof. Several of us have searched for evidence of his gravesite. Jerry was the first; it was 1961. Nephews Allen and Bruce on a summer archeological dig in Israel around 1971 searched the hillside in vain. Then in 1984 Marcia and I spent two hours climbing like mountain goats on the steep hill, managing to find an area containing many graves from 1915 to 1920. None had names even closely resembling Zeyda's. It was evident that many tombstones were missing or in shambles, or had illegible inscriptions. This sorry state could have been caused by defective construction materials, centuries of freezing winters and south-facing sunshine, and Turkish marauders.

In 1993, the day after Pesach, my friend Rabbi Joe Heckelman and I visited the *Rabbinate* (the Office of Religious Affairs) in Safed. We learned that in 1964 an exhaustive combing of the cemetery had been conducted. Identifiable gravestones were codified and repaired; etched inscriptions were highlighted with black paint. Eventually all legible information was entered into a computer. We first looked through books of raw data to no avail. Then for a half hour we worked with a computer-savvy secretary, again ending up empty handed. We searched references to Chaimovitz, Haimovitz, Eliyahu Chaim, Adler (the name on the passport that Zeyda used to leave Romania and to enter Palestine), and Romania from 1912 to 1920, Botajan, Sivan, Dorahoi, and Yassi, the towns of Zeyda's origin. None of the cross-files gave any hint as to the life or death of my Zeyda. End of the line. Who knows? Maybe he went for mineral baths in Tiberias and died; the cemetery there has no record of him.

I would not call myself a mystical person but I feel Zeyda's presence when I'm in Safed and that Zeyda knows I'm there. Being a rational person, I feel strange as I write this sentence. As the confused prince says in the play *Amadeus*, "There it is." It also says something of my relationship with my father who was called Zeyda by his grandchildren that, of all the sons, only I, on becoming a grandfather, became "Zeyda."

Every year Marcia and I spend the last couple of days of *Pesach* in Safed; the last day is daughter Amy's *yahrzeit* (anniversary of a death). While there in 1992, we received a call informing us that our niece, Cathy, had died in an auto accident. Having free time after making arrangements to fly to Pittsburgh, I took a walk to the cemetery. As I approached its perimeter, a pious young man, noting my direction, asked me what my intentions were. I told him that I was on my way to visit my Zeyda. He reminded me that cemetery visits were forbidden on *Shabbat* and on holidays and "Besides, your Zeyda wouldn't be there on the holiday." Not wanting to offend my young authority or contravene religious practice, I returned to my hotel.

Later at the final *minyan* of *Pesach* I sought Rabbi Heckelman's reaction to the exchange near the cemetery. "Not only is your Zeyda not there today, he never is."

So, "Why," I asked, "do we visit a grave at all?"

"Because it's the last known address," he wistfully replied.

I know Joe to be right. When I visit Amy's grave at Millvale cemetery, I know that she is not under the weeds we slowly clear from among the flowers. It's just that there at that small plot of earth, I can focus my full attention on Amy. Occasionally I can pull a memory out of the air, an image, which restores her to me for a brief moment, narrowing the gap that inexorably separates us.

One more story about my Zeyda's cemetery. In 1991 Marcia and I took brother Irv to Safed. Again it was *Pesach*. We drove to the lowest section of the cemetery to look up to the area of Zeyda's "decade." While Irv and Marcia were discussing Zeyda, I wandered around looking for the graves of the twenty-one teenagers, victims of Arab terrorists in Maalot. In May 1974 a group of 120 high school students from Safed were on a field trip in Maalot. They were bunked in a school building. Three Lebanese Arab terrorists seized the building and held the children and ten accompanying adults hostage. A few managed to escape by jumping out of windows. The terrorists demanded the release of twenty Arab prisoners. When efforts to negotiate the children's release failed and after two sharpshooters wounded two of the terrorists, Israeli soldiers broke into the building killing the three terrorists but not before the latter had sprayed the rooms with bullets, killing the twenty-one teenagers, four adults and one Israeli soldier.

By chance, our car was parked only meters from the beautifully landscaped garden that encompassed the graves of the young victims. All the low tombstones had names and ages inscribed. One boy was next to his sister. Another, a soldier killed soon after, was beside his brother.

The following morning, a young nurse from my hospital sat next to me on the bus to work. Knowing that she was from Safed, I related the previous day's emotional experience. "You know," she interrupted, "my girl friend and I told the terrorists that we had to go to the bathroom. After we feigned distress, they gave us permission. We jumped out the window, three floors. I broke both legs but my father was there and took me to the hospital. Those were my classmates who were killed. I can't give you details because hypnosis treatment for nightmares has blurred my memory."

I like to think that my Zeyda is comforting the souls of those righteous youngsters.

BROTHER JERRY, THE PACESETTER

It is evident that I structured my professional life parallel to Jerry's. Two forces came together: my intellectual and emotional attraction to medicine and my profound respect for Jerry. My relationship to him was like that of son to his father but unencumbered by Freudian pressures. I looked upon Jerry's life as the best that I could achieve.

He specialized in internal medicine; so did I. He trained at Lahey Clinic in Boston; so did I. He elected to do solo practice in a small town; so did I. He chose a dwelling with his office attached to his living quarters; again, so did I.

It wasn't as though we ever sat together to discuss what I should do, whether or not to take the premed course at Geneva College in Beaver Falls, Pennsylvania, or even to continue on to medical school. We really hadn't spent much time together in my youth, Jerry being thirteen years my senior. I just got on his track and didn't get off – until the move to Israel.

Jerry lived at home from the time he entered general practice in Aliquippa, Pennsylvania in 1939, until he reported for military duty in 1942. His busy day left no time for little brother. I do remember being intrigued by the medical-supplies salesman's metallic wares spread out on our front porch and Jerry's finesse as he ordered "one of these and two of those." I wish I could say that I witnessed one of his many home deliveries of a baby or even his setting a broken bone but I never did. Nor did I accompany him on his daily visits to Rochester General Hospital.

Jerry married Irma Goldstein in June 1942 soon after he entered the Army Medical Corps. They were able to live together outside the army base until Jerry shipped out to England.

Although the horrors of war were amply demonstrated by our brother Allen's death when two B-24 planes collided during training, I never considered Jerry, as a doctor, to be in danger. It was only after the fact, that we learned that he was in the second assault wave of General Patton's Armored Division in France in June 1944. He looked like an over-age Boy Scout in a picture of him digging a foxhole. Jerry survived unscathed. One of the last to return from Europe, he was ordered to California to join the fighting in the Pacific. By the time he arrived at the army base, two atom bombs had been dropped and Japan had surrendered.

When Jerry returned home, he showed me a Luger pistol he had brought from Germany. It was a frightening object. Years later I learned that members of the local B'nai Brith organization added it to other weapons they shipped to New York. From there, concealed under farm equipment, these were surreptitiously (avoiding an arms embargo) shipped to the *Haganah* (prestatehood army) in Israel.

Still in uniform, Jerry came to the Peter Bent Brigham Hospital in Boston to interview for a fellowship in pathology, considered at the time essential training for an internist. I arranged an interview with my pathology instructor, Thomas Kinney. Kinney's Sewickley, Pennsylvania, background gave them instant rapport.

After six months at the Brigham, Jerry moved to Lahey Clinic where he continued for two years as a fellow in internal medicine. Those two years coincided with my last two years at Harvard Medical School. I had many dinners with Jerry and Irma but unfortunately, these came when I was less in need, that is, after my first year's doldrums had passed. Irma was plagued with gynecological problems. All the sadness related to miscarriages evaporated when in 1949 she and

Jerry adopted Susie, at day ten of her life, followed eight years later by the adoption of Mark.

In June of 1948 Jerry and I attended a rally at Boston Garden in support of Israel. Independence had been achieved only the month before but deadly battles continued until January 1949. Those were both heady and ominous moments as we learned of Holocaust survivors pouring in from camps in Europe and Cyprus while Arab armies were attacking across all of Israel's borders. Egyptians had captured the northern Negev town of Beersheva and were bombing Tel Aviv. Jerry and I cheered the guest speaker, Moshe Shertok (later, Sharett), Israel's first foreign minister and second prime minister.

One month before Jerry completed his stay in Boston, Irma left to set up housekeeping in Sewickley. At that same time I was finishing my medical school days. One night Jerry and I went to the red-light district in Scollay Square to see Boston's famed tassel queen. It was my first venture into burlesque. The show's innuendoes concerning homosexuality went over my head – at age twenty-two I was that naive. In later years we shared more pro-Israel experiences, but not burlesque.

That we would practice together eight years later, upon completion of my training was taken for granted. I couldn't imagine a more gratifying professional life style. Jerry engaged an architect to draw plans to enlarge his office. Marcia and I had even paid one month's rent on a Sewickley apartment. Yet, it was a dream that only came close to fruition.

One day soon after I met Marcia, she spoke with a college friend, a Pittsburgh socialite. When Marcia described my intention to work with Jerry and live in Sewickley, her friend blurted, "Marcia, your boyfriend is a liar. There are no Jews in Sewickley!" Actually, there were two Jews on the local hospital's staff but such was Sewickley's reputation at the time.

Soon after, – it was April 1956 – Dad and Jerry came to Boston to announce the collapse of Jerry's plans. The attempt to enlarge his office had been thwarted by Sewickley's zoning commission. It was irrelevant that I had received no answer from Sewickley Valley Hospital to my application for staff privileges. I'm still waiting.

More than once have I pondered the question, "Why did Dad accompany Jerry to Boston?" I can only assume that Dad thought that there would be a falling out of his boys and he wished to be around to prevent that from happening. I do believe that over the years both Jerry and I were able to prove to Dad that his adage, "whatever happens is for the best," was valid. "God will help," he would add.

I will not rewrite history and deny my disappointment that the proposed partnership with Jerry was aborted. However, I was also relieved, knowing that I had a challenging fallback in the soon-to-be-opened Aliquippa Hospital. I also recognized the need to be on my own. Best of all with the separation, we would never run the risk well-known in partnerships of jeopardizing our personal relationship. We could act independently in our individual hospital's affairs. Jerry would never have to feel compelled to repress me. Nor could our wives complain, "You're working harder than your brother," "He's taking too much time off," or "He's slighted Mrs. So and So," which could only refer to me since Jerry never slighted anyone.

In the days when the concept of psychosomatic disease was popular, two personality types were described: the "A" personality, prone to develop peptic ulcers, was ambitious, competitive, and punctual. The "B," free of ulcers, was congenial, contemplative, and relaxed. Jerry was a solid "B" personality. Did he own a watch? Of course, he did; he just never felt compelled to look at it. When he was with a patient, his only concern was this patient. People might wait in the office for hours, at times past midnight, but they knew that once sitting in front of Jerry, they had his undivided attention, without any limitation of time. He made hospital rounds at least twice a day, virtually tucking his patients in at bedtime. This at times wreaked havoc with his family's schedule but his loving patients knew how fortunate they were to be in Jerry's care. And how fortuitous for Jerry to have a wife like Irma who accommodated to this predictably unpredictable lifestyle.

It has been several years since Jerry died on December 15, 1996. Were he alive, I could not have been as frank as I will now be. What I have to say would possibly hurt him for, in truth, I was relieved not to be going to Sewickley for additional reasons. I harbored much animosity toward Sewickley Valley Hospital and was dismayed that Jerry would knuckle under to their blatant abuse of him. For he too, initially, had been denied acceptance on the staff. In time he was allowed to admit patients but only under another doctor's name. Jerry, with the patience of Job, accepted this backdoor, second-class citizenship until after a number of years, he received a staff appointment.

In the last three months of Jerry's stay in Boston, he took a grueling course in electrocardiology (ECG) under the famed Louis Wolff at Beth Israel Hospital. Diligent as ever, armed with a wealth of lecture notes, he prepared to teach this relatively new science to his colleagues. This is exactly what he did over the years, possibly receiving thanks from friends but no official role in Sewickley's ECG department. Title or remuneration? Don't be naive. You must excuse me for making a boastful comparison, but even as the initiator of the cardiology department at Aliquippa Hospital, I shared the cardiology services and their remuneration with other qualified doctors.

Every year Jerry conducted one of the finest medical review courses in the Pittsburgh area for the Sewickley staff and for many physicians from surrounding hospitals. I was proud of him and pleased for him – but a bit dismayed – that he could carry it off free of discomfort in Sewickley's anti-Semitic milieu. But that was my brother; he could not bear a grudge.

It is doubtful that I would ever have been at ease at Sewickley Valley Hospital; I had neither Jerry's patience nor his apolitical stance. What made me more feisty, more ready and anxious than Jerry to do battle with bigots? Was it the position of number five among my brothers and the optimism of guaranteed success that accompanied that status? Was it the validation that came from being a Harvard man? Did it come from growing up in a changing attitude of Jews about themselves and of gentiles about Jews? Did the Holocaust and the establishment of Israel strengthen my ego?

And in Jerry's defense, well, he was thirteen years older, that is, we were half a generation apart. Weren't our times different? Wasn't getting along in a Christian world more important then? Hadn't Dad joined the Masons for that reason? And Jerry, too? And maybe because Irma was raised under the same set of circumstances, she sided with Jerry in not making waves. It is also possible that because of Jerry and Irma's quiet patience, years later young Jewish families found Sewickley a welcoming community.

One thing I can say for certain. Our ties became stronger and richer. Not being partners, we were free to take courses together, to travel to conventions while leaving each to arrange coverage in his own hospital. And I was free to branch out on my own whether it was into nuclear medicine or cardiology and eventually to make the move to Israel. As a partner, leaving Jerry behind in America might have been an impossibility.

I believe that Jerry and I were a great pair. We loved and admired one another. Jerry gave evidence of this in a letter he wrote in August 1991. "I must tell you that one of the crowning experiences of my life was being exposed to that medical stardom – the Peter Bent Brigham Hospital (see chapter, *Giants Come in All Sizes)* – during my six months in pathology, which gave me so much time to go to the marvelous clinical and radiological meetings . . . . THAT WAS LIVING! Best of all I had you to turn to, to share the excitement and the heady atmosphere of Harvard and Boston . . . for after all, who else but you would understand my wonderful feeling of nostalgia . . ."

Jerry and I even resembled one another. One afternoon he entered our house wearing, as usual, a fedora, hiding his baldness. Raina, age eight, rushed down the stairs and, mistaking Jerry for me, jumped into his arms.

Jerry at times had a sobering effect on me. Once I told him with jubilation and pride of my autopsy-confirmed diagnosis of an atrial myxoma, a tumor within the heart. With present-day imaging techniques this is no great triumph but in those days it was. I was walking far off the ground, that is, until Jerry's response following an initial compliment: "Pile up your successes one on top of the other. With your next failure they'll all come tumbling down."

Jerry would start every phone conversation with "*Dovid HaMelech*" (David the King). When we would get into a car or on a plane, we would say almost in unison, "Who's first?"; we had so much to share with one another. Whether it concerned patient care, hospital politics, medical economics, or our children, we could go on for hours. And how Jerry worried about Irma. So many times over the years when she was hospitalized, Jerry would say to me, "I think we're losing her." And, of course, Irma's stroke with near-total paralysis of her right hand was a tragedy also for Jerry. Being her husband/doctor compounded his frustration and anguish. Three months later as she sat in a wheelchair next to Jerry's virtually lifeless body, Irma lamented, "I was supposed to go first."

United Jewish Appeal, Israel Bonds, civil rights, and golf, all these passions I shared with cousin Sidney Eger. Not that Jerry didn't participate in most of these; they were just not high priority items with him. Also, I was involved with the Aliquippa-Ambridge synagogue and the Conservative Movement regionally and nationally; he, with the Reform Temple in Coraopolis.

Jerry devoted himself to the struggle of the Pennsylvania Society of Internal Medicine to bring equity to Blue Shield physician fee schedules. In those days compensation for surgical and diagnostic procedures was inordinately higher than for the internist's time-consuming and basic function, the consultation. In this pursuit he was most effective. Though proud of Jerry's achievements, I never sought to get into that fray.

Though I enjoyed having a life close to and in parallel with Jerry's, why didn't I consider options other than practice in Sewickley or Aliquippa? Why did I not direct myself toward remaining in my medical mecca, Boston, that I loved so much? Was there no place there for me? Did I feel I would be over my head, outclassed by all my great teachers? Or was it that Jerry innocently placed a ceiling on what I might expect of myself. Maybe I was just truly realistic about my potential.

This last statement was tested around 1972 when I received a letter offering me an appointment at Albany Medical School in the Department of Internal Medicine. I considered a career change for about two seconds; I was having too good a time practicing medicine in Aliquippa and besides, let's face it, I enjoyed being home.

Is it to be expected that our relationship should have existed without conflict? I can recall one major confrontation. This took place in 1974 during the interim between Dad's death and burial. Jerry requested that I ask Cliff Smith, an esteemed high school teacher and friend, to give a eulogy at the funeral home during visitation the day after Dad died. Adhering to the customs of Conservative Judaism, I developed antipathy for visitation other than for an hour before the service prior to departure for the cemetery. And I certainly couldn't accept the additional variance, a eulogy delivered a day before the funeral. I turned down Jerry's request, incurring his wrath. "Our father was a very special person," he said. Of course I agreed but said that this wasn't the proper moment to express it. "Everybody's father is special." Adding to the division with my brothers I opted not to be present at the evening visitation. I just could not bring myself to stand before Dad's coffin and be greeted. My brothers never criticized me for creating this disunity.

For years I reflected on my intransigence and Jerry's anger with me. In 1996, a week after our brother Irv died, – Jerry was to follow him in another seven months – Jerry and I had our customary lunch at a restaurant in Pittsburgh. It was then that I finally got up the nerve to apologize to him, regretting my having opposed him. Guess what? He remembered nothing of the incident! I should have predicted this since, as I've already mentioned, Jerry never bore a grudge. And all those years I was torturing myself with remorse and guilt. (Neither did Jerry recall another event, crystal clear in my memory. Jerry, then about eighteen years old, was lying on his back on the living room floor. I came running from the front hall and jumped on his abdomen. He let out a screech. I rolled off him, terror struck, thinking that I had ruptured his appendix. I can't recall Jerry's reaction but there were no untoward effects.)

There were other disagreements, particularly concerning Irv. The details are unimportant. Suffice it to say that in one instance Jerry showed his mettle by reversing a strongly expressed earlier opinion.

After Jerry's retirement and move to Pittsburgh at age seventy-four, he and Irma became involved in various activities at Rodef Shalom Temple. They participated in courses and volunteered as guides in the Temple's biblical garden.

A high point in Jerry's life was having a second *bar mitzvah* at age eighty-three – 70 + 13 – a custom not commonly observed, certainly never before at Rodef Shalom. In 1971 we had arranged a *Shabbat* morning second *bar mitzvah* celebration for Dad. This consisted of his being called to the Torah to recite the *Haftarah,* the supplementary reading. Services were followed by a light lunch in Dad's honor. It was a uniquely happy occasion. Unlike Dad who needed no preparation for his second *bar mitzvah*, Jerry approached his as the diligent student he was. He chose the same *Shabbat* as he had celebrated seventy years before and even managed to find the *bar mitzvah* speech his teacher had written for him.

His Torah portion dealt with God's refusal to allow Moses to enter the Promised Land. Jerry was unhappy with God's decision. "After all, how could God turn down his best friend?" Jerry sought out several rabbis for their reaction to his dilemma. He was obsessed with his quest for answers, so much so that Irma was prompted to say, "I never would have married him if I knew this would happen." The subject even dominated Jerry's frequent telephone calls to me. In one response I quoted a scholar-friend who said, "Tell your brother that Moses was God's servant. Abraham was God's friend."

Marcia and I returned to celebrate with Jerry. (Actually I had also been at Jerry's first *bar mitzvah*, albeit, *in utero*.) His rabbis finally acquiesced to Jerry's request to read with his Ashkenazi accent rather than the Sephardic accent popular in the temple. Prior to the temple service Jerry gave a scholarly class detailing his search for answers. Sitting with the rabbis in the chapel, Jerry wore a *kipah* and *tallit* (head covering and prayer shawl worn in more traditional synagogues). These were the same rabbis who would conduct Jerry's funeral service in this same chapel one year later.

In retirement Jerry had no trouble occupying his time. He delighted in expanding his knowledge of astronomy through courses at the University of Pittsburgh. This had been a lifelong interest. He used to take Bob and me to a dark field above Aliquippa High School where we lay on a blanket as he pointed out constellations with a flashlight. And I admired him for taking Mark to Cape Canaveral to watch the lift-off of the first manned rocket to the moon in 1969.

At last, there was time for leisurely visits with his children and grandchildren. He also pleased Irma by joining her in bridge lessons. But his obsessive drive for excellence marred his pleasure, prompting him to give up the game.

His interest in medicine never ceased. He continued to attend Grand Rounds weekly at the medical school. He recorded every lecture so that he could play each back, hearing them better via the tape than in person; he struggled with two hearing aids.

In Jerry's study there was much to attest to his scholarship. At Irma's request after Jerry died, it fell to me to throw out "everything," a painful experience. I found notebooks full of lecture notes on astronomy, bridge, and Judaica. His medical folders were filled with up-to-date articles as though he were planning to give a lecture the next day. Most fascinating were his daily notations of the time of sunrise and sunset, recorded for years. All of this I tossed. Family tree data I saved for whomever might use them; at least that would have pleased Jerry.

On a Friday Bob called to say that Jerry was to undergo an urgent coronary bypass operation. By the time I got to Pittsburgh the following morning, Jerry had awakened from successful surgery. The next five days were a gift to me. I spent hour after hour assisting him in small ways. Mainly he either slept or we talked, covering numerous subjects, some taking us into more personal areas than we had ever before ventured. It was as though we were once again on the road traveling to a meeting in a distant city, grateful for quiet time together.

Then came the scene forever engraved in my memory. Jerry asked me to help him sit up so that he could shave. During the attempt he slumped backwards, lapsing into a coma that continued until he died three days later. I have ruminated on whether we were too hasty in removing Jerry's life supports? My rationale came from knowledge of the site and extent of the infarcted brain and the overwhelming odds of imminent death. Further, Jerry and I had discussed two horrible "recoveries." One was cousin Saul Eger whose stroke left him totally paralyzed and aphasic; all he could do was cry in frustration. The other was a colleague who did better; he could sit in a wheelchair but not communicate. "I wouldn't appreciate living that kind of life." If Jerry were to recover at all, it would have been in that mode. Jerry's family, Bob, and I consented to the doctors' desire to desist.

The burial service began in the late afternoon at the temple. Mark delivered a brilliant and soulful eulogy. "So many times you tucked me in at bedtime and kissed me goodnight. Now I'm doing it to you." He ended with, "You used to say, ?My son, my son.' Now I'm saying to you, My father, my father." Jerry was buried in the dark and in pouring rain. It should have been under a starlit sky with at least one shooting star to announce his arrival.

Early after Jerry's death I had dreams, good visits with him. In one I was assigned to tell him that he had died; my pillow was soaked. How often I've wanted to call him on the phone to discuss my life or just to hear him say one more time, "*Dovid HaMelech.*"

BROTHER ALLEN, A LIFE TOO SHORT

At this moment I sorely wish for a hypnotist to take me back at least to ten years before Allen's death in 1943.

Memories of Allen have passed into oblivion leaving me only gleanings from others' memories, from photographs and 8-mm. movies, from recordings of his voice, his letters to Mom. But, alas, nothing specifically relating to me. Though I have mentioned the four of us – Jerry was already away at school – lying in one bed in the summers tickling each others' backs, Allen was only amorphously one of the other three. Oddly, I remember the ring that Uncle Dave Eger gave him (and each of us) for his *bar mitzvah* with his Hebrew initials and a tiny diamond. I see him wrestling with Irv on the living room floor; that still leaves me anxious that one of them would be hurt.

Photographs and movies reveal his sparkling, strikingly handsome face, his square chin with deep cleft, and his dark, wavy hair. He was about five feet seven inches tall like the rest of us; only Irv was taller by two inches. Cousin Bernice Eger Miller sent movies to brother Jerry. These were of her brother Milton acting up with Allen, both in uniform in Florida; they were doing a quick-march drill routine.

Pvt. Allen Chaimovitz on leave, 1943.

Unlike the rest of us, Allen never had any intention of being a doctor. During the year after high school he worked in Uncle Bill Eger's jewelry store in Leechburg, Pennsylvania so that he could be close to his girlfriend Helen Slomoff who lived nearby. He loved the business even though Uncle Bill was a hard taskmaster. The following year he joined Irv in entering Geneva College in Beaver Falls to prove, I believe, to Mom and Dad, that he was no dummy. That he did, with a "B" average. But one year was enough; he returned to the jewelry business, this time in Uncle Herman and Aunt Sarah's store in Aliquippa. In another year, 1942, he volunteered for the Air Corps.

Thanks to Norman Thomashefsky, Allen's voice was recorded at a farewell party in 1942 as he bid good-bye to Mom; he was being sent to Atlantic City for basic training. Oddly, he was billeted at the palatial Claridge Hotel where Mom and Dad had stayed not many years before. When Mom heard the recording, she was moved that he had asked her to sing from time to time one of our favorite, albeit tears-evoking, morbid songs, *Just For the Sake of Society*. The song tells of a woman whose children die in a fire while she's out playing cards with friends.

The whole family visited Allen early in his training in Atlantic City. How handsome he appeared in a starched khaki uniform. I believe that's a true memory but who's to say that the scene in my head doesn't come from a painting? A boardwalk artist made pastel crayon drawings of both Allen and Irv. This is the only souvenir that remains from my last contact with Allen.

Allen was sent to radio-gunner school in Alamogordo, New Mexico. Fate stepped in one day in June 1943 to get him to replace a previously assigned airman on a training mission. His B-24 was flying in formation and collided with another B-24; both crashed, each with a crew of ten young men on board. One airman survived.

Bob and I received the call at Geneva and came home immediately. Dad cried pitifully. Mom was pale and mute; she did not dance again until Bob's wedding in 1951 nor cry again until 1967 when we visited Rachel's tomb on the road to Bethlehem.

We were in limbo for two or three days until the flag-covered sealed casket containing Allen's remains arrived. At the time it seemed irrelevant to ask the accompanying airmen how he died. Had the planes exploded into flame? Had Allen suffered the awareness of his imminent death as he plummeted to the earth? The casket was placed on the dining room sideboard. Who knew what or who was in the box? I would stare at it, numb as I envisioned Allen falling from the sky. In retrospect it reminds me of the epitaph on Amy's tombstone that we quoted from one of her poems: "O May my falling be but a bow to you upon your altar, earth." She, too, fell, though only ten stories, to her death. Sometimes seeing Allen's shape walking on the street, as was to happen later with Amy, I would fantasize that Allen, not really dead, was a victim of amnesia, wandering, lost, somewhere in this world.

The United States flag that covered Allen's casket until the moment of interment was given to Mom. It lay on her piano until both she and Dad died in 1974. Subsequently the flag went to Irv and ultimately to his son Allen. I have two of Allen's medals, one each for marksmanship and for good conduct.

During the *shiva* (initial week of intensive mourning) I remember sitting in our cozy, blue breakfast nook upset that people were laughing as they discussed the Pittsburgh Pirates. How insensitive, how disrespectful of Allen and of me, I thought. How young and naive I was regarding the bereavement process. I remember sitting there also with Helen Slomoff, Allen's fiancée; a year later she was to marry Irv.

There were many who wished to perpetuate the memory of Allen. Norman Thomashefsky was the first to name his son for Allen a year after Allen died. Cousin Bernice Eger Miller followed suit in 1947 and brother Irv, in 1950. Allen's Aliquippa friends named their newly formed Jewish War Veterans Post 225 after "Allen H. Chaimovitz." (We surviving brothers changed the spelling to Chamovitz in 1948.) When this post was disbanded in April 1983, the $679 remaining in its treasury was donated to the Israel Defense Forces Medical Corps. A letter from Surgeon General M. Revach indicated that the money would benefit "wounded and sick soldiers recuperating in the Military Convalescent Home in Haifa." This letter and one of the dark blue overseas caps inscribed with Allen's name and worn by the Post's members were sent to the Jewish section of the Pennsylvania Historical Society in Pittsburgh.

Though I have demonstrated amply in my writings large gaps in my memory, it puzzles me that Allen has slipped so far away from me. Why am I left so bereft of even a single word between us, a single smile? Certainly he must have been one of my supportive big brothers.

In 1998 I was visited by Mickey Thomas, a close friend of Allen's and brother to Norman Thomashefsky mentioned previously. Trying to retrieve at least a fragment of a memory, I asked him to tell me something negative about my brother. "I can't. He was a completely lovable guy."

BROTHER IRV, MY BEST MAN

"Irv and Helen," was the answer when I asked daughters Raina and Amy their choice of guardians if the need arose. The reasons came easily. Uncle Irv and Aunt Helen were affectionate and incredibly cheerful despite the emotional burden of cerebral palsied Stuart and deeply retarded Laurie. Their house was a hubbub of excitement with sons Allen, Bruce, and Richard's friends and various nephews and nieces camping out, needing a change of venue under nurturing eyes.

Irv was number three of us five boys, born 364 days after Allen. Despite their one year difference I remember much more about Irv than I do about Allen. For example, I remember him getting long trousers, earlier than was the custom as an inducement to stop biting his fingernails. It was during a family visit to a winter Boy Scout camp that Irv prevailed upon Mom and Dad to let me remain one overnight; my tears alone had not been successful. And it was Irv who substituted for brother Bob as best man at my wedding; on duty in the Navy, Bob couldn't get leave. Irv, a believer of preventive medicine, alerted me, "Don't be overly concerned if you get nervous before the wedding. That's normal." For several anniversaries I called Irv, "When do I start getting nervous?"

It was during the third year at Geneva College that Irv decided on a medical career. He was accepted at Louisville Medical School in Kentucky under the auspices of ASTP, the army's special training program, which financed medical education in exchange for subsequent army service. Despite this financial assistance, Irv helped Dad by working summers, doing hard labor on the railroad. He would come home exhausted, covered with grease and coal dust after eight hours of laying railroad ties. This was in sharp contrast to Bob and me, who with summers filled with accelerated medical programs, earned nothing.

1944. After two years in medical school Irv married Helen Slomoff. This was a year after brother Allen was killed in an air force training accident; Helen had been Allen's fiancée. Irv and Helen were a "love match;" the marriage did not arise from any sense of religious obligation on Irv's part. July 1, the day of their wedding, found me in Boston for the opening day of medical school. But I did get to Irv's graduation. During the party that followed I remember dancing with Aunt Jenny Young. She scarred me permanently with, "You're a boring dancer." She was right.

During my third year of medical school, Helen brought their firstborn, Naomi, to Children's Hospital in Boston for an assessment. The diagnosis of hydrocephalus with severe brain damage was confirmed. No treatment was available for Naomi. She was placed in a chronic care facility where she died four years later.

Irv served in the Army 1949 to1951 in Cheyenne, Wyoming. Mom and Dad visited them when their second child, Allen, was born. Touring with Irv and Helen, they got to visit the sites of two of Dad's charities, the National Jewish Hospital (for lung disease) in Denver and Father Flanagan's Boys Town in Omaha.

The next couple of years Irv trained in pediatric neurology in Chicago at Bob Robert's Hospital under a world famous mentor, Douglas Buchanan. In my estimation this was one of medicine's most challenging specialties. An understanding of neuro-anatomy and working with the afflicted children and their parents require wisdom and compassion. In those respects, Irv was not to be excelled.

How fortuitous for me that the years of my army service in Fort Knox, Kentucky overlapped with Irv's residency at Bob Robert's. Chicago was an easy 200-mile drive away. I visited many weekends. It was there in 1953 that Irv and Helen saw me through a broken engagement.

Irv returned to Children's Hospital in Pittsburgh as its first pediatric neurologist. Building a practice was not to be as easy as Pittsburgh colleagues would have had him believe. Several of them had promised to refer all their epileptic children to him but when Irv opened his office, the promises turned into revelations that, "I've begun to enjoy taking care of epileptics." Nevertheless Irv slowly built up a large cadre of referring pediatricians and adult neurologists. Under his administration the hospital's electroencephalography department flourished.

Irv's family also blossomed but not always in a happy fashion. Following the birth of a healthy second son, Bruce, Stuart was born, afflicted with cerebral palsy and mental retardation. A few years later twins arrived: Richard, healthy and Laurie, severely retarded.

After a few years Irv was asked to go full-time. University salaries in that era were unacceptably low and Irv's family medical expenses were high. Accordingly he declined the appointment. Over the years time conspired against Irv. The hospital hired young pediatric neurologists while at the same time, Irv's grateful and faithful referrers retired or died. Irv was gradually squeezed out. One day during this later period I called Children's Hospital and asked to speak with Dr. Chamovitz. The telephone operator asked, "Can you spell it?" As is written in Exodus, "A king arose that knew not Joseph."

To take up the slack in his income, Irv found jobs at Crippled Children Association and at state institutions. For the latter, Irv was required to travel great distances and occasionally to remain overnight to complete his work. This proved especially exhausting as his strength failed in the last three years of his life.

Irv and I have both gotten into trouble with our style of humor. It didn't take him long to lose Marcia's sister Elaine's affection. It was at our wedding that Elaine was describing to Irv how wonderful I was with children. It was true that her daughter Vicki, age five, and I had hit it off. Irv couldn't escape from the gushy accolades for his kid brother. He finally retorted, "No wonder. He's got a child's mind."

Rather than appreciating his sense of humor, she took his remark as an insult to me and to her; she never forgave him. Some years later at a benefit for Children's Hospital Marcia and I were seated next to parents of one of Irv's patients. The mother was regaling me with compliments for Irv's handling of her and her husband. Finally, and only for Marcia's ears, I said, "No wonder. Irv's got an adult's mind."

In time we experienced for ourselves the aptness of that mother's compliments when Irv helped us with the care of Dan's febrile convulsion and during Amy's psychiatric admission to Homestead Hospital.

And then came the day I learned from Helen that their marriage had serious problems. Ten years later they legally separated but never divorced.

In 1991 three years after the separation and soon after the Gulf War, Irv spent three weeks with us. We toured much of Israel including our customary end-of-Pesach visit to Safed. There we visited the cemetery where our Zeyda is presumed to be buried. Farther north we took him to the Good Fence in Metula where Lebanese passed back and forth for jobs and health care. In Jerusalem at *Yad Vashem*, the Holocaust Memorial, Irv was drawn to the statue of Janusz Korczak, the martyred pediatrician, from the Warsaw ghetto, the "Dr. Spock" of Poland. Dr. Korczak, though not selected for deportation to Treblinka, chose to accompany the children of his orphanage into the gas chamber.

During that visit Irv formed a warm relationship with Yakov and Yardena Yalon, the parents of our daughter-in-law Shira. They guided him around Jerusalem, including another visit to Korczak's memorial. Irv subsequently reciprocated by escorting them for three days in Washington, D.C. To show their gratitude, they bought him a book of Klimt's paintings, which was constantly open in Irv's apartment. Irv loved visiting museums, and was himself a talented person with a sketchpad.

Whether by phone or in person, with every contact Irv would say to me, "I love you." How uncomfortable that made me. How was I to respond? I really didn't know. It just wasn't my other brothers' style or mine, to mouth this phrase. If the feeling was true, as I assumed it was, it sounded phony and needed no expressing. But what if not true? Then any words of love would be false. Well, I eventually got the words out that Irv was requesting but, in pausing, I probably failed his test, proving his suspicions that he was unlovable. I hoped the large block of time that we spent together on our frequent trips to America gave adequate testimony that we were loving brothers. He enjoyed taking us to the Three Rivers Art Festival, showing us the new subway, and taking me shopping for clothes; I trusted his selections.

During Irv's last few years he fell the victim of complications of cancer of the prostate. He suffered the side effects of pelvic irradiation and the hormone therapy that followed. Over the next few years the disease caused blockage of both kidneys and eventually his large bowel. These required external drainage operations and constant care of three "stomas" (surgically created openings leading from both kidneys and the large bowel through the abdominal wall). All this, Irv handled without complaint although he relied heavily on brothers Jerry and Bob, especially for urgent trips to the emergency room.

Irv and I said a tearful good-bye in his Presbyterian Hospital room about two months before he died. He eventually became comatose and died three days later; it was Thursday May 9, 1996. We got the call that night and arrived in Pittsburgh Saturday afternoon. Saturday evening Bob's wife Sheila made dinner for the three Chamovitz couples, Bob's daughter Julia, and her fiancé Brad. After dinner we recalled happy memories of Irv. Irv would have felt loved. That was until Jerry related sadly that two or three weeks earlier, Irv had asked Jerry to hug him. Jerry, who loved Irv and had devoted himself to Irv for months to the point of neglecting Irma, confessed that he couldn't and, therefore, didn't. Bob on the other hand indicated that Irv made the same request of him. "I hugged him even though I wasn't comfortable hugging on demand." It is so sad that such a simple exchange of affection with Irv became so emotionally loaded.

Irv was laid to rest at the New Kensington cemetery alongside his children Stuart and Laurie. Irv and Helen's close friend Rabbi Walter Jacob officiated, appropriately chosen since he had shared the personal tragedy of sick children with Irv and Helen. In addition he and Helen were principal movers in developing Horizon House, a residential home for children with severe mental retardation. The mother of one of Irv's patients, who himself was present, speaking for scores of grateful families, described Irv's compassionate care. Bruce described Irv's reaction to Bruce's smashing a new car; "As long as you're O.K., all's well." Richard conveyed the beauty of the moment watching his father shaving. Helen asked Jerry to speak; he was eloquent. "I'm speaking for Irv. There is no question in my mind that in his own way Irv loved Helen and his boys to the very end."

That evening and for the next two, *minyan* was held at Bruce's home. Danny Slomoff, Helen's nephew, conducted knowledgeably and soulfully on the second night. Bruce asked me to lead services on the last. I started by relating how Irv, as my best man, had alerted me to the probability of getting nervous before my wedding and how on each anniversary I would call him and ask, "When am I supposed to get nervous?" I confessed, "Well, at this moment I finally am."

At the end of a three-day *shiva* I asked Richard if I could have the Klimt art book that Irv had received from Shira's parents. Richard brought it to me but to my astonishment, in addition, he brought a stack of letters that I had written to Irv from 1988 to 1995. This tells me, I choose to believe, that he, too, treasured our relationship and that for him "I love you" was genuine.

BROTHER BOB, "SO CLOSE AND SEPARATE"

I was born the last of five boys – alas, not the daughter my parents wanted so badly. By definition that made me the *mazinik* (the youngest child). I usurped this title from Bob, arriving fourteen months after him. I also pushed him off the breast – not letting go for two years. Was Bob jealous? If so, I never felt it.

We weren't a verbally analytical family and yet on March 18 1996, the night before Bob was to undergo back surgery, he penciled a brief note to me. It read, "People would ask me why I never had many friends. I tell them I had David. Lucky to grow up so close and come out close and separate, too." That was a rare moment within a family that displayed but seldom spoke of affection.

Both Bob and Jerry, my oldest brother, grinned when I asked them why they never told me they loved me. We do sign our letters, "With love," but never, "I love you." It took two years for me to tell Marcia I loved her although I had made it clear from the first moment.

On the other hand, assisting one another financially was effortless. There was no feeling of imposition for Jerry and me to send Bob money while he was doing a gastroenterology fellowship in Philadelphia. Nor can I forget the $1,500 check that Bob sent me in Israel for plane fare to attend his daughter Julia's *bat mitzvah*. He assumed that the expense was preventing me from coming. Actually, the reason was the same as for my not returning to America for my father-in-law's funeral: I was beginning to study Hebrew, and, doing poorly, I was terrified of flunking out of *ulpan* (intensive Hebrew course for immigrants) and, consequently, out of Israel. I am being melodramatic; no one flunks.

I'm not so naive as to deny internecine conflicts. One I do remember. During high school days Bob and I climbed 208 steps up a wooded hillside in the morning and at noon, a third time if there was an evening activity. Especially after lunch we would scamper in order not to be late. Bob delighted in provoking me as he would speed ahead, stop, and block my upward progress. Lucky if that's all I can remember. I forgive you, Bob.

And imagine this nightly scene. We four boys – Jerry was out of the house after my fifth birthday – would sleep in one bed. Before falling asleep we tickled each other's backs in two shifts; we vied for the end position that was tickled last in the second shift. That lucky guy could fall asleep without further responsibility.

Living reasonably close to one another in adulthood, my brothers and I shared holidays and life-cycle events. Passover *seders* (ritual meal) were held mostly at either Jerry's house or ours. If at Bob's, he would play the *kiddush* melody on his flute and make soulful introductory remarks. Chanukah parties featured the giving of gifts and Chanukah *gelt,* briefly rehearsed skits by the children, and playing *dreidel.* For Succot *(the Feast of Tabernacles)* we had Bob's carpenter duplicate the *succah* (a wooden booth used during the holiday) he had constructed for Bob.

Sadly, there were too many opportunities to comfort one another as with Irv's loss of three children, the deaths of Bob's Cathy in an automoble accident, and our Amy.

In our youth Bob and I were inseparable, playing baseball, softball, and football in the sloping lot next to our house or in a larger, hillocky field a block away. We attended *cheder* both at our Aliquippa *shul* and later in West Aliquippa, requiring a streetcar ride plus a mile's walk.

AM

We also went to Saturday morning services in the latter *shul* where its aged congregation treated us like honored guests. We shared the activities of Troop 412 of the Boy Scouts of America which included weekly meetings at the *shul*, weekend hikes, and, especially, the fourteen-mile hike to Camp Umsteader, needed for a merit badge. We never confessed our failure to make the fire for cooking a meal; every twig was soaked from the previous night's downpour. Bob went on to become a First Class Scout, while, having failed semaphore signaling, I never advanced beyond Second Class.

And so many other activities. We played tennis well enough to be asked to join the Plan 6 tennis team. We could play on their court but Jews couldn't live in that part of town.

Almost every summer day we walked a mile along streetcar tracks overgrown with weeds and bushes to the Plan 12 swimming pool remaining there until dusk. We reveled on the steep sliding boards and, growing older, we graduated to the diving boards at the deep end of the pool. In those days it was an all-white pool; in our youth this moral issue was of no concern.

We worked together in Dad and Uncle Harry's shoe store. Our starting position was stock boy, dusting shoeboxes. Later we shifted stock, meaning we collated scattered styles into their respective groups. More exacting was stock controlling: when shipments of new shoes arrived, it was our task to fill out forms with size, style number, cost, (in code, to which we were proudly privy) and to put this form into the shoe box. In later years we became salesmen. How professional we felt as we checked our fittings by having the customer place his newly shod feet into a fluoroscopic machine. Little did we know how much radiation we were delivering to the customers and to ourselves; it wasn't many years later that this promotional gimmick was deemed a health hazard.

Even greater fun was passing bills. Newspaper advertising must have been too expensive. In its place prior to a seasonal shoe sale, handbills were printed and these we placed in mailboxes in one neighborhood after another. With eight of us working out of two cars, we would cover the whole town in one day. I can still taste the egg sandwiches and chocolate cream-filled cupcakes we consumed along the way. The only untoward event was my being bitten by a bulldog.

Our most exalted role in the shoe store was to be checkers for the twice-a-year inventory. The salespeople would record the number of each shoe style and multiply that number by the shoe's cost. After they filled a page, Bob and I would spring into action; we checked the multiplication figures and were paid a nickel for every mistake we found. Some days we made the grand sum of one dollar. Dad taught us not to be satisfied even if the variance was a penny: "There may be two large mistakes that nearly balance one another."

We made money in other ways. We sold flypaper in the days when poor general sanitation encouraged growth of the fly population and houses were inadequately screened. We frequently accompanied Dad out to the mining communities where his customers would buy the flypaper from Morris's cute little boys. The story goes that I once offered "two for a nickel, three for a dime."

In 1932 Bob and I started selling newspapers on Aliquippa's Franklin Avenue. It was in 1933 that we made thirty-four cents selling an extra. "Extra. Extra," we shouted. "Read all about it! Dillinger killed in Chicago!" Dillinger was the FBI's most wanted criminal. In later years we went house to house selling Spic and Span, a cleaning powder, making a profit of twenty-five cents a box.

In high school we sang in the Bach and a cappella choirs and played in the orchestra and band, Bob, the flute and I, the bassoon. In later years Bob studied the flute with his friend, Marty Lerner, who was second chair flautist of the Pittsburgh Symphony.

Friends smirk at my saying that I'm not a competitive person. It doesn't matter to me whether I win or lose at tennis or bridge as long as I've played well. I truly believe that I was not competitive with Bob. In truth, he was better than I at golf, tennis, and skiing. I remember being pleased that I made it to the tennis semi-finals in high school and that Bob made it to the finals. I doubt that it would have bothered him had I been better than he.

Nor did I resent him when I was passed over for the eighth grade American Legion Award which Bob had received the year before.

I confess. I *was* jealous of Bob's ease with girls. He would be out on a date while I would be mooning on solo strolls, not even knowing what I was missing. Blue-eyed Bob was the only blond in the family and women fell for his wistful, good looks.

Bob entered Geneva College in Beaver Falls, Pennsylvania, a year before me. We did overlap for one semester before he transferred to Bethany College in West Virginia under the Navy's V-12 college-assistance program. We entered medical school in the same year, he in Baltimore at the University of Maryland, I, in Boston at Harvard. I remember Bob visiting me in Boston in 1945. We were walking along the Fenway with our arms across each other's shoulders, Bob dressed in his Navy white sailor suit. The driver of a passing car shouted at us, "Hey, that doesn't go in Boston." We had never before felt self-conscious about body contact, to wit, the nighttime tickling. For me it was a moment of rude awakening to the world of homosexuality akin to Adam and Eve suddenly sensing their nakedness in the Garden of Eden.

For a month at the end of our first year in medical school Bob and I took an elective in radiology at Cleveland City Hospital under Dr. Harry Hauser; it was arranged by cousin Dan Jackson who was a resident in lung diseases there at the time. We spent our time going through x-ray teaching files and playing tennis.

Bob also visited me during my fourth-year rotation at McLean Psychiatric Hospital. He attended staff conferences with me and we played golf on a mangy course on the grounds which no one else used, least of all, the patients from blue-blooded Boston families.

I, in turn, visited Baltimore a couple of times where Bob arranged dates for me; having a limited number of female acquaintances, I could not have reciprocated.

We attended each other's graduation ceremonies, which fell a few days apart. Subsequently we interned in Pittsburgh, Bob, at Montefiore Hospital, I, at Presbyterian Hospital.

In 1949 we both got fellowships in Boston; Bob, in pathology at the Peter Bent Brigham Hospital, one of the most prestigious hospitals in the world; I, in nuclear-medicine research at the Beth Israel Hospital. We lived together in a rooming house, within walking distance of our jobs. Painting our one large room, three walls white, one, maroon, was an attempt at sophistication. Though we did enjoy many ski days together, we led separate lives, working very late hours. The following year Bob returned to the Montefiore Hospital in Pittsburgh, while I moved into the Beth Israel as a medical resident.

Subsequent years of training and military service found us in different parts of the country. I got a pass from the army to attend Bob's wedding to Florine Robbins in 1952 in Pittsburgh. Stationed in Cheyenne, Wyoming, he on the other hand was unable to be at my wedding in Brooklyn two years later. However, Bob did visit us soon after our honeymoon. Still, his absence at my wedding taught me to make every effort to attend family life-cycle events; viewing photographs is a poor substitute.

With encouragement from Bob, I introduced Marcia to skiing, giving her an initial lesson on the snow-covered Aliquippa Golf Course. Thereafter the four of us shared ski vacations at Seven Springs in the Allegheny Mountains and in Aspen, Colorado. It was during these trips that we became aware that Bob and Florine were having marital problems. When they finally separated after sixteen years of marriage, Bob led an unsettled life. For a while he even moved in with Irv and Helen. Subsequently Florine moved to Colorado. Their daughters Maxine and Cathy remained in Pittsburgh with Bob.

A new chapter began for Bob when he met Sheila Leff. Marcia gets credit for shortening their courtship. For a number of reasons, mostly relating to their age difference – Sheila was twenty-two years Bob's junior – Bob procrastinated. Sheila had planned a visit to her sister in London but was afraid of losing Bob if she went. Marcia said, "Go." After a two-day separation, Bob called London to ask Sheila to come home to get married. Together, they hosted a wedding in Sheila's family's backyard with Rabbi Leonard Winograd, Sheila's cousin, performing the ceremony. Those friends, who were concerned about the age differnce, worried in vain; as of this writing, the marriage has thrived for thirty years and has produced Julia and Max.

Both Bob and I volunteered at Hadassah Hospital in Jerusalem. He fulfilled a requested three-month stint in the gastroenterology department soon after its chief died, while I, a couple of years later in preparation for *aliyah*, gave five months of service over a four-year period in the nuclear medicine department. We both gave talks on behalf of Hadassah after our return. Bob, in his talk, contrasted the tall smokestacks at Jerusalem's Holocaust Memorial and Shaare Zedek Hospital, the first commemorating the Nazi death camps, the other, a life-giving institution.

Of all the family, Bob and Sheila have visited us in Israel the most. On one of these trips, because of Sheila's involvement with the American Jewish Committee, they were guests of King Hussein's brother Crown Prince Hassan of Jordan in 1987. Theirs was the first Jewish group to have an official tour of Jordan.

Bob made a generous donation to my isotope lab at Wolfson Hospital in Holon, Israel. More than the desire to help me buy equipment was his ploy to impress the hospital administration with my value as a fundraiser.

Neither Bob nor I feel comfortable expressing pain or guilt but, at least, we shared, even without words, each other's sadness over the deaths of Cathy and Amy. Otherwise, there isn't much that Bob and I haven't discussed – financial responsibility for the children, estate planning, the practice of medicine, tennis, our bad backs, and our prostates.

So, I too, have considered the absence of any best friend in my youth. Bob is correct. I didn't really need friends; I had him, and I still do.

COUSIN SIDNEY. "NO PROBLEM"

I ask, "How many friends do you have who will stop you on the street to enjoy the following exchange?"

"You owe me ten dollars."

Paying, I ask, "What *mitzvah* (good deed) am I sharing?" Obviously, Sid had donated twenty dollars to a worthy cause.

This chapter is about my cousin Sidney Eger. It comes on the heels of the chapters concerning my brothers. And well it should. It is no exaggeration to say that he was like a brother to me. In fact, our lives dovetailed in many spheres not shared with my brothers.

Sidney was born in 1917 and grew up in Aliquippa, living just a block away from us. As youngsters we were in and out of each other's homes. He loved my parents, especially my father, since his own father, Uncle Jake, half brother to my mother, was especially tyrannical towards Sidney. His mother, my Aunt Sadie, though a good friend to my mother, was a critical person. In such a household it was surprising that Sidney had such a pleasant disposition. Others seemed to harbor resentment of one kind or another. Saul, the oldest brother, for example, frequently, understandingly, expressed bitterness for having to settle for Hahnemann Medical School, at the time a school with a poor reputation; the enrollment was heavily weighted with Jewish students denied admission elsewhere because of rigid quotas.

How was it then that Sidney was everyone's friend? Growing up amidst this psychopathology, how was it that he didn't have a mean bone in his body? And how did he overcome his feelings of inferiority of being a storekeeper among professional siblings and cousins?

Sidney and I didn't begin a significant relationship until I moved back to Aliquippa in 1956. His hair had turned pale blond; in his youth my mother called him "Gingi" (redhead). He had developed a paunch. Sid's Home Supply store was next to Eger's jewelry store; I rented rooms above the latter for my first medical office. Sid provided items for the office as well as for our house charging me only his cost, maybe less. Whatever I needed, his stock answer, later famous throughout the community, was "No problem." I remember searching medical-supply catalogues looking in vain for a special concave neck pillow for patients with cervical arthritis. "No problem." Sid was able to supply them.

When I returned to Aliquippa, our old Orthodox synagogue on Church Street near Aliquippa's downtown was still in use but the move to build a new synagogue and to transfer affiliation to the Conservative Movement was already in the works. It was after this transition that I became involved on the *shul* board. Whatever the issue, Sid and I were always in agreement. We resisted punitive treatment of "dues shirkers" or those, obsessed with decorum, who tried to exclude children from religious services. We always supported the various rabbis, shielding them from petty detractors, though this support did not extend to one rabbi who was emotionally unsuited for the pulpit.

One Yom Kippur eve Sid and I incurred the wrath of the congregation by auctioning various honors (such as being called to the Torah or to open the Torah Ark) ordinarily distributed randomly. We had no thought of reviving this grossly undemocratic practice. Rather it was an attempt to offer a bit of nostalgia for those older members who remembered this as an amusing interlude during the High Holidays in the old Church Street synagogue. The result? Apathy for most but anger for a vociferous few. There was a paucity of bidders; several members stomped out of the synagogue. It was a terrible blunder. Although the ritual committee had given its approval, we obviously had not prepared the congregation.

Sid and I rotated from year to year as ritual chairman. In this capacity we saw to it that the services proceeded smoothly, preparing members as we distributed honors and maintaining decorum within very lenient limits. We were hardly uniformly loved, but no one rushed to replace us.

Sid and his wife Rose took Marcia and me to our first United Jewish Appeal (UJA) function, a Young Leadership Mission weekend in Cleveland. Rabbi Herbert Friedman, a charismatic speaker, hooked and reeled us in. From that moment Sid and I were prime movers in both the local UJA activities and the promotion of the sale of Israel Bonds. (In those days, ninety percent of UJA funds went to Israel or to meet other world Jewry needs, whereas at the present time, over fifty percent remains in the USA, primarily for education.) Frequently we teamed up to solicit tough prospects who were nongivers to UJA. We "struck out" with otherwise good-hearted Barney Snyder, a junk dealer. "I wouldn't give nothing to those Israelians." He complained that not enough had been done for his aunt when she made *aliyah*. Years later Barney began buying Israel bonds and even later still, became a significant contributor to my nuclear medicine department in Israel. Barney's having a generous Zionist wife might have been the key.

While Sid and Rose traveled to Israel and Europe in 1964, their children Jeff, seventeen, and Bonnie, sixteen, lived with us. I still wear a ski sweater, which was one of their gifts.

Years later, serving as master of ceremonies at an Israel Bonds dinner, Sid fumbled with his glasses. He adlibbed, "See these glasses? They cost me $50,000." These were the first prescribed by Jeff, by then an optometrist. Jeff expressed bitterness that his father hadn't mentioned that the debt had been repaid.

Sidney's good deeds were performed without fanfare. One especially bears noting. Sid and Rose had been close to our cousin Ruth Eger Levenson and her husband Fred, even more so once Ruth became housebound in 1981 from multiple sclerosis. Mindful of Fred's tremendous expenditure of energy to attend to Ruth's physical needs and later the high cost of her medical care, Sid wrote a letter to members of our Eger family. It was a beautiful request, reminding us when, years before, the family had pulled together to help defray the financial outlay for the care of Bobie Eger. Stressing that the initiative was totally his, he emphasized Freddie's discomfort with the gesture. The response was magnanimous in terms of money – around $8,000 – and in accolades for Sidney. Uncomfortable receiving praise, Sidney would sheepishly reply, "Who is likened unto me, Oh Lord?" Only one cousin complained: "We have our own problems." And when Sidney felt that a conversation was becoming distateful, he would say, "Next case."

Playing golf with Sidney was pure joy. His banter was cheerful and capricious. Neither of us was competitive; we were happy for one another after a good shot. Sid would say, "It's my therapy." He played the buffoon with the golf-course crowd, enjoying the warm reception, and ignoring occasional anti-Semitic innuendoes.

We frequently ate in each other's homes and we socialized together with mutual friends. But it was plain to see that Sid was overwhelmed by Rose's neurotic behavior. She had had emotional problems since childhood and was frequently in need of psychiatric care. She was a constant source of embarrassment as she drove away old friends. Yet Rose was a wonderful hostess to the family. She succeeded in getting a BA degree from Geneva College in Beaver Falls, Pennsylvania after years of part-time study – she and Bonnie graduated together – and she became a bubbly kindergarten teacher.

Shortly after Sid suffered a mild heart attack, he focused more and more on his unhappiness with Rose. Doubtlessly the heart attack raised the specter of a life cut short. As Sidney's doctor I suggested a diagnostic psychiatric interview. Aware of the psychiatrist's (Karl Lewin) success with two close acquaintances, he leaped at the suggestion.

At the end of the first hour Karl gave Sid three options: 1. Leave Rose. 2. Take a mistress. 3. Accept the present situation. The result was magical. Sid realized that no way could he adopt either of the first two options. Therefore option number three was all that was left. His free-floating anxiety dissipated.

On time for his second session, Sid kept pressing Karl's doorbell.

When Karl was finally free to answer, Sidney quipped, "What's the matter? Need a hearing aid?" For the next hour they discussed Sid's unbridled sense of humor. When Sid related the subject of the session, I begged, "Quick, tell me what he said." It was evident to many that I suffered from the same malady. Karl discussed with him the elements of inferiority and hostility in sarcastic humor.

The day we moved into our house, a stone's throw from the hospital, a stranger came to our front door and asked Marcia, "Is this the Aliquippa Hospital?"

Marcia reacted instinctively, "Tell Sid Eger to stop with his jokes." The stranger, nonplussed as he realized his mistake, retreated to the somewhat bigger building up the road.

One of the happiest days of Sidney's life was his sixty-fifth birthday. For weeks, cousin Evie, Marcia, and I planned a surprise party. Sid and Rose came to our house ostensibly to drive Marcia and me to *shul.* When he heard "Surprise!" he uttered something akin to "Jesus Christ." Hugging and kissing took up the next half hour. Bonnie had come from Atlanta with her two boys, Jeff, from Arizona. Guests included Sid's sister Dorothy, numerous cousins, friends from the Jewish community, UJA, and Israel Bonds, business friends like Steve Plodinec, and Sid's golf course buddies.

Marcia had prepared a couple of her famous musical parodies. She, Evie, and I sang her words to "Tit Willow": "On a tree by a willow a Sidney bird sat, singing, 'No problem, no problem, no problem'," ending with Sidney's oft-repeated risqué expression, "That's just what the girl told me last night."

The pièce de résistance was a belly dancer, a gift from Evie to her favorite cousin. Sid sat regally in a high-back chair with a grandson on each side. The performer, a professional, skantily attired, young woman went through her routine directly in front of Sid. Sid who frequently talked "dirty," – he was a one-woman man – blushed like a teenaged boy and was as excited as if he had hit a hole-in-one golf shot. Grandson Steven said to Bonnie, "This isn't good for Grandpa; he'll have a heart attack." I don't know who was more ecstatic, Sid or Evie.

One sad day two years later in 1984 Sid admitted having a problem with his right leg while driving the car. "It just doesn't seem accurate." A CT scan diagnosed a brain tumor. The prognosis was terrible. There was no way to cure him and even the options presented to him were spoken with little enthusiasm. The neurosurgeon however pontificated, "We must do everything we can on the outside chance of giving Sid more meaningful time." He suggested a craniotomy to remove as much of the tumor as possible and then follow-up with chemotherapy. How could Sid's family say "No" to that? Jerry's gut reaction – and mine – was to let the disease progress without adding the side effects of treatment since at best, with or without treatment, Sid would have only a few months to live.

After the surgery, though fully aware of his surroundings, Sid lost much of his ability to communicate. Never again did he walk unassisted. He needed a full-time nurse.

One afternoon I concocted a marvelous plan. (Permit me to brag.) First I alerted John Darak, the golf pro. With the help of the nurse I got Sid into my car. Johnny, riding a golf cart, met us at the golf course parking lot. We maneuvered Sid onto the cart, propping him up by sitting on each side of him. For the next half hour we rode up and down the fairways, stopping long enough for Sid to be greeted by his friends and for him to smile in return. He was elated; I was teary-eyed. It was beautiful, Sid saying good-bye to a significant chapter in his life.

It wasn't long after this that Marcia and I moved to Israel. Two months later, Sid was dead. Just as I had elected not to return for my father-in-law's funeral, so, too, I could not free myself from my Hebrew studies for Sidney's. Jeff couldn't appreciate how depressed I was over the prospect of "flunking" out of *ulpan*. Bonnie tried to assuage my feelings of guilt.

A couple of months later Marcia took a picture of a store near our apartment. It was called – in Hebrew of course – "No Problem." She sent it to Bonnie. Bonnie subsequently related to us how wonderful brother Irv was to Sidney during his final days and how comforting he was to her during the *shiva*. She quotes herself saying to Irv, "You're your brother David in another body."

Sidney, the son who was victimized by his parents, who didn't have a profession, who didn't go to college, who didn't serve in a political office, and who was not a fire-brand merchant – all this in contrast to his siblings – was outstanding as an exemplary husband, a loving father, an active participant in the community, a friend to all, and a performer of countless good deeds. In Mom's words Sid was a *shteck golt* (a piece of gold). In my words he was a *lamed vovnik*, one of the anonymous thirty-six righteous men on whose sanctity the world exists.

RAINA. "IT'S A GIRL AND HE WEIGHS . . ."

For Marcia and me to bear children was mandated by the same confounded logic which rushed us into marriage four months after falling in love at first sight. Raina's birth one day after our first wedding anniversary gave testimony to our undaunted intention to experience all that the good life would allow us. And with Raina we hit the jackpot.

Raina was born by caesarian section on March 15, 1955 in Boston. A few minutes after, I phoned my mother with the news: "Marcia had a little girl and *he* weighed 8 pounds 13 ounces." I don't remember Mom picking up on my Freudian slip but just as soon as the words had left my mouth, instant replay revealed my unspoken disappointment. Having been raised in a world of brothers only, I had not even contemplated the possibility of a daughter. Even Marcia had toyed with names of boys only. Dr. Samuel Gargill, a Beth Israel Hospital teacher, diagnosed my mood saying, "How lucky your first-born is a girl, if by chance you'll have no more children" – he had three daughters. And he was right; the first time I held Raina all disappointment vanished.

After two months a friend thought it necessary to encourage me, "Wait till Raina is two years old. Then you'll begin to enjoy her." Ridiculous! We were enjoying her responsiveness from day one, possibly, in part, because she was two to four weeks post-mature. Over the next few weeks we evoked coos and giggles unprecedented in the history of the world, or so it seemed.

I remember well when Raina was three months old rocking her in my arms in our living room in Boston while Marcia was in the kitchen preparing dinner. I looked into Raina's brown eyes and said aloud, "I'll kill the son of a bitch . . ." referring, of course, to a guy who on some future day would hurt my Raina. Marcia laughed hysterically.

Raina was a gratifying nurser and sleeper, that is, once she got to sleep. My mother-in-law Madge started the practice of patting her to sleep. Try as we might we could not alter this pattern. When we tried slowing the rate or reducing the intensity of the patting, Raina would go, "Uh, uh," to let us know that she wasn't asleep. Finally one night during our first month back in Aliquippa when Raina was fifteen months old, we let her scream it out, our hearts pounding as we clutched one another for support – or was it to restrain one another from rushing into her room? The next night the crying period was brief and from then on, she went to sleep without tears and alone in her crib. I'm reminded of Karl Lewin's book, *Heritage of Illusions.* He defines the critical moment that unconditional love from a parent ceases to be when Mother says, "No, not in your diaper. In the toilet." For Raina it was the night of screams.

Under the category of "Children Say the Funniest Things" came the following incident – Raina was two. I was standing at the bathroom sink using shaving foam. Raina reached up for the can and started ejecting foam from it. I reacted, "Did you ask my permission?"

Raina looked up to the ceiling and asked, "Permission, may I use Daddy's soap?"

Amy was born eighteen months after Raina. How impressed I was with Madge when she orchestrated placing Amy on Raina's lap the moment of Amy's arrival from the hospital. Did this lessen the blow to Raina? Raina confessed years later that though she may have hidden her jealousy, she did tease and poke Amy when we weren't looking.

By the time Amy grew out of infancy she and Raina were inseparable. What we did with one, we did with the other, whether it was building a snowman or playing "fox and geese" in new-fallen snow, skiing at Seven Springs Resort, or horseback riding within the confines of a corral. And when Marcia was away for Hadassah conventions, the three of us would have a "date," dinner and a movie in Pittsburgh. How fortunate I felt with a daughter holding each of my hands, walking, even occasionally skipping, along the city streets.

Raina entered first grade at age five and a half. To us she seemed socially mature enough to be among the youngest in her class. An evaluation at the Sewickley Children's Guidance Center confirmed our assessment. As years passed we were less confident of our decision. Being older than her classmates might have bolstered her ego. She might have resorted less to overeating; in her teenage years she did not succeed in fighting a weight problem. It was only after she graduated from college, moved to Israel, and had a gratifying job, that she slimmed down to a size that satisfied her.

When Raina was eight, Danny was born. Their bonding occasionally left Amy an outsider.

In 1966 we ventured out for a four-week station wagon trip to California. Raina was eleven, Amy ten, and Danny three. At our first stop, at the home of the Margolins in Cincinnati (Gordon had become my friend during basic army training at Fort Sam Houston in Texas), our children played quite naturally with their two deaf children. On the second day driving west, Danny asked, "Does this mean we're never going home forever and ever?" It was a pleasant surprise that even the children enjoyed Independence, Missouri, its Truman Library, and walking around Truman's white clapboard house.

And what good sports the kids were, when after a 500-mile drive to sweltering Goodland, Kansas, we learned that the one reservation made without prepayment was not honored. We all were glum as we drove away, gazing back at the swimming pool, sliding board, and all. And the next available lodging was another eighty miles away.

I was sorely tested as we sat in the elegant restaurant at the Broadmoor Hotel in Colorado Springs. What was I to do as I looked at my festively dressed family watching me when I learned that our inflated room rate did not include meals? Get up and go to a diner? I eyed each of them, looked at Marcia for support, and said to myself "Oh, what the hell!" The food was almost worth the extravagance.

Of all the visits, Mesa Verde stands out. Climbing in and out of Indian cliff dwellings added reality to an educational experience.

In Hollywood we acquiesced to the girls' wishes to linger at the home of David McCallum, TV star of "The Man From Uncle" though he was nowhere to be seen. We did the obligatory Disney World and Universal Studios, lifting virtually weightless fake boulders. The children tolerated the long waiting lines with adult patience.

Four weeks together can be a challenge to the equanimity of any family especially when attempting to juggle the interests of the eight-year age span of the children. Boring parts of the day's travel were broken up by filling in a chart containing the names of the fifty states when we encountered that state's auto-license plate. Passengers in the car from Maine must have thought us crazy as we waved and jumped about, filling in the final missing check mark. Marcia had one break from us; at Tahoe, under the cover of going out to do the laundry, she sneaked away from the laundromat to gamble at a roulette table – the laundry costs were higher than anticipated. Except for Dan's infected nose, causing us to return home a day early, the trip exceeded our expectations.

The following summer's programming was our next agenda item. Raina's cousin Vicki, older by six years, impressed us with a description of her Camp Ramah summer experiences. Marcia and I were anxious to expose our girls to the same Jewish enrichment program. The Ramah Camp for the Pittsburgh area was in Utterson, Ontario. Both girls balked at the idea, especially, Raina. "I want to spend the summer here with my school friends." Our compromise was that they would go to Ramah that summer but need not return in subsequent years.

On visitor's day half way through the summer, Raina and Amy met us as we drove into the parking lot. "We're coming back next summer." There were so many positive experiences, even observing the sad Jewish holiday, *Tisha b'Av,* which commemorates the destruction of the first and second Temples. Stan Sperber, now director of the Haifa Symphony, was the music counselor; they both fell in love with him. Raina's summer was somewhat marred by Amy's homesickness and yet the following summer it was only Raina who stayed home, getting her wish to be with her friends. The next summer she did return to Ramah.

I've described our family trip to Israel in 1967 in detail (*Going Up in the World)* but one event most significant for Raina bears repeating. Soon after checking into the Shulamit Hotel in Haifa, our first evening in Israel, we put my mother to bed and took a walk. We heard dance music and traced it to a school building. Young teenage scouts were having a Hanukah party. Looking through a window, Raina and Amy were noticed and immediately invited inside. Lo and behold, within hours of arriving in Israel my girls were dancing the *hora*, competently because of Ramah. Raina's reaction? She wrote in her diary that night, "One day I'm coming back to live in Israel."

A few months before this trip to Israel Raina celebrated her *bat mitzvah*. Her talk, including her analysis of the *Haftarah* and expressions of gratitude, was delivered in excellent Hebrew – for herself – and in English – for the rest of us. Several years later during a Brandeis University semester in Israel an event occurred which validated her adeptness with Hebrew. She came to stay with us when we were guests at the Dan Hotel in Tel Aviv. In need of stamps, Raina went downstairs to the concierge. "Sorry, I don't have any." As Raina was walking away, she overheard a hotel guest making the same request. The concierge promptly pulled out a folder and filled the order for stamps. Raina indignantly returned to the concierge to do battle. "But young lady," he explained, "these stamps are for tourists only."

Raina replied, – the entire conversation was in Hebrew – "But I *am* a tourist."

The concierge gave Raina one of her most memorable compliments. "Not true. You're a *sabareet* (a native-born Israeli)." Though not convinced, he reluctantly sold her the stamps. Raina returned to our room triumphant.

Raina's Ramah experience was tarnished by the personality of its director. In 1975, he rejected her for a job as a counselor. He was prejudiced against her since her early Hebrew study had been in a tiny congregation school. "As I remember, your Hebrew isn't very good." She fumed when he denied her the opportunity to demonstrate her fluency. Subsequently, to our delight, Young Judaea Camp in Hendersonville, North Carolina hired her. She spent a summer there, the same time that Danny was a camper.

Another conflict concerned her schedule in eighth grade. Raina had elected a study hall as her choice for a daily free period. Though the study hall was meant for performing homework, it amounted to little more than fun and games. We put our collective foot down and said, "No." After pulling out the "I'm old enough to decide" stop, she finally agreed to take chorus; I doubt if this did much more for her development than study halls would have, but the point was made that learning is a serious matter.

Basically cheerful, Raina struggled and fretted primarily about her excess weight. It didn't help that we thought she was beautiful. She would express her frustration to Marcia with whom she also had scenes about her haircuts and clothes. Conflicts with her, however, were few; she somehow knew our limits.

After the sophomore year at Hopewell High School, Raina applied for transfer to Sewickley Academy, a prestigious private school across the Ohio River. One of her best friends and a cousin were already students there. Raina sensed that they were stimulated more by their studies than she was. At the interview with the headmaster, Mr. Cavalier, Raina's first comment was, "Cavalier. Like the Cavaliers and the Roundheads of the English Revolution?" The headmaster was impressed with her knowledge of history. She concealed the fact that she encountered the name while reading a torrid novel, "Forever Amber." Mr. Cavalier commented during the interview that with the Academy's high standards, Raina's class position might be lower than it was at Hopewell High School. "Why is that important?", Raina asked. We were proud of having reared our daughter so that she was naive about the importance of class standing in being accepted by colleges. How nice that our children could excel without the incessant prodding some parents initiate in first grade.

My impression of Raina's Sewickley Academy experience on balance was favorable. Without a doubt she was challenged intellectually more than if she had remained at Hopewell. But there was the abusive, politically right-wing, athletic coach/history teacher who delighted in goading Raina. Finally, when we felt it was time to intervene, the three of us went to Mr. Cavalier. With a hand on Raina's shoulder he said, "Well, Raina, one of Mr. Webster's problems is being confronted by a student from a home where politics are discussed freely and especially from a liberal perspective. Many of our students are reared by household help while their parents are either busy or on the Riviera." Raina and we, too, were complimented and, as always, impressed with the Academy's good fortune to have such a stellar headmaster. And after that, Mr. Webster behaved.

Although Raina's was the marijuana generation, we never raised the issue with her. We were oblivious of her experiments at B'nai Brith Youth Organization (BBYO) functions and at Sewickley Academy where the practice was rampant. We were naive as to why Raina seemed "high" at her graduation. Fortunately for Raina, though subsequently not so for Amy, there was no progression to another level of potentially addictive drugs.

Raina spent three summers at Camp Ramah in Canada. At age sixteen she toured Israel on a Ramah program. Unfortunately there was no Ramah carryover into the school year. The vacuum was filled by BBYO but we were disappointed in its goals and achievements; they fell far short as compared to those of Danny's subsequent Young Judaea experience. It did provide activities with Jewish teenagers when her school friends were all Christian. Her summer visit to Israel in 1972 was disappointing because of an incompatible traveling companion; Raina hadn't anticipated her friend's low energy level, her slow pace, or her lack of enthusiasm for their Israel adventure.

It was while Raina was attending a BBYO weekend in New Kensington that I was awakened late at night by a phone call. It was a hospital emergency-room nurse, trying to tell me something about Raina while in the background I could hear Raina making efforts to take the phone from her. Raina had learned the difference between a potentially traumatic call from a husband saying, "Honey, I'm feeling O.K. but I'm here in the emergency room" rather than from a nurse saying, "We have your husband here in the emergency room." The problem was no more than an irritation from a contact lens. I was relieved and proud of Raina's judgment.

Visits for college interviews were Marcia's province. Amy managed hers on her own, while subsequently with Dan we divided the responsibility. What a pleasure it was for Marcia to show off Sarah Lawrence, her college, but Raina was not attracted to the student body or maybe she was avoiding comparison with her mother. On the other hand, she was attracted by an air of excitement at twenty-five-year-old Brandeis University (in Waltham, a suburb of Boston). It was small and open to change. One week after matriculating, Raina called to register pleasure with her choice of colleges and her love of the city, "Why did we ever leave Boston?" (when she was one year old).

I did very few things alone with Raina. I knew it was special when I traveled without Marcia to Brandeis to witness her installation as a Phi Beta Kappa (a prestigious honorary national college society) in 1975 at the end of her junior year.

A year later along with Marcia's parents we attended Raina's graduation. Commencement speaker Texas congresswoman Barbara Jordan asked, "Where have all of you been these last four years? Previous classes used to be at my door protesting this or demanding that but not a murmur from this class." The truth was that Brandeis was reeling from bad publicity caused by civil rights activist Angela Davis, a Brandeis student a few years before Raina. The selection committee did a 180-degree about-face, accepting only safe applicants such as Raina and yeshiva graduates – no rabble-rousers. Amy probably would not have stood muster. Raina developed a fighting spirit only after entering college.

Raina's saga leading to medical school is described in detail in the chapter, "Inherited values, not inherited professions." Suffice it to say that she started out as a pre-med student. During the first semester she witnessed with abhorrence the merciless competition among her fellow pre-meds fighting by any means for top class standings. Developing an antipathy for these combatants, she switched to psychology.

On the positive side at Brandeis, Raina became intimately involved in two subjects that subsequently assumed much importance to her successful *aliyah*. First, was the Student Sexual Information Service which offered 24-hour/day call-in, walk-in advice. From the training she received and the experience she accumulated, Raina was able to give lectures in Israel to classes of female soldiers, to mixed groups, and even to young married couples. Once on our visit in Jerusalem Raina asked me to buy a *Playboy* magazine. She wanted it as a prop in a seminar conducted jointly with a Pittsburgh-Brandeis friend, Steve Kaplan. Raina was to say to Steve, "Look what I found under *your* son's pillow! What are *you* going to do about it?"

When Raina was a young teenager, I gave sex talks to youngsters from Aliquippa's Jewish Sunday School (and even to teenagers from St. Titus Catholic church). I shudder to recall my Victorian concepts. Once on discussing mutual respect between boys and girls, I made reference to sex without respect being equivalent to "using a sheep." Soon after, at a BBYO party one of the boys approached Raina and bleated, "Baa-baa;" she blushed, fully cognizant of its reference. Despite this, my girls were proud of my being an early advocate of enlightened sex education.

In truth even though a few years separated our involvement in sex education, as a teacher Raina was a generation ahead of me. So it was natural that soon after making *aliyah* in August 1977, she volunteered for service to Shilo, an organization – the first of its kind in Israel – to help infertile couples as well as young women with unwanted pregnancies. After one year Raina became Shilo's executive director, continuing for three years until entering medical school.

The second subject that Raina mastered at Brandeis was Re-evaluation Counseling, also called Cocounseling. At first a grateful participant, she eventually became a leader and teacher of this psychological support system. In Israel it not only gave comfort in the early, lonely years of her *aliyah*, but also was crucial at two critical moments in her life. The first incident occurred late one night at a woman's conference in Paris during a confrontation with a group of her cocounseling friends. Out of it came the realization that she, herself, wanted to be a doctor and not from any parental pressure. That night she decided to apply to medical school. The second significant moment was at a weekend cocounseling conference when she received the news of Amy's death. For a few hours after she made arrangements to fly to the United States, numerous friends, using cocounseling techniques, helped her grieve.

Fate was working overtime one night in Jerusalem when one of her cocounseling students brought her brother Zvika to Raina's class – and not with emotional support in mind. There was instant chemistry between him and Raina. Two weeks later Raina flew to the United States for Thanksgiving, bursting into tears the moment she saw us at the Pittsburgh airport. The problem? "What shall I do?" A firm cocounseling rule forbade any fraternizing between participants. This was to free the handholding, important to the cocounseling technique, of any lustful implications. "If I date Zvika, I'll have to leave the cocounseling community. Oh, me." The solution seemed simple enough. Zvika's sister obviously brought him to have a look at Raina and not particularly for him to join the class. In any event, rules be damned: they married.

In my chapter about Amy I describe Raina's return for her funeral where she gave a tearful eulogy; a year later she returned for the unveiling of Amy's gravestone. It was following the latter ceremony that we had a ski week in Vail, Colorado. One sign, that all four of us were now able to get on with our lives, was the continuous laughter on the slopes, at mealtime, and at the erotic movie, "Ten." That the trip was restorative is documented by a poster-sized photo of the four of us grinning at the top of Vail Mountain.

I've already written (see chapter, "Inherited values . . .") about Raina's crestfallen state when I reacted coolly to the announcement of her intention to apply to medical school. The misreading of my expectations of her has now been corrected. For the record I can here relate my admiration for Raina, for being accepted into the prestigious Hadassah Medical School, Israel's first medical school, she as their first primarily English-speaking student. I also admired her trudging through the six-year college-medical school program, having already completed four years at Brandeis. Along the way she picked up a second bachelor's and a master's degree. How proud I was to learn in the first year that she had led an effort to halt cheating on exams. Apparently no one in authority was impressed.

I respected Raina's opting for an internship at Shaare Zedek Hospital, a teaching hospital under Orthodox auspices, rather than at Hadassah Hospital, both in Jerusalem. She based her decision on the former being more family-friendly to the house staff. Hadassah interns and residents seldom arrived home before 10 PM.

Initially Raina thought of entering practice after her internship or after no more than an additional year of residency partly to begin earning money and also to have more time for her family. Zvika wisely convinced her that with competition from the influx of a vast number of general practitioners from the then USSR, jobs would be scarce. She therefore elected to continue training toward specialization in family practice.

Over the years, reports of growing respect by patients and colleagues have trickled in. For example, one day Raina received a call from a former teacher, one of Hadassah's most illustrious oncologists. "Raina," he asked, "Would you consider becoming my eighty-five-year-old mother's doctor?"

Raina thanked him for the honor of his request but indicated, "I'm sorry but I'm afraid my patient load prevents me from taking on any new patients."

"But, Raina," he persisted, "I like the way you don't give up on your aged patients." Only the day before, he had seen Raina in the outpatient department accompanying an aged patient during a treatment-planning discussion with an oncologist. How could Raina then refuse her caller's request?

The latest compliment came via Danny's father-in-law Yakov. At a swimming pool in Jerusalem, a friend complained about not feeling well for an extended period. "Why don't you go see your doctor?"

"That's the problem. My doctor is away and no one else is half as good as she is."

"Your doctor sounds like Raina Rosenberg."

Danny and Raina, 1996, at Maia's Bat Mitzvah party.

"How did you know?" Yakov went on to explain his relationship to her and to update him on Raina's sabbatical year in Pittsburgh. (This was 1998. Raina had a fellowship at St. Margaret's Hospital in Pittsburgh on teaching family-medicine residents. A more important motive for the year abroad was to expose her daughters Maia and Tamar to a year of English-speaking schools.)

Raina is aware of my pleasure when she calls to describe a patient's problem or when she calls to consult me with a question relating to cardiology or nuclear medicine. On the other hand, more and more I lean on her for personal medical advice. It is beyond my comprehension how she can manage all the responsibilities of being a physician, wife, and mother. I say this knowing that having a helpmate like Zvika has been crucial to her success. In my own career I had only me to take care of. Another comparison. In the realm of family doctoring, I have no doubt that Raina surpasses me. From her innate talent plus her pursuits prior to entering medical school, she has developed into a better listener and a more directive counselor than I am.

I cannot quantify the love I feel for my first-born or the gratitude I feel toward her for much of the good in my life. I do believe we programmed one another so that we would be living together in Israel; I for taking her on her first trip to Israel in 1967, and she for preceding me by seven years in making *aliyah*.

Now tell me, are we and the world not better off for our having brought Raina into existence?

AMY

I am unclear as to my motivation for writing an autobiography. So how baffled, incredulous, I am that I would attempt to deal with our daughter Amy, dead by her own hand at age twenty-two. This chapter will serve as a memorial to her for those who loved her and for those who would have, had they known her.

Amy arrived September 5, 1956 by caesarean section a year and a half after Raina. That she was different from her sister was soon evident. Amy was generally more passive. Not a good nurser and preferring a bottle, she gave up the breast at three months. Amy was intellectually precocious, understanding language and mimicking our finger games before six months. She was a fatter baby and was a better sleeper than Raina. Early on she became a thumb sucker and relied on her security blanket.

Her senses were fragile. Marcia took the girls to the Heinz factory when Amy was three. The smell of vinegar distressed her terribly but what could she do? Both of her hands were occupied, one holding a banister, the other, her security blanket. Raina, walking alongside her, saved the day by pinching shut Amy's nostrils.

Many textures were offensive to her. She would often change her clothes because the material didn't feel good. Her frustration threshold was very low. One day when Amy was three, as my brother Jerry and his wife Irma were preparing to leave after a short visit, Amy awoke from a nap. Realizing that she had missed the visit, she pleaded, "Start all over again."

It was not easy to deal with Amy's whining. At age six when we were skiing at Bear Rocks in the Allegheny Mountains, she complained of pain in her leg after a gentle fall. I looked at the leg and found nothing unusual. Thus her complaining didn't find very receptive ears. She appeared content to sit out the remainder of the afternoon. When we got home, I grudgingly performed an x-ray in my office. Imagine Amy's vindication and my shame when the film showed a long spiral fracture of her tibia. I felt minimally exonerated when after a glance at Amy's legs, the orthopedic surgeon asked, "Which one?"

On a trip to Bridgeport, Connecticut, at one point on the highway we heard a loud thump in the back of the car. Marcia reprimanded the girls, "Stop fooling around." Amy replied in defense of them both that something had fallen off the roof. Marcia ended the discussion with a, "Yeah, yeah." Stopping for gas an hour later, I discovered that a suitcase, indeed, had fallen off our luggage rack. Amy for a second time in her life felt vindicated and in subsequent years never lost an opportunity during a dispute to remind us, "Remember you didn't believe me when I told you . . ."

At age three or four Amy described something on the horizon as a "loptical pallusion" (optical illusion) and at the end of a recording of La Bohème, she announced to Marcia, "Mimi's dead." What a good laugh we had at Niagara Falls when Amy was four. Entering the boat, "The Maid of the Mist," we were each handed a large, hooded raincoat. As we approached the Falls, she asked Marcia, "What will we do with our old raincoats?"

Pace was a serious issue. Being on time was important to us. Raina and Danny had no problem adapting to our tempo, to our scheduling. But, this created a mold too constricting for Amy. Surely she felt the tension as we would stand at the front door calling, "Let's go, Amy."

At age seven Amy had considered changing her name. The four of us (Marcia was pregnant with what we presumed would be another girl) were sitting in a restaurant discussing names for the new baby. Marcia, thinking of my grandmother Bobie (Rebecca), suggested

"Betina." This caught Amy's fancy. "I know what. Let's name the baby Amy and I'll take Betina."

Amy was as beautiful as she was brilliant. Both adjectives were emotionally charged words. Beautiful? Even with emerald green eyes and dark blond hair she never felt it; she would have preferred brown eyes rather than being different from the rest of us. Brilliant? It only kept her from sharing intimately with a girlfriend. At age eleven she wrote from Camp Ramah in Canada, "At last I have made a friend who's as smart as I am." She was so competent: she took piano lessons; she played the flute and, years later, the lute which she constructed; she could do macrame by the hour; she filled notebooks with her poetry and prose; she grew bean sprouts in every vacant, dark corner in our house.

When we moved into our new house, Raina and Amy shared a large room. By the time they were eleven and ten years old, we divided the room making two singles. It was at this point that it was evident that Amy loved order, lining up her dolls and generally keeping a neat room. This contrasted with the bedlam in Raina's. Amy followed her sister into activities at a younger age than we had permitted Raina. Accordingly, she, being precocious, associated with, and was welcomed into Raina's cluster of older friends. She dated at a younger age, and, as we found out only later, experimented with sex at this early age.

Amy's feelings for Raina are best described at age fifteen in her going-out-of-office speech as president of regional B'nai Brith Youth Organization. This is how she wrote it: "there is someone i always avoid speaking seriously of or to, because the prospect of losing her soon is too much for me. she is my complement in every way. she is pisces and I am virgo. she is dark and I am light. she is gentle and I am rough. she is always imposed upon, i am always imposing. she is calm, at times to the point of lethargy and i am nervous, at times to the point of hypertension. she is my voice box when I have no voice. she is the one to whom I run to whisper and giggle over things no one else would understand. she is my sister in blood and my sister in spirit . . ." (During this same speech Amy read, "whoever said you can't teach an old dog new tricks, never met david chamovitz.")

The sixties and seventies were a period of terrible foment with race riots, the Vietnam War, and Richard Nixon's chicanery. Add to this the flourishing drug scene and one can imagine the unrest and confusion among teenagers and even us adults. Amy's idealism found expression in many ways, not the least of which was wearing army fatigues, the uniform of war protesters. With cousin Mark Sherman on Earth Day she demonstrated on behalf of the environment. Both she and Mark were arrested in downtown Aliquippa for soliciting donations without a permit. They were detained at the police station for an hour.

On Mobilization Day, protesting the war in Vietnam, she wore a black armband to school to the scorn of our redneck community. Our family was among the first in our town to criticize our government in this travesty and to turn against Nixon. Even I, experiencing discomfort with my colleagues, stopped eating lunch in the doctors' dining room.

Amy was heartbroken when she didn't receive the American Legion Award given to the most outstanding eighth-grade student. Several years later we learned that one teacher, an advocate for Amy, spoke up at the award committee meeting. "Let's face it. Because of her political views, we are denying a thirteen-year-old an award she deserves." Amy felt less isolated when she heard of this knight in shining armor.

A problem for her and us was Amy's multiple interests and her compulsion to be at two places at the same time. We scrambled to accommodate her. For example, she loved being a cheerleader but she also loved Camp Ramah. Training camp for cheerleaders overlapped with the last two weeks of Ramah. Accordingly we drove to Canada to bring her home before camp ended in time for "cheering."

Others among Amy's friends were equally rebellious. On a vacation at Lake Chautauqua she and a friend were gone for hours at night while I frantically searched the town's deserted streets. At Snowmass Ski Village she would find friends and be absent for hours. During that ski week she even got a job working in a vegetarian restaurant. In Washington for a few weeks one spring she worked in a similar restaurant.

At B'nai Brith Starlight summer program in the Pocono Mountains at age sixteen she learned about mysticism, Cabala, and Hinduism. She returned to the Pittsburgh Airport dressed in hippie style. I swallowed hard during a lunch stopover, listening as this beautiful child tried to explain herself to me.

And just as she met truly unusual, positive role models at Starlight (like the director Danny Thurz), so did she start to collect gurus in the trappings of Jewish scholarship. She met Jewish intellectuals at a commune where it was customary to participate in a pre-*Shabbat* co-ed *mikva* (a ritual naked bath for men and women, separately!) in a creek. In Winnipeg, Canada she first met Rabbi Zalman Schachter who helped her look for her own "center." To accomplish this, Amy and others she admired, used LSD. Her misfortune was that while these gurus were gifted intellects, some were also struggling to find the meaning of life – and all of them were so much older than Amy. They loved her but I believe they failed to protect her. (While in Winnipeg, Amy helped at the birthing of a friend, burying her placenta in the garden as an ecological gesture.)

She went to a yoga conference in Jamaica. God knows what she encountered there. Did we know what was going on? Were we too insecure to investigate? Could we have maneuvered differently? If so, who's to say she wouldn't have run away from us? At fifteen Amy wrote in praise of Marcia and me: "Don't listen to those old and insecure folks who tell you it's dangerous to give your kids too much freedom. I'm the only fifteen-year old I know who has been given the freedom to be herself."

In 1973 at age seventeen Amy went away to Hampshire College in Amherst, Massachusetts. It was a new, small, innovative school. Before a week had passed, we got a call from her sounding very shaky, saying she felt she might jump out of a window. Marcia flew to Amherst, calling me to come after she found that Amy had inflicted superficial cuts on her wrists. Finally, we knew that Amy, and we, were in trouble. I immediately got in the car, arriving in Amherst late that night. The next day we started a painful trip home with our depressed daughter, who presumably, was having LSD flashbacks.

The following morning we had an appointment in Pittsburgh with Gerald Sandson, a psychiatrist. As we prepared to leave the house, Amy's reactions were bizarre and she became somnolent. I assumed she was acting up and, accordingly, rejected the fleeting thought to take her to the Aliquippa Hospital emergency room only two minutes away. As soon as Dr. Sandson saw Amy in the car, he told me to drive her to Homestead Hospital. She was quickly intubated; stomach pumping confirmed that she had taken an overdose of sedatives.

Amy remained in a coma for two days during which time I was unable to leave the hospital. I just had to be there should any complication develop and also for the moment she would awaken. Following this hospitalization, she was treated as an outpatient by a psychologist she had gone to while in high school. With an illness like Amy's (manic depression) it's not for me to criticize any therapist, but I do believe he had been too impressed by her intellect while being totally unaware of her use of drugs. Relapsing after living at home for three months, she was admitted to the St. Francis Psychiatric Unit. Even there she managed a serious suicide attempt.

It was then decided to admit Amy to Western State Psychiatric Hospital in Pittsburgh for a thirty-day sleep-study, which included continuous nighttime recordings of electrical brain waves. At its completion the department director Dr. Tom Detre sat with Amy, Marcia, me, and a resident physician. He blurted out without any preface, "If this were my daughter, I would take her out to Synanon (a therapeutic community for hard drug users which Amy wasn't) and drop her there." I was flabbergasted.

"Do you really mean that?", I countered.

Detre lashed back, "And who do you think you are, God?" I was shattered. Detre's resident escorted us from "the courtroom" and sat us down. "Don't pay any attention to him. He's a cruel son-of-a-bitch." (At least that's how I interpreted his assessment.) He thereupon directed us to Gould Farm, a therapeutic, in-patient setting in Massachusetts.

After a short time, Amy functioned well enough for us to agree to let her go to Israel to live with a boyfriend. We took comfort from the fact that Raina was there for a college semester and would be able to check on her. After two months when Marcia and I visited Israel, Amy seemed fragile. A poem she had just written should have given us further concern:

Song to the Setting Sun

Good bye Sun
I know you'll come up again
I don't know when

You fall behind dusk's hills
leaving me alone.

Blow wind, chill me to my bones
I shake like the reddened cliffs
You go and they lose strength to stand up
They want to fall into the winding wadi

Fill my cup,   Sun
with your last light
before you leave
and I fall
fall
fall
I long to sup
at your table Lord
God of all.

O May my falling be
but a bow to you upon your altar earth
O may this dying be
but the death before rebirth.

A brief diversion regarding "O May my falling . . . ." Amy's attraction to high places stood in contrast to my marked discomfort with heights. Twice, at age ten, she caused me to panic. The first episode occurred at Red Rocks, Colorado. High rocks formed natural acoustical enclosures for this mountainside amphitheater. Amy climbed to the top of one, sitting there until she finally responded to my order to come down.

The second incident occurred in Pittsburgh at a family party on the top floor of the Hilton Hotel. Amy went out on a narrow balcony, which was actually more of a ledge, although it had a railing. This time Marcia calmly requested that she return to her table. Maybe Amy was fantasizing that she could fly.

Amy getting in Shabbat mood, 1976.

In Jerusalem Amy resumed therapy with a psychologist. Another two months later I received a frantic call from her therapist beckoning me to make haste in retrieving Amy as the manic phase had returned. That plane ride home with Amy acting erratically, at times jumping up from her seat shouting incoherently, was my longest.

We next took her to the Country Place in Connecticut where Phyllis Beauvais became her therapist. Moments prior to our departure we saw Amy and Phyllis smiling at one another as Phyllis began, "You must tell me about your dreams." On the drive back to Aliquippa we felt optimistic for the first time in months. Amy progressed and was soon well enough to come home for what proved to be a delightful Passover *seder*. Amy related the Passover story to mental sickness and health. She equated crossing the Red Sea with the gamble of therapy, of risking the unknown rather than staying in a safe, stuck place of mental illness.

After six months at the Country Place, Amy moved in with a friend in New Haven. Both were involved in a yoga group. Amy had weekly sessions with Phyllis. She supported herself giving massages at the Jewish Center. Wanting to be a nurse and beyond that, a midwife, she applied to Simmons College Nursing School in Boston. This almost materialized even to the point of Marcia's helping her find an apartment. A week before college was to begin Amy suffered a relapse and was readmitted to the Country Place. Phyllis Beauvais resumed as her therapist continuing even after opening her own therapeutic residence, Wellspring, also in Connecticut.

There were many drives to visit Amy or to take her to treatment centers. Each time, I felt decimated as I despaired of any improvement in the quality of her life. More than once I stopped by the side of the road a few moments after hugging Amy good-bye, a torrent of tears covering my face as I beseeched God or anybody for help. This was strange behavior for a rationalist, who doubted the existence of any supernatural power. Nor did this philosophy stop me from inserting notes on Amy's behalf in the Western Wall in Jerusalem.

I won't write about Marcia's reactions and feelings but I can quote Libby Elbaum, one of Marcia's many Hadassah friends in Pittsburgh who said after Amy's first breakdown, "Marcia, be careful. Mental illness in a child can be a terrible threat to a marriage." Her admonition kept us on guard during our worst moments.

While an outpatient in Connecticut, Amy went to a retreat in Philadelphia under the auspices of Rabbi Zalman Schachter. Soon after returning, she had an acute psychotic break requiring four extremity restraints at Waterbury Hospital. I called Rabbi Schachter asking, confrontationally I'm sure, if they had used LSD, which he denied.

Amy's flashbacks were typical psychedelic reactions according to her doctors. The only happy note from this setback was that Amy reestablished contact with Rabbi Joe and Tzipi Heckelman. Joe by chance had been on chaplaincy rounds when he encountered Amy. Their son, Josh, had been one of Amy's companions in the quest for the truth and for peace of mind. And Tzipi, a kindred spirit, had encouraged Amy to be faithful to the treatment program with lithium. As a token of gratitude as a guest at their seder, Amy wrote a poem for the Heckelmans, which I've reproduced for this book. Each year during Pesach Tzipi posts it in her living room.

Lithium, which moderates the extreme mood swings of manic depression, turned out to be a godsend, at least for a while. It had to be discontinued when it caused abscesses on Amy's face. With Phyllis Beauvais's help, Amy seemed to be in control. Living in Emunah Farm, a religious commune in Massachusetts, she began a relationship with Jeff Bolotin who with Amy's encouragement accompanied her into the Habad (Lubovitch) movement. We have lovely photos of their subsequent delightful engagement dinner at a restaurant in the old Pittsburgh and Lake Erie railroad station in Pittsburgh. Their wedding on Aug. 30, 1978, conducted by a guitar-playing rabbi, took place in the yard of a synagogue in Amherst. Photographs show a number of guests holding handkerchiefs, not because of emotion, but rather because of the ragweed that filled the yard. (The building had once been a church where Emily Dickinson, a nineteenth century poet, had worshipped.)

A month later in the hectic automobile motorcade transporting Marcia's mother to her burial site, it was Amy who got out of her Volkswagen van at a traffic light and ran to catch up to the lead car to scold the driver for not being more attentive of straggling vehicles. It was typical of her to try to bring order to the world.

Neither marriage nor religion solved Amy's problems. On one occasion Amy went to a woman's religious weeklong retreat in wintry Minneapolis. While there, she entered a psychotic phase, wandering thinly clad for miles on a highway. Again it was necessary to retrieve her for hospitalization. As she improved, she was transferred to Wellspring. In time she was permitted weekend visits home with her husband.

During Passover Phyllis thought that Amy could handle the holiday in her apartment in New Haven. We had first *seder* with her and Jeff. Amy sheepishly showed us her meticulous Passover preparations, which included silver foil on the tables, the sinks, and the refrigerator trays in order to cover any breadcrumbs she may have overlooked with her cleaning. I noted the picture of Rabbi Menachem Schneerson, revered by his followers as the messiah, on the wall behind their bed. I experienced a sense of revulsion and foreboding.

For whatever role it played, Amy stopped using laxatives and bran during Passover as was decreed by her rigidly shortsighted Habad rabbis. Lithium was very constipating, and within days Amy became more deeply depressed. On the final day of the holiday, April 19, 1979, Jeff was worried enough about her to consider not going to morning prayers. He chose to go. And, alone, Amy made her way to a tall building in downtown New Haven and from a high floor jumped to her death. The rabbis said she "slipped" from the ledge after changing her mind; this interpretation allowed her burial as a nonsuicidal death in a Jewish cemetery. Actually Amy died about the hour Marcia and I were reciting memorial prayers for our parents in the Aliquippa synagogue.

Jeff followed the ordinances regarding holy days to not call us until after sundown. I was home with Danny when word came. We retrieved Marcia from a visit nearby with friends. Holding Danny, we sat stunned on the family room couch. In truth we were not surprised. After all, Amy had made at least three previous attempts to end her life.

Raina was living in Israel and was attending a cocounseling conference when word came to her. She was fortunate to receive consolation both from her group and on the plane from her seatmate Fred Goenne, a lovely elderly man who himself was grieving the loss of his wife. The memorial service took place at a funeral home in Pittsburgh with hundreds of grieving relatives and friends present. The ceremony was brief with Raina's eulogy having us visualize Amy walking away, up a grassy hill, stopping at the top to wave good-bye.

At the New Light Cemetery Amy was carried to her grave by cousins and laid to rest in the six-person plot already housing the remains of my parents, brother Allen, and Naomi, Irv and Helen's first child. Rabbi Marty Sofer officiated, grieving like a member of the family. We all participated in filling in the grave. Cousin Mark Sherman, a sufferer like Amy, later said that during his turn he vowed to straighten out. Marcia's nephew Dennis Appleton kept shoveling until his hands bled.

During *shiva* week there was a constant flow of people, returning again and again to share our grief. Marcia's father, brother, and sister-in-law remained the whole week as did Marcia's cousin Ronnie Birnbaum. They were a constant source of comfort and, at appropriate times, humor. Each night Marty lead prayer services following which, he spoke words of Torah.

Our children were a comfort during *shiva*. Danny had always been such an easy, cheerful youngster. And yet in retrospect we thought, how could such sophisticated parents not have anticipated the trauma Amy's illness inflicted on him? When Amy first got sick, he would, at age ten, spend hours in his room holding his dog, listening to radio music in order to drown out the noises of Amy's hysterics. He must have heard Amy in the bathtub screaming at me, "You'll be better off with me dead." Maybe Danny was like children of Holocaust survivors who, to their detriment, were reluctant to raise their own problems and thereby avoid adding to their parents' heartache.

How can I ever forget friend and colleague, Steve Zernich? He's tough and competitive, and a superb surgeon generally not known to be very sensitive. He sat quietly opposite me watching me cry as a steady stream of friends came to offer sympathy. After five minutes he got up, came over to me, and said, "Why in the hell don't you get out of here and go back to work!" No kinder words were ever said to me. They were in contrast to those offered by a minister who one month later encountered me in a hospital corridor when I was again functioning well. "Oh, how I meant to visit you and tell you how bad I felt."

It took me another week after *shiva* to return to my practice. My self-confidence was shattered. I experienced difficulty making decisions and held back from getting involved in personal discussions with patients. When one of the patients in the cardiac care unit was about to die, I could hear the family crying. I returned to the nursing station, alone, and shed tears for myself.

Although only one month of *kaddish* (prayer for the dead) is mandated following the death of a child, we opted for the eleven months required for a parent. Our standing alone to recite this prayer reminded the congregation that we were still fragile and deserved not to be harassed over synagogue politics. Music was a strange phenomenon. I found that I could not sing the familiar melodies of the synagogue service; I just choked up. Two months after Amy died, at a Pittsburgh Symphony concert, Marcia and I sat side by side, tears running down our cheeks. And for several years, attending weddings was traumatic.

I had been planning to volunteer at Hadassah Hospital for the summer of 1979. During the week of *shiva*, we got a call from a real estate agent in Jerusalem indicating that she had located a desirable apartment. We made the decision to follow through with our original plan. Accompanied by Marcia's father, we spent July and August in Israel. The days were filled with novel experiences, therapeutic beyond measure. And since Dan was in Israel on a Young Judaea summer program and Raina lived close by, the five of us helped heal one another.

Amy's gravestone was subsequently inscribed with a closing line of her poem: "O may my falling be but a bow to you upon your altar earth." She had acted out her poem.

Almost yearly since we've lived in Israel, we have spent Amy's *yahrzeit* in Safed with Rabbi Joe and Tzipi Heckelman. Their synagogue is appropriately named *Kehillat Shalva,* meaning Congregation Serenity. The last day of Passover, the day Amy died, is celebrated on the eighth day of the holiday outside of Israel. The holiday lasts only seven days in Israel; Joe declared it acceptable to observe Amy's *yahrzeit* on the last day of Passover wherever we are.

How often I had dreams of Amy. I would wake up sobbing, the pillow wet with tears. At first I found the dreams painful, until I came to realize that good or bad, each was a visit with her. Marcia learned not to wake me or hold me, lest she abort the visit. I haven't had an Amy dream in over three years; I wish I could have another and another.

It is ironic that Amy's death freed us to make *aliyah*. Had she been alive, we could never have lived 7,000 miles apart; we would have perpetually been on call. In addition, I would have had to continue earning enough money to pay for her expensive medical care and to provide an endowment large enough to cover her needs after Marcia and I died. How I fantasize trading Israel for my Amy.

Am I scarred? Of course. Am I not a less cheerful person than before? Without a doubt. Fleeting reflections of Amy's existence and her demise insert themselves unendingly. Every event that should make us rejoice is clouded by thoughts of a future fraught with dire possibilities. Even though Amy's illness is now considered, at least in part, to be genetic in origin, I still ask, "Do I feel guilty?" The answer? "Of course. After all, am I not Amy's father and a good doctor?"

DANNY AND I TEAM UP

One evening in 1962 after a concert in Pittsburgh, Marcia and I were at a restaurant with friends. I sat next to a woman, a complete stranger. A psychologist, she began quizzing me about my relationship with my daughters Raina and Amy, then seven and six years old, respectively. "Do you take them to Pirate games?"

"No, I stopped being interested in baseball years ago."

"Do you take them to Steeler games?"

"I never was much interested in football except touch football when I was a kid."

And then came the reproach, "Well, if you had a son, you'd become interested."

I dismissed her criticism as so much party patter. Obviously, she stung me for soon after, and repeatedly over the years, I would ask Raina and Amy if I had short-changed them. "Daddy, don't be ridiculous," they reassured me. "Baseball and football don't interest us in the least. It would be an imposition if you asked us to go with you to a game and, besides, didn't we spend a lot of time together skiing?"

Then, a year after the psychologist's rebuke, along came Danny. The pregnancy had not been planned, since following a life-threatening miscarriage of twins, Marcia and I had decided not to have a third child. Though not anticipating any difference in parenting, I was naive not to be ready and not just because of the psychologist's prediction.

A forerunner of my intense feelings for Danny was manifested at his *brit milah* (circumcision). The moment the deed was done I released a torrent of tears. Relief that all went well was only the trigger for other undefined feelings.

I won't say I put sports equipment in Danny's crib, but it wasn't long before we acquired baseballs and a bat, fielders' gloves and catcher's mitt, and a football. The initiative came from Danny; in me he found a receptive partner. He and I would practice throwing a baseball or a football in our front yard before supper. We saw our Pittsburgh Pirates play once at Forbes Field and numerous times after they moved to Three Rivers Stadium near the Point where the Allegheny and Monongahela Rivers meet to form the Ohio River. We knew the batting averages of our favorite players and we bought chewing gum to collect the accompanying cards with photos of major league baseball players.

One afternoon Danny and I went to a Pirate's game with Danny's best friend Roger Morris and Roger's father David. In the middle of the seventh inning David boasted to the boys, "Watch how I can get the crowd to do what I tell them." Whereupon he stood up and shouted, "Everybody, stand up!" Within seconds everyone in the stadium did his bidding. Danny was astonished and Roger swelled with pride; the boys were obviously unfamiliar with the traditional seventh inning stretch.

As the years rolled by many heroes entered the scene. Danny's mood, and mine, rose and fell with the Pirates' league standing and with the performances of Willie Stargell, Al Oliver, and Roberto Clemente. We grieved when Clemente died in a plane crash while in the Caribbean for a benefit on behalf of children's sports in Nicaragua.

I was taking a cardiology course in Indianapolis in 1972 during the National League playoffs between Pittsburgh and Cincinnati. As soon as the Pirates' final losing game was over, I phoned Danny to commiserate with him. He was inconsolable. I thereupon committed the blunder of the century. "Just think of the happy kids in Cincinnati." I was trying to remind him that the Pirates had recently won so many World Series.

"Dad, (pronounced, 'Daaad') that's stupid." And it was.

He loved looking for the umpteenth time at the 8-mm movie I took at Forbes Field October 13, 1960 at the climax of the deciding game of the World Series between the Pirates and the awesome New York Yankees. It was the last of the ninth inning; score tied, 9-9. Our Bill Mazerowski was the lead batter. With the count one strike and no balls, Maz hit the next pitch over the left field scoreboard. Pandemonium broke out. Standing with the screaming fans I held the camera over my head and aimed it down the third base line as Maz rounded third base and headed for home. Throngs of spectators raced onto the field slowing his forward progress. I don't know if he ever reached home plate. It didn't matter; we Pirates were the champs!

And, of course, as soon as the baseball season ended, football season was in full swing. Danny grew up in the era of the unbeatable Pittsburgh Steelers. The quarterback Terry Bradshaw, the impregnable defensive line, "the Steel Curtain," Mean Joe Greene, and Lynn Swan, who studied ballet in order to improve his moves for catching passes. "We" were Super Bowl champions three or four times. When we watched a game on TV, we shouted like rednecks at a bar. How convenient it was when during a ski-week in Snowmass, Colorado, I strained a leg muscle. Danny and I took the next day off and just incidentally watched the Super Bowl between the Steelers and Minnesota. The Steelers rewarded us with a victory.

Mention fishing and Raina and Amy would make faces and utter sounds like "Yeech." Danny was hooked when he reeled in his first catch. As I was. My own interest traced back to my childhood when Uncle Herman Eger took my brother Jerry to Canada on a fishing trip. How I envied my brother! My first and most disappointing experience occurred at Milton Dam, Ohio; I was seven. Before dawn I was searching for worms in the yard just below Uncle Harry Jackson's bedroom window. Even with the aid of a flashlight I failed to find a single worm. Uncle Harry heard me muttering, "Doodie (my childhood nickname),

Doodie, dumb Doodie." This expression became a tame way of teasing me.

One night a friend described for us fishing with his Polish barber Walter Walters. The latter had a summer home on French Creek in Cambridge, Pennsylvania. The following week I called Walter and received an invitation for us to spend a couple of days with him. His house was quite small. Danny and I were billeted in a hut behind his house on the bank of the creek. A flock of sheep were housed on the ground floor bleating all night long, while upstairs there were cots and a sink. An outhouse was a few steps away as was the dock for Walter's rowboat, which was outfitted with a small motor. A barber by profession, Walter was self-educated and sophisticated; he talked nonstop – an occupational attribute. He was attracted to us, especially to Danny, guiding us through the awkward first steps of assembling fishing rods, attaching hooks and sinkers, and baiting hooks with worms and lures. Walter taught us how to remove hooks as painlessly as possible at least from the throwbacks, fish too small to keep according to the game commission. We trolled the creek catching a variety of fish. Each catch gave a sense of competence, of controlling nature.

On the second afternoon while Walter was napping, Danny and I ventured out on our own. Within minutes Danny landed a muskie, a ferocious fighting fish. Once we netted him into the boat our troubles began. His teeth were formidable. He flopped from side to side avoiding blows with an oar until a few whacks with a bottle subdued him. We thought we had caught a monster. "Isn't he a beaut?" asked Danny displaying our trophy to Walter.

"He sure is, Dan, except that he's four inches under the twenty-four-inch acceptable limit. If he weren't already dead, he would be a throwback." Walter's wife Martha scaled and gutted our catch, the first of many we brought home for our maid Racheal to cook.

We continued to correspond with Walter even after he entered a retirement home. Twenty-five years after we first met, I still send him our annual letter and, in turn, receive a handwritten postcard. Walter is a goodhearted soul. I think of him when I repress the telling of "Polish jokes." But an incident with one requires telling.

Marcia, Danny, and I were seeing Raina off at Greater Pittsburgh Airport, she returning to Israel after the *shiva* for Amy. It was a difficult moment, especially for Raina who was sobbing nonstop. Wanting to cheer her up, Danny said, "Raina, I have a Polish joke for you."

Raina expressed consternation with her kid brother, "Danny, you know I hate racist jokes."

Undaunted, Danny blurted out, "Did you hear about the Polish lesbian? She liked men." Raina pelted him with soft cuffs, angry with him for making her laugh at a joke both racist and sexist.

When Danny was eleven, he went to summer camp, Young Judaea, in Hendersonville, North Carolina. From camp we took him to Florida. One morning at Daytona Beach, Danny and I took a walk on the beach. There were numerous people riding motorcycles and, of course, Danny asked if we could do likewise. I responded, "Danny, you know how I feel about motorcycles" – I had always forbidden Raina and Amy to get on one.

"C'mon, Dad." Finally I relented and asked the rental agent if I could take a trial run. Well, it was no challenge at all, so with Danny sitting behind me, off we went. The cycle had a governor which limited its speed to seventeen mph. For thirty hilarious minutes we rode up and down the beach. "See, Dad? Don't knock it till you try it."

From there we went to Pompano Beach. I looked up Deep-Sea Fishing in the Yellow Pages. The next morning Danny and I were in a fishing boat out on the Atlantic Ocean. Expectations of struggling to bring in a record-breaking marlin were dashed, especially for Danny. From the first moment on the water seasickness overcame him; he lay down the whole four hours of the outing. Sitting in a very professional armchair, I managed to catch only a lazy throwback hammerhead shark. So much for blighted dreams.

Cousin Elmer Eger recommended a fishing camp on the Georgian Bay in Canada. It was located on an island called Burritt's Bay, 200 miles north of Toronto. By prior arrangement we met George Chesne – he and his wife Connie owned the island – at a marina where we left our car. George transported us away from civilization. Each time we took this twenty-five-minute boat ride, there was the same excitement as the first.

The camp never accommodated more than fifteen guests. There was a common dining room – Connie did the cooking; she even broiled the kosher steaks we brought – and rustic cabins with spring cots, oil lamps, and a woodstove for heat. There was no television and only one telephone on the island. Connie provided us with a motorized rowboat and a French-Canadian beer-drinking guide, Rege, who maneuvered us around the bay eight hours a day. He knew how to avoid rocks and where to find good fishing. Rege untangled our lines, helped extricate lures from snapping jaws, and cooked us "shore lunches." After three hours of fishing he would dock at one of thousands of islands; many with makeshift fireplaces. While Rege readied the ingredients for lunch, including breaded fish Connie had prepared from the previous day's catch, Danny and I hunted firewood. Only once on all our trips was it necessary to catch our lunch; there had been insufficient fish in the previous day's catch. After lunch Marcia fed the seagulls with leftover scraps of food.

And the fishing itself? The first year was the best. We each caught ample numbers of northern pike and bass. Marcia would lie across the middle of the boat, feet up, with a book in one hand and a fishing pole in the other. She would exclaim, "Oh heck!" when a fish interrupted her reading by taking her line. The fish seemed to favor her, knowing that among us she was the least eager for a catch.

While Danny was satisfied just to let his lure troll behind our slowly moving boat, I had to be more active, casting from side to side. I was the least successful. With any nibble on a line the boat would come alive with rapid chatter. It would be chaotic with each of us shouting directions to the lucky angler in order to share the thrill of the catch. Between times hardly a word was spoken other than to say, "Look at the heron!" And if hours went by without my catching anything, *dayenu*; it was enough just to savor the ambiance.

At the end of the day there was the traditional fisherman's photo of the happy anglers holding the ends of the string of the day's catch, in our case, about ten beauties. Connie took what was necessary for the next day's shore lunch and the rest she froze for us to take home to Racheal.

What a great experience it was to be fishing out in the rain! Connie had provided us with rain gear. On that first trip we even managed a swim during a lunch break in cold, unpolluted, even drinkable, water. The fresh air, the quiet, the sounds of the birds, the carefree hours out in the boat, our zesty appetites, the plethora of stars at night, and the total freedom from responsibility were incomparable.

A day's catch! Canada 1988.

In July '85 the whole family returned to the states to ship our household goods to Israel. While Marcia and Raina did the packing,

Raina's husband Zvika, Duba, Zvika's Israeli friend, Danny, and I took off for Canada. Zvika and Duba were usually in one boat, Danny and I, in the other. Zvika's guide, drunk but competent, spoke only in cuss words. Playing horseshoes was our evening activity. The place got into Zvika's blood; "For that alone I would return to America."

During a visit to the States in September '88 I drove from Pittsburgh to Toronto where I met Danny who had flown directly from Israel to Toronto. What was his first request as we began the drive north? "Dad, can we stop at McDonald's for a Big Mac?" It was his first in three years. This was to be our last fishing trip. In 1998 Connie answered my inquiry, saying that she and George had given up Burritt's Bay. End of an era.

There were so many sporting activities that Danny and I shared, some more frequently than others but none without immense pleasure. Take horseback riding, for example. As with fishing the idea to ride was first planted by my brother Jerry. I would watch him putting on riding breeches and polishing his magnificent riding boots. This was 1939 to 1942 while Jerry was in practice in Aliquippa.

I got the family started when Danny was still an infant. There were riding stables in Independence, ten miles from Aliquippa. Raina and Amy would ride around within the confines of a corral. When Danny was three, we took a trip out West. In Colorado Springs we were disappointed in the old mares we hired. In Cheyenne, however, we encountered a riding stable that gave us children-safe, but splendid, horses that we rode freely on an open plain. With Danny sitting on the saddle in front of me, I felt I was the best father in the world. I even managed to find a rodeo which excited Danny and me, but not Marcia or the girls.

Several years later – Danny was ten – I learned about the U T Bar Ranch in Colorado. The owner was Fum McGraw, a onetime famous football player and coach. In the summers he opened his ranch to dudes like us.

How could I resist a ranch vacation? For the first week we – Marcia, Danny, and I – visited Yellowstone National Park. We toured three different stopover stations. At each we managed two-hour horseback rides to prepare ourselves for U T Bar.

We drove across Wyoming to the ranch near Ft. Collins, Colorado. Fum and his family were gracious and supportive of us city slickers. Our bunkhouse was rustic, smelling of old wood. The mess hall was crowded with boisterous wranglers recounting the day's excitement.

On the first morning, horses were selected for us, matching our appearance, our experience, and our age to the characteristics of the horse. Each morning we rode for three hours, returned for lunch and a rest, and then hit the saddle for three more hours. On each trip we headed in a different direction. True, the riding was tame enough. The real thrill was seeing the surroundings: the forests, the hills, the prairies, the mountain streams. As there were no roads or even paths, only backpackers experience this wilderness. A highlight was our encounter with a herd of yearlings. These colts were allowed to roam free during their first year. They trotted up to us, happy to be visited by their parents.

Returning to the ranch at the end of one day, we were caught in a rainstorm. It was the one time we were allowed to gallop or was it that our horses were scurrying barnward for shelter? We gave ourselves to the downpour in utter abandon. What a shock when we undressed! Our skin and underwear were dyed blue. Little did we realize in those days that new blue jeans required presoaking. Different eras bring new problems; tourists wearing Levis in Moscow have only to worry about Russians trying to buy them off their bodies.

Danny, the new cowhand, was ecstatic. And how proud I was of Marcia, a Brooklyn gal in blue jeans, not jodhpurs, happy in the saddle. Being short was a little handicap but with a hoist she mounted, displaying a professional carriage. As for me, anyone who spent as many nickels as I have in the shooting galleries (movie houses that showed Westerns) or who sat twice through cowboy double features, could appreciate my fantasy life as I roamed the Rockies. Protecting Marcia and Danny, I scanned the horizons for bandits, horse thieves, train robbers, and damsels in distress. I knew that movie heroes Tom Mix and Buck Jones were riding alongside should I need help. In their day right always triumphed, God-fearin' farmers could keep the cattlemen out of their crops, and the handsome cowboy always got the girl. No complex psychodrama and, thank God, no sex.

Tennis would require a chapter by itself because of its importance to my life in Israel; Danny and I didn't really play together that much. But this is a good a time to discuss winning. Speaking to my athletic, surgeon-friend Steve Zernich, I once complimented someone for being a good loser. Steve corrected me, "There is no such thing. Just winners and losers. What's this business of shaking the hand of the guy who just beat you? Break your racquet." That's the kind of a guy I want if I need surgery but not for a tennis partner. No one believes, that win or lose, I could be satisfied if I played my best; most people need to win.

When Danny was a youngster, no matter what sport we played, I did my best to encourage him by letting him win, albeit by a slim margin. One summer – Danny was about eight – we were playing shuffleboard at a resort, Bedford Springs. An older boy observed that I was committing intentional errors. He shook his head, saying to Marcia out of earshot of Danny, "My dad would never, never let me win."

Ping-Pong was another matter; I resolved that I would not let Danny win. We had a regulation Ping-Pong table in our cellar. Over the years Danny did progress but remained below my level. When he was twelve, I teased him by saying, "The first time you beat me, I'll give you fifty bucks." Well, one afternoon three years later, wasting shots, I found myself falling behind. By the time I decided to take back the advantage I had allowed him, it was too late; he beat me 21 to 19. Remembering the earlier promise, Danny asked for his fifty dollars and got it.

Danny had called us up on another perceived promise years before when he was six. In September '68 he first asked for a dog. Marcia had casually intimated that the summer, when his sisters would be away at camp, would be a good time to get a puppy. Nothing more was said, that is, until June '69. We had been to niece Vicki Wolfson's wedding in Connecticut. At LaGuardia Airport we put the girls on a plane to Toronto where they would be met and driven to Camp Ramah.

We then drove home. About an hour east of Pittsburgh without any preliminaries and to our surprise, Danny asked, "Are we getting my dog today or tomorrow?"

That evening we looked in the local newspaper and found an ad by a family wanting to give away a beagle-basset puppy. We called the owners and within the hour Danny had his first dog; he named him Shroeder from the Peanuts cartoon. After a few years, Shroeder, and the next dog, Popeye, were killed by eating poisoned meat a neighbor had placed in his yard. Danny was heartbroken each time. He challenged us, "Do something." Another neighbor who similarly had lost a police dog, his palsied son's best friend, did threaten the culprit. Danny's third dog, Daphne, escaped harm.

When the time came to move our household goods to Israel in 1985, we had to decide what to do with Daphne. We knew that Danny would be living in a dormitory and Raina, being a medical student and a mother, couldn't take on more responsibility. Marcia and I would be renting an apartment. Besides, we, I especially, couldn't take care of the dog; psychologically I just didn't have the energy. Marcia and I decided not to take Daphne to Israel. We were especially relieved when good friends from Pittsburgh accepted Daphne into their home. Well, Danny let us, mainly me, have it. "How *could* you make such an important decision without asking me?" He was right. We really hadn't taken into account how important Daphne had been to him. Though the final result might not have been different, the decision would have been so much less traumatic if Danny had been consulted. I believe this event will forever remain the most significant downward blip on our otherwise smooth history.

Skiing is a great family sport. I got started as a student in Boston. Encouraged by my brother Bob in 1961, I gave Marcia her first ski lesson one wintry day on the Aliquippa Golf Course. Thus began an exciting part of our life. We would ski for a day or an overnight at Seven Springs in the Allegheny Mountains. It wasn't long before Raina and Amy joined us. Frequently we would pack their ski clothes, pick them up after school, and drive to the slopes an hour and a half away. On the way we would stop at Howard Johnson's Restaurant for a snack and for the girls to don their ski clothes. Night skiing was glorious. My gang collapsed on the way home.

One afternoon at the bottom of a slope at Seven Springs with Marcia pregnant with Danny and feeling my thirty-eight years, I asked Marcia, "Who will teach him (generic) to ski?" Well, Danny started at two and a half, and quickly, like his sisters, became an independent skier. Though proficient at every sport he played, as a skier he became an expert, and even a teacher.

New Year's holidays at Seven Springs became a family tradition. We joined Bob, his girls, and numerous friends. On New Year's Eve we all partied, the youngsters in one motel room, we adults in another. On one occasion Marcia and I cleaned up sprayed champagne from the ceiling of our room; the kids had shaken the bottle before we opened it.

On one particular overnight ski we took nephew Mark Chamovitz, cousins Mark and David Sherman, and a friend. Danny was six while the others were five to six years his senior. Danny by then was a competent skier while the others had never been on skis. The first evening we spent outfitting the boys in rental ski equipment in preparation for the following morning. As we started the drive to our motel, Danny asked, "Well, guys, how do you like skiing so far?" This became a classic for our family. No matter the destination or the purpose of a trip, the competition was to see who would be the first to ask, "Well, how do you like ___ so far?" Fill in fishing or boating or Canada and you're a winner.

Marcia and I loved our first ski week in Snowmass, Colorado. We returned almost yearly for the fifteen years before moving to Israel; the children occasionally joined us. We entered them into ski school and it wasn't long before they could handle even difficult slopes. Actually, the uniqueness of skiing as a family activity is that we could ski together on the same slope albeit at different speeds and with varying pitch of the turns.

Only once did Marcia remain at home; she was needed by Amy. On that trip Raina, Danny, and I encountered six consecutive blue-sky days. Together we attended the traditional Saturday amateur night where guests volunteered to sing or play instruments. Remembering this, Danny had brought his guitar; he had been taking lessons for a couple of years. At that time he was eleven. As it was late, I asked the emcee if Danny could be the first contestant. Nervously, Raina and I watched Danny approach the performer's stool opposite two microphones, one at guitar level, the other for his voice. Danny sang his own composition, titled, "Tumbling Down on Campground" (a very challenging slope at Snowmass). The several verses described a previous year's fall with lurid, exaggerated injuries. Danny got a rousing ovation from the beer-drinking crowd of skiers. The emcee bantered with him giving compliments and making remarks such as, "Hey, Kid, I'm going to break your knuckles. You'll be too much competition for me."

Danny was asked for an encore. At that point my nervousness soared. "Raina," I said, "he doesn't know anything else." Wrong! What he sang I don't remember but he carried it off well. Departing, we walked on air; Raina and I with pride but neither of us as elated as Danny himself.

We frequently skied at Vail, Colorado, either as a day's stopover on the way to Snowmass or for a ski week there. Vail was fashioned after a Swiss ski village. One afternoon Danny, Marcia, and I stopped at a pizza pub after a great day of skiing. That we were high was not unusual. At first we were the only patrons. We ordered a large pizza. When we were well along with our snack, two middle-aged couples walked in and sat at an adjoining table. Since there were two large untouched slices of pizza remaining, I offered them to the newcomers. One couple sneered at my offer while the husband of the second couple, hesitating a moment, said, "Thanks," and took the pizza.

After the two pieces were consumed (by all four), I asked, "Was it good?"

"Fine, thank you," one replied to which I retorted, "Then that will be one dollar." The sneering couple made an expression of disgust while the other couple laughed heartily.

Meanwhile, Danny was mortified, wanting to dissociate himself from his father. Then the elongated, "Daaad!" At the door of the pub two or three steps up, we waved good-bye while I threw out, "Spongers!" Outside, Danny was embarrassed but Marcia and I roared over my spontaneous craziness. Danny relates years later that after teasing a waitress he said, "Oh, my God, I'm becoming my father."

Not only did Danny inherit my sense of humor but also my looks (and my Dad's). One day in New York City when Danny was on a bus in the vicinity of Columbia University, a middle-aged stranger approached him. "Tell me, is your father David Chamovitz from Aliquippa? I went to high school with him and you look exactly the way he looked then." Danny's New Yorker roommate, sitting with him, was flabbergasted. "All my life I've been riding city buses; no stranger has ever recognized me."

On another evening in Vail I really erred at Danny's expense. We were eating at Pepy's, a very high-priced restaurant. I had felt abused by having to pay an exorbitant sum for bad-tasting fish, which was served in skimpy portions. This put me in a dour mood. When it came time to order dessert, Danny requested the most expensive item on the menu, baked Alaska. I jumped on him as though he was the most spoiled brat. Heaven knows he never was. I'll never live it down, nor will he forget. Offering Danny baked Alaska many times over the years hasn't erased the memory of that dinner.

The day after unveiling Amy's gravestone, the four of us survivors – Raina had come from Israel – left for a week's vacation in Vail. Whatever the reason, maybe the passing of this emotional milestone, it was a week of continuous hilarity. The first night was our anniversary dinner. I slipped a small box on to Marcia's plate, a ring Danny and I had bought. "Was that the lump in your pants pocket on the plane?" Marcia asked. The children arranged for a cake; they kept kicking the waiter from under the table as he almost gave away the surprise.

The following evening we went to see the movie, "Ten." Even in line for tickets we were acting crazy, unashamedly. The movie began with credits. When up popped "Music by Henry Mancini" (from Aliquippa), Marcia and I applauded. Thereafter, with each credit, even "Gaffer," the audience took over with unruly shouting. Raina and Danny slid low in their seats, pretending to be embarrassed by their parents.

That night the kids stood outside our bedroom door singing the "Bolero," the movie's sensuous theme.

On the last ski day Danny and I skied together and were at the bottom of the slope when down came Marcia and Raina beaming. Why? On the previous run, they had raced to the bottom of the lift, just in time to catch the last chair to ascend. None of us wanted the week to end. It really hasn't since we each have a poster-sized photograph of the four of us taken at the top of Vail Mountain. It reminds Marcia of cousin Evie's question – Evie hates cold weather. "Tell me the truth, Marcia. Don't you go skiing just to please David?" The smile on Marcia's face gives the answer.

The last time Marcia and I skied was with Danny and his wife Shira in Jan. 1992 at Mt. Hermon on the Syrian border. We went for two days. Shira watched three-month-old Eytan on the first day while Marcia took the duty on the second. The ski conditions were ideal; Marcia and I skied with abandon. "Look at my old parents," Danny shouted to friends. When Marcia and I returned to Tel Aviv, we each came to a decision that, rather than wait for a broken limb, it was time to give up our favorite sport.

Golf was a less frequent experience since I had resigned from the Aliquippa Golf Club when Danny was about ten. My foursome was being interrupted with increasing frequency by emergencies in the Cardiac Care Unit. But wherever we played, it was four hours of togetherness and friendly competition. We knew how to nurse one another through moments of frustration such as when we would hit a ball out of one sand trap into another.

In 1974 we arranged a five-day vacation at Greenbriar Resort in West Virginia. Danny had a full set of clubs given to him by Marcia's brother-in-law, Bernie Wolfson. Splurging, we rented two golf carts on each of the five days. After one particular round on a hot, muggy day, Marcia downed two beers in rapid succession. At that point Danny whispered to me quite seriously, "Mom's becoming an alcoholic." He had never seen Marcia drink even one beer.

I have asked myself, "In what ways, other than sharing so many sporting activities, did my relationship with Danny differ from that with Raina and Amy?" An easy first answer: I never took my girls shopping for clothes. Danny and I went to Kaufman's in Pittsburgh for his *bar mitzvah* suit; it was rust colored. He loved it especially because of its vest, which allowed him to use Dad's pocket watch with a dangling chain.

It was even more fun shopping for his college wardrobe. I felt that I was shopping for myself but had no memory of wearing clothes at Geneva College that differed from what I wore in high school. I should emphasize that in contrast to my shifting from one mill town to another when I went to college, Danny was moving up to the Ivy League; Aliquippa *shlumperie* (rags) just wouldn't do. He gleefully selected a suit, sport jacket, shirts, etc., all conservative in style. By the time Danny was to pick out a wedding suit, styles had changed but my taste had not. Nothing he and I looked at pleased him. A few days later, accompanied by Shira, his bride-to-be, he choose a dark suit with a flashy vest. And it matched him.

As to visiting colleges, for Raina and Amy I played no role. With Danny I participated with the first half of his long shopping list of colleges. It was the fall of 1980, Danny's senior year in high school. Our itinerary took us first on a ten-hour car ride to Boston; we stopped at a roadside picnic area to eat sandwiches and to toss a baseball.

Our first visit was to Brandeis University, Raina's alma mater. Danny found it too bland. Next he had an interview at M.I.T.; the campus scene with students playing frisbee was like a Seurat painting. We then went to Harvard College. There was the statue of John Harvard holding court over "The Yard" and the magnificent Widener Library with its Gutenberg Bible; I showed him the medical school as well. Danny also visited Tufts College in Medford, Massachusetts. Most memorable there was a flaming, orange-leafed tree in the middle of the campus.

I had the pleasure of showing off Danny to my teacher, Al Freedberg and Al to Danny. Danny was forewarned to bridle his inherited teasing nature.

Our last school visit in Boston was to Boston University. Neither of us was impressed. It was Danny's fallback.

From Boston we drove to Providence, Rhode Island to visit Brown University. Danny loved the ambiance. Already biased in favor of Brown, Danny decided it would be his first choice. After that visit I turned my budding collegian over to Marcia in Bridgeport, Connecticut and flew home. They continued on to Sarah Lawrence, Columbia, and Penn.

The bottom line was that Danny was accepted by Columbia and Boston University; he chose the former. At the end of the first school week, he called home extolling praises of his choice: "How could I ever have wanted to live in Providence?" So much for a kid who would have been happy wherever he went.

Danny, like Raina before him, was never openly rebellious. Neither of them made unreasonable requests of us. Danny, on the other hand, did con me into buying him a car in Israel. A year after we arrived, Danny, who had been getting around Jerusalem on a bicycle, called to say that he was taking instructions in driving a moped. (He only recently confessed to having flunked the driving test.) He knew that I forbade my children to ride a motorcycle. I swallowed hard and asked him to price a secondhand car. This isn't quite as Danny recalls the exchange but he did say he hung up and rolled on the floor in laughter, telling his roommate that he had just manipulated his father.

In one other way Danny's growing up did differ from the girls'. As a child I remember my Dad talking about sleeping in a *succah* with his father in Romania; he never did with me or with any of my brothers. Only with Danny and not the girls did I revive this custom; I assume that I thought of this as a father-and-son activity. The gesture was meaningful, connecting us to my *Zeyda*. Danny subsequently continued the tradition with his sons.

The length of this chapter speaks to the strong bonds that exist between Danny and me. Our relationship was intense, but never stifling or oppressive. I can't imagine that there could be a more honest relationship, or a child with better judgment as to the use of the freedom that he was given.

Marcia's mother Madge had always criticized her for making "too much of a fuss over Danny." While on a trip to Israel in 1978 with my in-laws and Danny, Madge was silently overwhelmed by Danny's maturity – he was only fourteen – as she observed his patience with the adult tour group, his helpfulness with luggage, and his cheerful demeanor. During this trip she confessed to Marcia, "You know, he really is a very nice boy."

This nice boy went on to transfer to Hebrew University in Jerusalem after two years at Columbia University. After obtaining a BA degree, he continued on to obtain a PhD in genetics. Surprisingly while contemplating the post-doctoral track, Danny applied for a two-year program leading to a job in the Israel Foreign Service. At the end of a six-month testing period, Danny was one of the twenty successful applicants out of over 750. After the first day's orientation when the proper way to shake hands was taught, Danny dropped out of the program. He decided against the foreign service, at least, because of its requirement to move his family every three years. When I asked why he had even been considering giving up science for which he had a special aptitude, he replied, "Lab work is boring."

"What is there in favor of science?" I asked.

"I love designing experiments, I love writing papers, and I love teaching."

"But Danny," I said, "that's a lot of loves for one profession." He spent the next three postdoctoral years at Yale University in New Haven, Connecticut. On returning to Israel he received an appointment as Senior Lecturer in Plant Biology at Tel Aviv University where his scientific, teaching, and organizational skills have received recognition.

When people would ask my mother how she could raise five such nice boys, she would reply, "Luck." On the other hand as Marcia once replied to her mother's compliment, "I don't want credit for the good or blame for the bad." Modesty would have her say, "Some kids are just congenitally easy." We were lucky and Danny was easy.

A KINGDOM FOR A KIDNEY

Friends have asked, "David, how can you write your memoirs and not include, or better yet, start with, a chapter about the most significant person in your life, your wife?"

"But," I defend myself, "Marcia appears in just about every chapter I've written. There are few facets of my life that she hasn't shared and often inspired. A chapter dedicated to her would be redundant. Besides, to do it justice, it would have to include the intimate aspects of our courtship and marriage that we prefer not to share with anyone." Equally important, reader appeal for marriages made-in-heaven is low; credibility for my accolades would be suspect. "No marriage is that good. How saccharine! What's he hiding? No woman is that beautiful, that kind, that smart."

Hold on. At least, the last I can defend with facts. In high school Marcia was a Regent's Scholar, the most prestigious high-school award given in the state of New York. She was a winner on the intellectual television quiz show "Jeopardy," which requires knowledge of a myriad of facts and their rapid recall. She completes the Sunday *New York Times* crossword puzzle, in ink.

And yet one momentous, seminal event characterizes Marcia more than any other aspect of her life. It is this event which prompts me to break the self-imposed restriction on writing about her.

M

I was introduced to Marcia by her sister, Elaine. As the story goes, one of the reasons I married Marcia, is that I was infatuated with Elaine's five-year-old daughter, Vicki, so bright and vivacious. At our wedding Vicki preceded Marcia down the aisle, strewing flowers.

Over the years Marcia was intimately bound with Vicki. She seldom missed being present at Vicki's life-cycle events. More importantly Marcia was constantly in the wings ready to give Vicki unconditional love and attention. To a significant degree Vicki was responsible for the direction of our children's lives. It was her enthusiastic response to the summer Camp Ramah experience that impressed Marcia and me. We entered our children on this same track; it ultimately contributed to our *aliyah*.

Vicki's scholastic achievements were stellar. She emulated Marcia by attending Sarah Lawrence College and went on to earn a doctorate in psychology. She subsequently achieved a reputation as an excellent diagnostician of children's behavioral problems and as an adult psychotherapist.

In 1969 Vicki married Marius Pessah who became a kidney specialist in Long Island, New York. The son of a rabbi, he is a Jewish scholar as well as a classical guitarist. They have two sons, Michael and Adam.

In 1975 Vicki developed abdominal pain due to polycystic kidneys. Over the years her kidneys became massively enlarged and her kidney function deteriorated. Finally she reached end-stage renal disease, a death sentence before the days of dialysis and renal transplantation. Dialysis, a system for filtering Vicki's blood to rid it of the lethal levels of urea and potassium, required a surgical procedure in which a connection (a shunt) was made between a vein and an artery in her arm. After a few weeks when the shunt was healed, a nurse would insert needles into this shunt; the dialysis machine then received Vicki's blood, filtered it, and returned it back to her with healthier levels of urea and potassium. Unfortunately Vicki's shunts were frequently complicated by pain, local infection, and blockages; new shunts were required. Knowing that these shunts were all that stood between her and dying, she was in constant fear that they might close off completely.

Initially the three-times-per-week dialysis treatments were done in the hospital outpatient department but later at home after a dialysis machine had been installed. Looking out at her landscaped yard or watching television did little to distract Vicki from agonizing pain; she couldn't control her sobbing during the three hours of dialysis, despite knowing the torment this caused Marius and her sons. And adding to her misery were the multiple attempts by lab technicians to take blood from her tiny veins; her arms and hands were constantly discolored from failed attempts.

Once permanent dialysis became necessary, Vicki's name was entered onto the roster of candidates awaiting kidney transplant. At the outset she was a foreboding number 2,000. She was told that the earliest she could expect to receive a cadaver kidney would be two years. Vicki never left the house without her beeper; she had to be ready at a moment's notice when a kidney became available. Both Marcia and her brother Bob offered to be tested for tissue compatibility but Vicki declined their offer. "I'm not going to endanger your lives. I can wait for a cadaver kidney." Her husband was found to be an unsatisfactory match. By the time the two years had passed Vicki was number 250. This number would have been even higher if many patients had not died for lack of a donor in time.

In the autumn of 1996 our daughter Raina, visiting from Israel, witnessed a dialysis treatment. Raina was appalled by her cousin's dire condition. On returning to Israel she described Vicki's plight to Marcia. "I'm going to have myself tested to see if I can give her a kidney."

Though Marcia was proud of our daughter, her instant reaction was, "Oh, no, you're not. If anyone will do it, I will." Marcia knew that as a match, she carried twice as many of Vicki's genes as did Raina.

What other possible donors were there? Our children and those of Marcia's brother Bob would all have volunteered. Vicki's father had died seven years before. Her mother Elaine, eight years older than Marcia, was unfit; at age seventy-four she had metastatic breast cancer. Her Uncle Bob at seventy-one was no longer acceptable. The truth was that Marcia wasn't going to permit anyone else to be the donor.

M

"Vicki is my niece. No one is more responsible for her than I. No one loves her more than I. Besides, I'm the best genetic match available."

Marcia's friends were dismayed by her cavalier attitude toward undergoing life-threatening surgery for her niece. "Why can't Vicki wait till her name comes up on the waiting list to receive a cadaver kidney?"

"Can't she buy a kidney from India?"

"Why you and not someone else in your family?"

"Is David really letting you do this?" Obviously I was not oblivious to the dire, albeit uncommon, risks. Yet I agreed with Marcia's Sarah Lawrence anthropology professor, Irving Goldman, who after praising her, added "But Marcia, you really don't have a choice, do you?"

Nor did the risks deter Marcia. Certainly she had no death wish but, to save Vicki, she felt any risk was worth it. "After all, I'm sixty-six and Vicki is only forty-eight." The problem was not new to Marcia. Her cousin Grace was fifty-seven when she gave a kidney to her son and had continued in good health twenty-six years later. Marcia was keenly aware that one could live as normal a life with one kidney as with two. The remote possibility of accidental injury to the remaining kidney didn't concern her.

The donor process got under way. First, Marcia called Vicki offering to be a donor. It was as though a volcano had erupted:

Vicki: "Aunt Marcia, you're the greatest but no way will I let you."

Marcia: "I won't take no for an answer."

Vicki: "I'm not going to let you put your life in jeopardy."

Marcia: "I'm healthy. We both know the risk to me is negligible."

Vicki: "How will I ever thank you?"

Marcia: "Letting me do it is thanks enough."

There followed repeated callbacks from Vicki and Marius with expressions of disbelief and overwhelming gratitude. Finally, "It's too good to be true."

The initial requirement was to prove a satisfactory tissue match between Vicki and Marcia. To achieve this, Marcia's blood had to be in the laboratory at Westchester County Medical Center in White Plains, New York, less than twenty-four hours after it was drawn. Two hours before departure of the 1:00 AM El Al flight, I drew blood from Marcia, enough to fill several vials received from the Medical Center. We drove speedily to Ben Gurion Airport and quickly approached a security agent. Marcia handed her our package. The agent began the usual rapid-fire security questions: "Who gave you this package? Has it been in your possession the whole time . . ." but stopped short when she realized the nature of Marcia's request. After heaping a cascade of blessings on Marcia, she initiated red-carpet treatment for the blood samples, personally handing them to the flight's purser. Eleven hours later at Kennedy Airport in New York he, in turn, gave them to a security guard, who passed them to Vicki and helped her avoid Customs and Health Department delays. An hour and a half later Marcia's blood arrived at the hospital well within the prescribed time.

The matching procedure took three days. The report indicated a "3 of 6" match (identical twins would be "6 of 6") "adequate for transplant . . . a little better than a cadaver." (I teased Marcia, "I always said you were a little better than a cadaver.") Marcia was now a major step closer to being an acceptable donor.

Soon we received instructions and numerous forms from the transplant center. Wishing to save valuable time, and since Marcia had no doctor who knew her medical history better, I wrote her medical history and performed a physical examination. This presented the usual dichotomy within me as an objective doctor and a loving husband who had to resist wishful thinking that there be no abnormalities. With each area I examined I said to myself, "Let it be normal." Actually the only item of note was a blood pressure of 160/80, on the high side of normal. "No problem," I naively predicted.

There followed a series of blood tests that were performed in Tel Aviv, including a test for HIV (human immunodeficiency virus that causes AIDS); no abnormalities were found. Ultrasound and an isotope study revealed normal anatomy and equal function of her kidneys. Thus ended the testing that was to be performed on this side of the ocean.

Finally, a time frame was proposed. Marcia would go to New York a week before the transplant to have final blood tests and a kidney angiogram. The latter study appraises the vascular anatomy of each kidney and indicates which kidney would be best suited for attaching its arteries and veins, to the appropriate vessels in Vicki's body. If Marcia remained on an approval track, I would join her two days before surgery.

Westchester Hospital was chosen by Marius. He was acquainted with the highly acclaimed transplant unit headed by Dr. Khalid Butt. He was also satisfied that Dr. Butt's associate, Dr. Leone (not his real name), who would be Marcia's doctor, was a superb surgeon. The plan was that Dr. Butt would remove Vicki's more pain-producing left kidney (rather than both or neither) and prepare the "bed" for accepting Marcia's kidney, while Dr. Leone took out Marcia's right kidney in an adjacent operating room. When a relative asked how Marcia's right kidney could be put into Vicki's left side, I quipped, "They just turn Marcia's kidney upside down. No problem, except that when Vicki pees, the foam will be on the bottom!"

All went smoothly. (Marcia even tried to be a matchmaker for the radiologist who performed her angiogram.) That is, until she encountered Dr. Leone. He was short, thin, probably in his late thirties. She knew that he would ultimately be the one to give the green light or to scuttle her efforts. He immediately became an adversary when, frowning, he commented, "We almost never take a donor your age (sixty-six)!" He next snapped, "How can your husband be so unethical as to do your exam?" He was not wrong except for his accusatory manner, not even asking for an explanation. When he finally got around to taking her blood pressure, at which time Marcia was boiling with anger, again he attacked. "Your husband lied. Your blood pressure isn't 160/80. It's 200/100!"

Marcia was in a panic. She was furious at this Napoleonic scoundrel but she had to placate him. Rather than scolding Dr. Leone for unprofessional behavior, she countered, "Do you really think my husband wants me to die?"

He remained incredulous. His only moment of professionalism came when he said, "You know it's my responsibility to get you off the table (safely through the operation)."

Eventually, Dr. Leone pronounced Marcia fit as a donor. Surgery would proceed as scheduled. Marcia was relieved, though hardly placated. All of this I learned after I arrived at Vicki's house. Already concerned that Dr. Leone's attitude toward Marcia and me might affect her operation, I used restraint not to confront him.

The final night before hospitalization, Marius and Vicki treated us to a lavish room in a charming hotel in Great Neck. With little thought of this as the "Last Supper" we nevertheless reveled in the youngsters' romantic notions. This was not the last gesture of their gratitude. We kept reminding them that it was difficult to say who should be grateful to whom. Also I quoted my father who would say, "If you thank me, you take away my *mitzvah.*" The day after the surgeries, Vicki and Marius gave Marcia a magnificent Chinese jade brooch. Inscribed on the back were the words, "With gratitude from Vicki, Marius, Michael, and Adam." My present to Marcia was a Yemenite gold multistrand necklace.

The morning of surgery was suspenseful for us, not the staff. Except for their adulation for Marcia – they hadn't witnessed a sixty-six-year old donor before unless it was a parent – for them it was as routine as an appendectomy. At the same early hour Vicki and Marcia left their separate rooms – policy interdicted donor and recipient sharing a room. Marcia's brother Bob and his wife Helen, Marius, and I tried to distract one another. The absence of progress reports added to our anxiety.

A report finally came from the operating room indicating that both Vicki and Marcia were doing well and that fifteen minutes after the transplant was completed, Vicki's kidney (or was it still Marcia's?) was excreting copious quantities of urine; in the first day it amounted to a total of nine liters. It was mind-boggling to see a multiliter plastic bag ballooning with clear urine at Vicki's bedside. Within hours Vicki's kidney tests approached normalcy. Imagine her elation after the catheter was removed to be able to urinate freely and in normal quantities; she hadn't put out more than an ounce or two a day for a couple of years.

Vicki's mother Elaine wasn't physically able to be at the hospital the day of surgery. Two days later, upon entering Vicki's room in a wheelchair, Elaine saw a woman standing at the sink washing her hair. She thought, "This must be Vicki's roommate." Of course not; it was Vicki.

My emotional lability on first seeing Marcia being returned from the recovery room said more than words. I was not as nonchalant as I may have lead the reader to believe. Fleeting thoughts of losing Marcia darted in and out behind my cool facade. I was ready to blame myself if anything went wrong which is partly why I panicked when on her second postoperative day, I noted her swollen right leg. Dr. Leone's flip reaction was, "It's almost always nothing." "Almost nothing" wasn't good enough for me. At my request Dr. Butt ordered a simple test that proved that it indeed was "nothing."

Marcia's recovery was otherwise uneventful. Most of her pain was related to having a rib removed to enlarge the operative field of view. Dr. Butt visited her soon after surgery. With a crisp, lilting accent he said, "My dear lady, what a beautiful kidney you gave to your niece!"

I said "uneventful" except for repeated confrontations with Dr. Leone. Departing from Marcia's room on her second postoperative day, he turned back saying, "And I still think you're secretly taking blood pressure medicine and that your husband wrote a false blood-pressure report." A year later he was no longer Dr. Butt's assistant.

Except for Vicki's distress with antirejection medication, a festive mood prevailed. Many of Marcia's cousins and friends and scores of Vicki's friends streamed back and forth between their two rooms. Of course they were happy for Vicki but their praise for Marcia was almost embarrassing; her room overflowed with flowers, fruit, candy, and from those who knew Marcia best, books and crossword puzzles. And I, too, got plenty of hugs.

Marcia loved sporting the green lapel pin that Dr. Butt gave her. Like the red pin to remind people about AIDS, this pin was to trigger discussion about organ donation. Signs in the department read, "**Don't take your organs to heaven. Heaven knows we need them here.**"

Marcia quickly returned to normal health. I remained with her one week after the surgery enjoying the role reversal of reading Marcia to sleep. She stayed another week at Bobby's home until Dr. Butt gave her permission to fly back to Israel.

Vicki, on the other hand, endured the extremely unpleasant side effects of medications taken to prevent her body from rejecting Marcia's kidney. (This latter event occurs in less than 10% of transplants.) She required frequent blood tests, changes of medications, and manipulation of drug dosage. It took a year before she was working full-time and before she ventured out alone for long drives. Catastrophes were no longer looming around the corner. And what a relief not to carry the donor beeper. Three years after the operation Vicki's kidney tests remained normal and the side effects of her medication continued at an acceptable level.

It is difficult for us not to be self-conscious about Marcia's *mitzvah*. The rabbinic injunction of performing a *mitzvah*, which cannot be reciprocated (*gamillot hesed*), fit Marcia's heroic act. It was as though it was her mission in life, to save her niece's life, maybe especially imperative because we hadn't been able to save our daughter Amy's.

We frequently talk about Marcia's donation of a kidney. If it appears to be self-aggrandizing, let it be. Our task is not to popularize the obvious benefit to the recipient but rather to tout the satisfaction of being a donor. How validated we would feel if just one person were influenced one day to lie on a table in one of two adjoining operating rooms. Can you not visualize the life force in a glistening kidney as it passes from one room to the other?

M

CAREER

ANATOMY OF A DOCTOR

"What made you want to be a doctor, David?" Probably every doctor since Hippocrates has been asked the same question.

Numerous motives have been suggested but who knows which or how many apply to me? These range from the idealistic of wanting to help mankind to the basest, of wanting to be rich. For some it may be the desire for power, for status, for rising above one's peers. For others it is the compulsion to please parents or an ego that requires being needed or loved. I know one young man who, responding to exhortations of his parents, entered medical school only to transfer to law school after one semester. I never felt parental pressure.

I do have an early negative memory that dates back to age five. I can see myself in a children's ward in Pittsburgh's Montefiore Hospital being forced to stand naked on a bedside table. Oblivious of my embarrassment, the surgeon poked my groin as he looked for, obviously in my mind, a monstrous rupture. I was exposed for all to view my shrinking manhood. Possibly I vowed then to join 'em in order to lick 'em.

At age nine, in fourth grade, I volunteered to man the first-aid station. The extent of my responsibility was applying tincture of iodine or mercurochrome and bandages (no Band-Aids in that era) to cuts and bruises caused by falls in the cinder-covered school yard. I tended at least one patient during every recess and wasn't sued once.

It was also about this time that brother Jerry was in the first year at Jefferson Medical School. Being thirteen years older, he was without doubt a significant role model. Sending his laundry home by mail (the cheapest way for Jerry to have clean clothes) implied an elevated status to me. Once he enclosed an ear from his anatomy lab cadaver. This startled but didn't disgust me.

There is no doubt that Mom and Dad as first-generation immigrants *shept nachas* (took great pleasure) from having a son studying to be a doctor. At that time (1934) the country was in the midst of the Great Depression and like almost everyone else, my family was hard hit. Jerry waited on tables in his fraternity house in exchange for meals; during summer breaks he performed hard labor at Jones and Laughlin Steel Mill in Aliquippa. Some of Mom's family gave a few welcomed dollars. I was thirteen when the whole family drove to Philadelphia for Jerry's graduation. Commencement was held in the Philadelphia Academy of Music, its seating resplendent with deep, red, velvet cushions.

In 1942 during World War II – I was seventeen – my homeroom teacher announced that future premedical students could leave high school a semester early in order to enter college. (The government reasoned that the war would be protracted and that the number of physicians would need to be augmented.) I grabbed the opportunity, and following the path of four brothers before me, I entered Geneva College in Beaver Falls, Pennsylvania in January 1943. It never occurred to me to apply anywhere else. Why not? I can only guess that then, and even subsequently, I allowed my brothers to set goals for me. Perhaps the goals became limits. It was only in my thirties that I began to break out of the mold. The most obvious and final example would be my move to Israel.

Medical schools were considering applicants after four semesters of college – traditionally four full years were necessary. I was accepted by Harvard Medical School (HMS) for the Class of Oct. '44.

I'll never know why Harvard took me. At Geneva I was an excellent student though hardly a stellar one. Dr. Theodore McMillion,

Professor of Biology and Dr. Allen Morrill, head of the English Department sent letters of recommendation. (Allen and his wife Eleanor became close friends and subsequently, patients.) The record of the two previous Genevans at HMS was mixed. One graduated magna cum laude; the other majored in bridge at the Copley Plaza Hotel and flunked out in his first year. My class was the last before women were accepted; I didn't have to compete with outstanding female candidates. Possibly I fell into a geographic selection. Doubtlessly, like other schools, Harvard had a quota for Jews – as best as I can estimate, we comprised about ten to fifteen percent of the class. (In 1999 I learned that a classmate with an Irish name is Jewish. Did Harvard know?)

Immediately after the government passed a law that only students enrolled by July 1, 1944 would be deferred from active military service, all medical schools adjusted by having their students begin on July 1. Most activated medical classes while Harvard sent its student body to the college in Cambridge. Some, like me, needed the time to complete medical-school requirements. Short one semester of French, I began a course at Harvard Yard but never completed it because of an emergency appendectomy. The appropriate conclusion is that I practiced medicine fraudulently for over fifty years.

Living in Cambridge was intoxicating. I ate my meals in Adams House where the Roosevelts, Cabots, Lodges, and Kennedys had also eaten. I took a class in art appreciation at Fogg Museum – no time for such luxuries at Geneva. I studied Plato with a philosopher who resembled Demosthenes. The historian Arthur Schlesinger Jr. gave a series of lectures. Best of all, I sculled alone on the Charles River, all the while pinching myself asking, "What is this nice little boy from Aliquippa doing here?" I didn't say "nice Jewish boy" for, at the time, my Jewish consciousness was hibernating.

One negative but medically useful experience deserves telling. Soon after arriving in Cambridge I developed lightheadedness, so much so that I feared fainting in Boston's subway. I remember studying at my desk, marking a calendar every time I burped. Any fourth-year medical student would have diagnosed this combination of symptoms as hyperventilation syndrome, a physiologic reaction to anxiety. The treatment is simple: know the disease for what it is and breathe as slowly and shallowly as possible. Unfortunately, the school doctor who examined me wasn't that smart. He did absolutely the worst thing: he ordered an x-ray of my head! I assumed naively, "That's for a brain tumor." A competent physician would have sent me to a psychiatrist (which might also have prevented my subsequent peptic ulcer). I improved despite my doctor.

Medical school began in earnest in early October 1944 opening with a two-hour lecture by my future boss Professor Herrman Blumgart. He held us spellbound and forever committed, as he described his joy at being a doctor. He demonstrated, cruelly I initially thought, a patient pushed to chest pain by doing a step-test (the forerunner of the treadmill). To my relief and amazement, the patient's pain subsided quickly with rest and with no ill effects, as Dr. Blumgart had anticipated.

Eugene Landis, Professor of Physiology, also on the opening day said, "We've invested much energy and money selecting each of you. We will do all we can to protect that investment." This was in striking contrast to some medical schools, which automatically lopped off the bottom one third of the class on completion of the first year. "Look at the person to your left and at the one to your right. One of you will not return next year." Even without this threat at Harvard, one of our class committed suicide the day before lectures began. I believe three students (out of 150) flunked. One was my lab partner in microanatomy who was sleepless and depressed from nightly defending Catholic dogma against a bevy of sneering WASPs. I wonder what kind of doctors the latter became.

The rest of the year was sheer terror. Writing all I knew, I finished a three-hour anatomy exam in one and a half hours only to discover first hand that the feared warning note, indicating a D, known as the pink slip, was white. I was never to receive another. Although I got A's in college chemistry, trigonometry, and physics, I really understood the basics of very little. Who can fathom double bonds, cosines, and electrons?

Despite the present theory of a bacterial causation of duodenal ulcer, I have no doubt that anxiety led to mine. I was referred to Chester Jones, Professor of Gastroenterology at Massachusetts General Hospital. Dr. Jones called the office of Professor Merrill Sosman who had performed my gastrointestinal x-ray at the Peter Bent Brigham Hospital. The secretary read, "a 5 cm. deep duodenal ulcer;" obviously a typographical error, it should have read, "0.5 cm." What Professor Jones said to me was a blur. What I heard was, "You know you're too young to be in medical school" – I had just turned nineteen.

"Here it comes," I thought. "He's going to tell me to pack my bags. I've disgraced my family. I'll never survive this failure." Well, I left Dr. Jones's office without such threats. He told me to drink milk and to chew antacid tablets. Presumably, his "too young" comment was meant to give me insight. It was too subtle for me.

The supportive therapy I didn't get from Dr. Jones came from Cy Rubin, a fourth year student. He took me for a walk one evening. We talked, but not a word do I remember. I only know that I went to bed that night confident that my world had not come to an end.

My next crisis was resolved by family. There I was in the biochemistry laboratory standing with instructor Dr. Westerman as he tried to explain the hemoglobin molecule to me. As he drew it on the blackboard, I grew increasingly panicky. I had just pleaded with him to go through the explanation a second time when out of the corner of my eye, I saw my uncles Harry and David with my aunts Rose and Fanny standing in the doorway. (These are the relatives who had contributed to Jerry's tuition.) I bid a hasty good-bye to my instructor and let my family wrap themselves around me. Probably I cried. Their visit was a turning point. I entered class the next day knowing that I would never understand hemoglobin but that I could pass a biochemistry exam. And my patients never need know. Thirty-three years later this scene was re-enacted in Jerusalem. This time it was Uncle Harry's son Daniel who surprised our daughter Raina in her office at a very low moment in her *aliyah*. She cried in Daniel's arms, restored after his visit. Both Raina and Daniel were aware of history repeating itself.

The second year included the first course on being a physician. It was given by Dr. Henry Jackson, tall, gaunt, bespectacled, looking like

Sergei Rachmaninoff. He taught by listing the causes, for example, of hemoptysis (spitting blood):

"1: Tuberculosis.

"2: Tuberculosis.

"3: Tuberculosis," repeated for emphasis until

"8: Cancer." That was 1946. Well, we loved the lecture and him.

Then, came the final lecture both to us and, after two decades, at Harvard. The subject: "What to tell the dying patient?" At last we felt privy to the clinician's world. The answer – and remember, those were the days before aggressive surgery and chemotherapy – was "anything but the truth." Dr. Jackson elaborated. "One day a patient came to my office two weeks after he had been 'opened and closed' for inoperable stomach cancer. We, of course, had told him that he had an ulcer. The patient asked if he could have a cocktail before dinner. I replied, 'Yes.' He then asked about wine during his meals to which I also consented. 'And what about a highball or two after?' I nodded, 'Yes, all you want.' Thereupon, the patient left my office, bought a revolver, and killed himself. Do you know who pulled the trigger? I did, for I let the poor devil know it didn't matter what he did, that he was doomed."

Well, I got the moral to that story and from 1956 to 1960 I also lied to my patients. (See chapter, "Down with doubletalk . . .")

At the end of the lecture, knowing full well that we had been let into the inner sanctum, the physician's sacred office, and knowing that greatness was about to leave the stage, we heard Dr. Jackson close, "It's not how can the students do without their teacher; it's how can the teacher do without his students." And, thus, he vanished from the lecture hall. There was no applause. In the silence I refrained from looking around to see who else might be wiping his eyes.

Since we were in the midst of a war, the usual four years were to be reduced to three, summer study making up the difference. If the school year had not lengthened when World War II ended, the absence of summer breaks would have created problems for some who needed free time to earn money for living expenses. Fortunately tuition remained $400 for each year though tuition for the next class jumped to $1,000. Living in Vanderbilt Hall in a three-man suite in the first year, and in a suite for four the next three years, helped keep my expenses down. Dad and Uncle Harry's shoe business began to thrive during and after the war, but I remained puritanical about spending money.

The third and fourth years were entirely clinical, relaxed and joyous. It became obvious that I learn best starting from the concrete rather than from the theoretical. Show me a chemical formula and I panic, but give me a patient with a problem and all my computer pathways are open. If grades are any criteria, I was in the lower part of the middle third of the class after two years and finished at the top of the middle third.

In the third year I was inducted into the prestigious Boylston Medical Society, founded in 1811, whose purpose was the exchange of ideas between students and faculty. It was expected that students would present progress reports on their research projects. I never did, since my research with spinal fluid floundered.

Of course, nothing helped when I was faced with my first patient on the ward at the Beth Israel Hospital. I had just turned twenty, was socially about sixteen, and here I was, assigned to perform a heart exam of an elderly woman with enormous breasts. I panicked. "How will I get my fingers and stethoscope, ah, er, near her heart?"

This formidable lady saw my dilemma. She confronted me with, "Why, I have children older than you!"

I assume that my blushing subsided as I countered with the mother-of-all non-sequiturs, "and I have brothers older than I." Thereupon she bared her breast and I dug in, never again to be intimidated by female anatomy.

Touching patients came naturally to me and was reinforced by a plethora of role models. Drs. Blumgart and Al Freedberg would place a hand on the arm of the patient whose history was being recited by an intern on the opposite side of the bed. This symbol of caring may not exclude nontouchers from the ranks of good physicians but I would guess that more of the latter became pathologists or anesthesiologists. I learned from Raina years later when she was teaching Re-evaluation Counseling that placing a hand on the client's arm was essential for facilitating the process of emotional discharge.

M

How validated I felt when I read the following in a speech delivered by Dr. Wood to a gathering of newly inducted members of the American College of Physicians: "There are two kinds of doctors, one an 'F.O.B.,' the other an 'S.O.B. .' The first is the professor who enters the patient's room leading an entourage consisting of an assistant professor, the chief medical resident, two interns, the head nurse, and a medical student. They discuss catecholamines, acid/base balance, and DNA. No one looks at the patient and the only one to touch him, and this accidentally, is the medical student while plugging in the x-ray viewing box. That professor is an 'F.O.B.,' a 'foot-of-the-bed' doctor. The second variety enters, maybe with a nurse and/or a medical student, pulls a chair to the bed, sits, and putting his hand on the patient's arm, asks, 'And how are you, Mrs. Cohen?' He's an 'S.O.B.,' a 'side-of-the-bed' doctor." Dr. Wood concluded, "So what kind of doctor will you be, an 'F.O.B.' or an 'S.O.B.'?" Parenthetically, I have added a third type, the "D.W." doctor: he passes the *d*oor*w*ay proclaiming to the patient, "You are feeling better today."

What a pleasant interlude I experienced on a ward at the Massachusetts General Hospital. I had compiled a table of significant words required for history taking. All I had to do was to fill in the appropriate words in Italian, German, Greek, Russian, Chinese, and other languages represented among the patients. Despite A's in Latin and French, languages were not my forté (as the reader will surmise when I discuss "My battle with Hebrew"). Nevertheless, my use of a word or two in a new patient's native tongue helped create an atmosphere of caring.

I vividly remember sitting between the beds of two Italian patients and posing the problem, "How do you ask a nice old woman (in Italian, of course) if she has seen blood in her stool?" Laughing hilariously while whispering each possible word to one another, they concluded that there were none that were acceptable. Presumably when the need arose, I could play charades.

The cumbersome use of language got me into trouble with "God" himself, Dr. Blumgart. It fell to me, as it did to one of the house staff every six months, to admit one of Beth Israel Hospital's most generous philanthropists, a private patient of Dr. Blumgart. His problem was "cancerophobia." It was our job to coordinate, in the three days that our benefactor would allocate to us, all the available tests that could disclose a hidden malignancy. My history opened as follows: "This fifty-six-year-old philanthropist is readmitted for tests that far exceed any medical indication." Presumably I added that these workups gave him several months of relief from his cancerophobia. I received a call – a summons – to appear posthaste before Dr. Blumgart. I remember standing as at military attention in front of his desk as his piercing countenance accused me of the worst insubordination. "Do you realize how insulting your history is to me?"

"But, Sir," I backpedaled, "I was only trying to justify all the exposure to x-ray, venipunctures, enemas, and endoscopies that it took to treat his 'cancerophobia'."

"Fine," Dr. Blumgart responded, "Now go and write that" as he tore up my initial composition.

Obviously, Dr. Blumgart was right. The lesson was also that an improperly, although accurately written history, may cast inappropriate blame on the referring doctor while touting one's own brilliance. How often the house staff would write, "This patient was treated (read mistreated) by his LMD (local medical doctor who obviously could never get into Harvard) at an outlying hospital (read enter at the risk of your life)."

Years later, on the occasion of Dr. Blumgart's retirement, his "boys" were asked to write letters of esteem. Mine was a tongue-in-cheek reference to my father's slowly developing anemia. It was only after Dad fainted that I detected his problem. With further testing I diagnosed pernicious anemia which responded dramatically to vitamin B12 injections. At the time I entered practice in Aliquippa, family doctors were routinely giving vitamin B12 injections as a cure-all for fatigue, depression, and menstrual symptoms. The patients came to rely on these once-or-twice-a-month shots. Knowing that the only indication for vitamin B12 therapy was pernicious anemia, I scorned the prevalent practice. I therefore wrote to my esteemed professor that had he not trained me to be so scientifically pure, my father would never have fainted. I hope he detected my irony and was complimented.

Another important lesson for teachers, doctors, parents, and everyone else was taught to my roommate, Garry Hough, and to me by a professor of ophthalmology. Within a few minutes of commencing clinical rounds one day, reacting to my question, he snapped, "That's the most stupid question I ever heard." He jumped on poor Garry only a moment later saying, "Don't you ever read the literature?" Well, even before being graded, we sent the S.O.B. (do not read "side-of-the-bed") a letter suggesting that "humiliating a fellow human being, under no circumstance was justified." There was no reply and we both passed. At the time we thought ourselves to be quite brave and self-righteous. It was years later that I learned, that although letters do let off steam, face to face confrontation is more effective and more gentlemanly.

Another negative lesson followed. When Marcia became pregnant, there was no doubt that I would request my instructor in medical complications in obstetrics to be her doctor. I loved his lectures although I did not love obstetrics. He was great to Marcia but I soon learned that he had no use for husbands. I was miffed that I couldn't be with Marcia in the labor or delivery rooms but this was not unusual in those days. Okay, not so terrible. After Marcia had been in labor for twenty-four hours, he had to resort to an emergency caesarean section. Again not so terrible. In fact my mother-in-law had requested that Marcia have a pelvic x-ray since Marcia's sister had required an emergency caesarean section. It made sense. So far I had not made comments or demands. After the delivery, my teacher came out to tell us that we had a little girl. He apologized to my mother-in-law for not heeding her suggestion. Before even thanking him or asking about Marcia, I blurted out, "Can we have any more children?" Inappropriate? That was what was in my head at that moment.

He glared at me and attacked, "Why is it that every time you ask me a question, you put a knife in my heart?"

I'll never know what there was about me that precipitated such rage, but the insult sits with me to this day. Nevertheless I remain grateful for the lesson he taught me, to keep a poker face when confronted with what would be considered an annoying question and to apprise students and patients alike not to be reticent – "No question is stupid or silly." I almost lapsed years later, when after detailing to a patient the precautions she must take to prevent radiation exposure to her children following her treatment with radioactive iodine, I was asked, "And what about my dog?" I contained myself and with the look of concern asked, "How old is your dog?"

Another instance of criticism came from a female staff member at Lahey Clinic where I was a Fellow. "Why is it that when you are in a room, you give the impression that you know more than anyone?" Yikes! What did I do to deserve that? She could not have been talking about me. Goodness knows, I have always been painfully aware of the limitations of my medical knowledge. Or does it mean that my professed humility is false, a delusion?

Isn't it convenient that fifty years after graduation from medical school, those I criticize so freely are gone to that "Great Boston in the sky." On the other hand, how wonderful it would be if those I describe with such high esteem, could read my laudatory and grateful words – Al Freedberg at age ninety-two has done so.

I was astounded by one of my classmates, who, never having contributed to the Alumni Fund, was referred to me for solicitation. His answer to my pitch? "Why should I? I paid my tuition. What did Harvard ever do for me?" Now that I have returned from the fiftieth reunion of my medical-school class, I have a simple answer to that question. Not only did the school mold me into the doctor I am, but also it reinforced my ego, enabling me to take unpopular positions, whether in the pursuit of medical excellence or of a more democratic society. I could not have asked for more.

DOWN WITH DOUBLETALK TO CANCER PATIENTS

"Are you thinking of killing yourself?" It was something in Sara's eyes that made me ask.

She shrugged, "What's the use of prolonging my suffering?" Unable to deny the logic of her response, I found myself, for the first time in my long medical career, aligned with a cancer patient who was defying the conventional wisdom – namely, that the doctor had to fight death until the patient's last breath and often even after that. Maybe this was finally the moment for me to join with those who were redefining the doctor's role in the care of the patient with terminal disease.

Yet, a dissenting opinion screamed within me, "Run! Leave Sara. Get away before you become so deeply immersed that you violate your Hippocratic oath to do no harm." How was I to choose between these two options?

Many years ago, Harvard Professor Herrman Blumgart wrote an article in the *New England Journal of Medicine* entitled "The Compleat Physician." He quoted an earlier source, Francis Weld Peabody, who said, "The secret of the care of the patient is caring for the patient." Over time, I learned that management of the patient with life-threatening cancer requires an extra ounce of that caring.

My introduction to patient care came in the second year of medical school during a lecture by Professor Henry Jackson. He confessed he had once led a cancer patient to suicide because he had not been a good enough liar. (Details of this lecture appear in the chapter, "Anatomy of a doctor.") His message was clear: the patient cannot handle the truth, unless of course, he needs to know in order to make financial arrangements to protect his family. Remember, it was 1946 before safe anesthesia and surgery, before chemotherapy and focused radiation therapy, before a wide array of antibiotics, and before adequate pain-control programs; none of these options were available for the patient and his physician to choose. I took Dr. Jackson's message as gospel and could find no reason to contradict it until several years after starting my medical practice in 1956.

Several patient encounters opened my eyes. The first concerned an elderly Serbian immigrant woman with inoperable cancer of the colon. Before I could form my own plan, the son and daughter, both schoolteachers, took me off the hook. "Don't let Mom know, and certainly, the truth will kill our father." Well, the patient died three months later. No problem as far as I knew. Then nine months later the widower, an uneducated mill worker, was admitted to my service with shortness of breath. Before I could begin a history and physical exam, he led me to the privacy of the visitors' room and began, "Doctor, I want you to know I'm very angry with you. What right did you have to hide the truth of my wife's sickness from me? Who gave you the right to confide in my children? I was her husband! It was for *me* to decide what to do."

If ever I felt chastised (Dr. Blumgart couldn't have done it better), if ever I realized that my role as a physician was being challenged, it was then. After my apologies, which seemed to satisfy him, but not me, we shook hands; I knew that something pivotal had occurred. Our relationship afterward was strong and warm.

Not much later I had the pleasure of being consulted by a close friend of our family. As a boy I remember watching Morry play first base for sandlot baseball. A successful grocery-store owner, he was extremely bright, winning many TV sets, as prizes from newspaper and magazine quizzes. His marriage to Rose was a love match generally acknowledged by the Jewish community. Well, with one hand on Morry's abdomen, I knew that he had cancer in the liver. Needle biopsy confirmed metastatic disease from the pancreas. I estimated that he had three months remaining. Rose and her two children met with me and begged me not to tell Morry the truth. We conspired to tell him that the gastrointestinal x-ray showed an "ulcer."

He did get some relief from ulcer treatment until six months later when he was admitted to the hospital with bleeding from the stomach. A repeat x-ray showed a malignant gastric ulcer, doubtlessly from metastatic disease. By this time one of the first effective chemotherapeutic drugs had become available. Finally, I took control and informed the family of my intention to be truthful with Morry.

It was 10 PM as we sat close together, Morry and I, in a darkened hospital solarium. "Morry," I said, "I must confess that I've been lying to you but I'm not going to any more. The truth is, you've had cancer all along. There's a new drug that offers hope . . ."

I don't remember how far I got before he took my hand, and lifting it to his lips, kissed it. This was even more remarkable since Morry was not normally a demonstrative guy. He exclaimed, "I knew something was wrong. Rose hasn't been talking to me. And the kids, well, it's sort of cold when they're in the house." Morry then asked, "How long do I have?"

"Six months. Six years. Who knows? You've already beaten the odds."

Morry lived another two years, looking emaciated but happy as he walked his daughter down the aisle at her wedding. Soon after, he died peacefully at home with Rose and me at his side. Rose shared with me then and repeatedly over the next thirty years, "What wonderful rapport Morry and I had during those last two years."

Finally, I knew that Dr. Jackson's admonition of 1946 to be a good liar no longer obtained for the 1960s. It took Dr. Kuhbler-Ross, author of *Death and Dying*, to reinforce my change of heart. She gave structure and a vocabulary to the process of dying with her "five steps." When she lectured at Beaver County Community College shortly after my experience with Morry, I was one of two doctors in a crowd of 200 nurses, social workers, and ministers. I braved a question: "But what's wrong with continuing with blood tests, for example, bilirubin in a dying patient with intractable itching, if it might prove jaundice and suggest a treatment?"

To the delight of the nurses Dr. Kuhbler-Ross replied, "Doctor, you don't get it. You've not learned to let go." And that was not, and still is not, easy to do. As to my question, both she and I were right.

At times a family would disagree with the honest approach; convincing them of its merit often took considerable effort. A famous gastroenterologist gave me his solution. "It's easy. I avoid the family, speaking first to the patient when he awakens from his anesthesia or as soon as a biopsy report returns. It is only then that I seek out the family. When, as is often the case, the family instructs me to be evasive, I tell them, "I'm sorry. I've already told him the truth." Though I agreed with the gastroenterologist's goal, I was appalled by his authoritarian style.

Physicians, including me, live in fear of not making the correct diagnosis, not only because of a potential lawsuit but because our professors, always figuratively peering over our shoulders, will judge us harshly, as if our self-judgment isn't hurtful enough. And if our therapy isn't working, nothing in our training assuages our feelings of guilt. If our patient is slipping away despite our best efforts, we are conditioned to feel like failures and, being failures, we could not face our patient. Goodness knows, what trivia, what banalities we uttered to fill up each dreaded visit with the dying patient. Such missed opportunities to provide consolation! Thus, before I could ever begin to deal with dying patients, I had to accept the reality of death and that the compleat physician remained responsible even after the last therapeutic card had been played.

If only I had read the following quote from Tolstoy's *The Death of Ivan Ilych,* my maturation might have hastened:

"What tormented Ivan Ilych most was the deception, the lie, which for some reason they all accepted, that he was not dying but was simply ill, and that he only need quiet and undergo a treatment and then something very good would result. He, however, knew that, do what they would, nothing would come of it, only still more agonizing suffering and death. This deception tortured him – their not wishing to admit what they all knew and what he knew, but wanting to lie to him concerning his terrible condition, and wishing and forcing him to participate in that lie. Those lies – lies enacted over him on the eve of his death and destined to degrade this awful, solemn act to the level of their visitings, their curtains, their sturgeon for dinner– were a terrible agony for Ivan Ilych . . . This falsity around him and within him did more than anything else to poison his last days."

I gave a number of lectures after my transition from a patriarchal physician to a sharing one, stressing the patient's right to know his diagnosis. As was to be expected, my colleagues responded with disdain and derision. "How can you take away hope?" A logical question. The answer in part is, first of all, you don't; all optimistic potentials are emphasized. Second, most patients *know* and by lying you only cut them off from meaningful relationships. Both patient and family have the need for opportunities to resolve conflicts, and ultimately in time, to make extended good-byes. Third, and legally correct, the patient has the right to know, to be a part of and to control decision-making. "Won't the patient commit suicide?" someone asked. A colleague's patient did. All I could say at that time was that none of my patients had chosen that path; I had yet to meet Sara.

In Israel the situation is somewhat different. The highly touted "patient's right to know" is less emphasized whereas in America every doctor is legally culpable if he doesn't reveal all. In addition there are large segments of society here that greet the word cancer with inconsolable terror. I therefore feel it my responsibility to analyze what the patient wants to know and how much he can handle. That's not easy.

My revised attitude toward the incurable cancer patient had to be evaluated in the light of possible secondary gain for me. There can be no doubt that I reaped tremendous satisfaction from the warm bonding that developed. The intense esteem I sensed was indeed seductive. Though not protected by psychoanalytic training as are psychiatrists, I always managed to keep from crossing the line. Nevertheless, I had to keep asking myself whether giving my patients so much information was for their benefit or mine.

And don't think that the word seductive is inappropriate. I remember reading a novel in which a doctor did lose control. He was so seduced by the relationship with an incurable cancer patient that he accompanied her to the Bahamas. Following a couple of passionate days, the patient swallowed a number of Seconal capsules. She and her doctor/lover then walked to a secluded section of the beach where she sat enveloped in his arms until she breathed her last. *Schmaltz*? Not to me; it's utterly conceivable.

How well I remember the near-terminal bedroom scene of my cousin's wife, Fern. She was skin and bones, tragically emaciated. Her jaundice was intense. How bad I felt not to be able to give her the hot dog she sorely craved. But how could I? Her husband, Milton, and his alternative-medicine advisers, remained rigid to the end in their attempts to cure her. I had such an urge to crawl into bed with Fern just to hold and comfort her – and me.

Another article in the *New England Journal of Medicine* spoke to the issue of doctors touching and hugging their patients. Why not, the writer proposes, if for an appropriate reason like news of a positive pregnancy test after years of testing and treating? He assumes that the doctor is comfortable and that neither he nor the patient has a secret agenda. In reference to hugs, a caveat: not pelvis to pelvis.

Not that all of my patients have been huggable. Take Bill, a derelict, an ex-convict. It was probable that his inoperable colon cancer would not give him much time to live. After he pressed me for the whole truth – at the time I was unsure what support system he might have since his family had disowned him – I leveled with him. His response? "Will you be my doctor till the end?" Holding his arm, I promised that I would. We subsequently had a number of intimate conversations. I don't think Bill ever had a friend from my "class," or I, from his.

While on the subject of unhuggable patients, I must confess that at times, on beginning an interview with a new patient, I find myself having entirely negative reactions. Whether it be a sorry state of physique, lack of cleanliness, or a cold, snobby facial expression, is unimportant. What becomes one of the major thrills of my medical experience is my own metamorphosis as the patient's story makes him or her come alive in my eyes. This moment that the patient becomes locked into my sphere of concern is cataclysmal, humbling, and beautiful.

I was enthralled by a story published in the *Annals Of Internal Medicine.* A professor one morning asked his hospital interns to present to him, not the usual dramatic problems, but rather the least interesting patient admitted during the previous day. They chose an old lady, dumped by neighbors in the emergency room; she lay apathetic in her bed. The professor began his history. "Ever been in a hospital before?"

"Yes."

"How many times?"

"Once."

"What for?"

"A broken arm."

"How did it happen?"

"A trunk hit it."

"How did a trunk hit it?"

"It fell when the ship hit the iceberg."

When it was reported in the newspaper that a survivor of the Titanic lay abandoned in the hospital, neighbors rallied to her support. A humanistic quality of life was restored to her. It would not be an overstatement to call this a cataclysmic teaching moment.

Back to patients with cancer. When I moved to Israel, I switched from cardiology to nuclear medicine and had no opportunity to serve as anyone's primary physician. There was one notable exception: Sara. This is what I wrote about her in a letter sent to my brother Jerry and to A. Stone Freedberg, my mentor during and since a fellowship in 1949:

Sara (not her real name), age 63, my patient for the past eight years, is going to die tonight by her own hand and with my acquiescence. You two have been my role models, so now I ask, "Have I put myself outside the pale?" What would Professor Henry Jackson, who taught us to lie to the cancer patients, say now that I have witnessed Sara and her daughter obtain a lethal dose of phenobarbital? (The faster, shorter-acting barbiturates are not available in Israel.) I hope that, at least, he would agree with Dean Daniel Federman who wrote in the Harvard Newsletter in 1991 that given an incurable disease in a patient who is suffering physically and emotionally, with a limited future, and who is fully aware of all information available, and not depressed or confused by organic brain syndrome, it is not immoral for a physician to assist that patient to commit suicide, though he is not required to do so.

I am one of many physicians, surgeons, internists, endocrinologists, oncologists, nuclear medicine specialists, and radiation therapists, who have cared for Sara since 1985. Her thyroid papillary cancer was treated by near-total thyroidectomy followed by treatment with radioactive iodine. Cervical lymph nodes subsequently appeared and were removed. Soon after, she received radiation to a mass in the left side of the neck. All was quiet for three years until she developed neurological problems – that was one year ago – and soon after, paralysis of the left vocal cord.

It was at this time that I became aware of Sara's desire to commit suicide. It wasn't a frivolous fantasy; not at all. A widow for ten years, she had for years verbalized to her daughter her reluctance to undergo a lingering, painful demise. I begged her to defer any further consideration of suicide, at least, until she would undergo an assessment at Memorial Hospital in New York. She consented though with little enthusiasm. I was gratified that my New York consultants proceeded to radical surgery. Sara came through a ten-hour operation but alas, the pathology had changed to "anaplastic." (This is the most aggressive form of cancer; such patients are usually dead within a few months.)

Sara had three to four months of respite, though never without some pain, until rapidly advancing paralysis of the left arm appeared. Computerized tomography showed a huge mass with destruction of the left half of C5-7 and D1 (upper spine). *Further radiation and chemotherapy were deemed futile.*

For the past month Sara has been lying in bed in her apartment surrounded and entertained by her daughter and numerous friends and their children. Hospice services are ideal and plentiful. Her support system is superb. She is wistful but not depressed.

Her pain is now excruciating with any movement despite large and increasing doses of morphine. Her breathing is occasionally labored. She can no longer swallow solids.

The subject of suicide has come up unrelentingly during her latest hospitalization and during my many home visits these last ten days. Sara expresses terror that her status will deteriorate to a point where she will no longer be able to perform "the job." She is pathetically aware that quadriplegia (paralysis of all her extremities) *and aspirating and choking to death are just around the corner.*

All of my "Yes, but why don't you . . ." entreaties in favor of allowing nature to take its course with guarantees of enough morphine to keep her "comfortable" (it really wasn't doing very much for her) have been exhausted. She and I exchange life stories, boast of our grandchildren, and laugh at our mutually sick humor. "Can't we, you and I, and your daughter have more enjoyable moments like these?" Sara doesn't comment but I feel selfish in the asking. "You're bored, aren't you, Sara?" She nods. Though I am ethically and legally restrained from assisting Sara in her plan, it pleases me that she knows that she finally has my approval.

Sara has chosen tonight. The phenobarbital tablets are at her bedside.

Unbeknownst to me, there is an equivalent to the Hemlock Society here, The Israeli Society for the Right to Die with Honor. Sara's daughter has received all the necessary literature from this organization. The "how to" book, "Final Exit," is available; Sara has a copy. Is it ever detailed! I sorely want to be with Sara during her final ordeal. This afternoon I contacted a lawyer, the founder of this "Right to Die" society to ask if my being present during my patient's "final exit" would be legal. His answer in effect was a request that I "go public." After a moment's reflection I respectfully declined, suggesting that he get an esteemed, native-born oncology professor to perform this noble service. I wish I were as brave as Dr. Timothy Quill who described in the New England Journal of Medicine his involvement with the death of the patient "Diane." As a relative newcomer in Israel, I believe there would be few to defend me publicly. A doctor participating in an assisted suicide (acquiescence may not imply assistance) could lose his medical license and spend three years in prison.

Two hours ago I said to Sara, "Good-bye. Have an easy passage."

"Is it far?", she asked.

"Only from here to there."

I am now home, standing by. I'll return to Sara's apartment when the deed is done.

I concluded my letter, my confession, *"Please write to label me a 'compleat' physician. God knows I feel I've done the right thing, but I need further convincing."*

The response of Dr. Freedberg, as would be predicted, was laudatory. He wrote, "At any rate, get over your period of grieving and carry on. You have acted in the full tradition of a compleat physician trying to cure if you can, benefit if you cannot cure, and finally, helping your patient cross the line from life to death. Maimonides would have approved, I believe. I certainly do. God bless you!"

Jerry's response was equally approving. "You are a great doctor." And "We've all been down that road for shorter or longer distances."

Addendum: Sara died peacefully in an apparent natural sleep. The doctor, who pronounced her dead, listed the cause of death, "Metastatic anaplastic carcinoma of the thyroid." I agree.

Some time has passed since Sara's death. Thoughts of her and her demise frequently surface. Marcia and I have visited her grave. No bolts of lightning have struck me nor have I suffered any nightmares or change of heart.

I do not advocate legislative changes for assisted suicide. I strongly believe that each physician who gets involved with a tragic patient like Sara should struggle and suffer, case by case, as I did during her last tumultuous months. In a recent article on the vexing question of assisted suicide, the writer claims that when the patient has a good relationship with his doctor, one he trusts to make the right decision until his last breath, the patient rarely asks for assisted suicide. I hope not to be placed in such a situation again.

Only once in my twenty-eight years of practice in Aliquippa was I asked to help a patient die. It was 1974. Dear Alma was a sixty-two year-old lady with inoperable cancer of the lung. She would occasionally appear in the emergency room pleading with me to stop her pain with an "overdose." Alma despaired of treatment which seemed to do no more than to make her bald.

One evening several months after she had received a combination of chemotherapy and radiation, I got a call from her. With an adrenalin surge preparing me for the worst, I asked, "What's the matter?"

"Nothing is the matter. I'm at my card club and I just wanted you to know that I'm having a wonderful time." Can you imagine that? Never have I received a more wonderful gift. And to top it off, several months later, a month after Alma died, her daughter brought me an afghan, crocheted for me by Alma. To this day I get a special warmth when, on a cold winter's evening, I cover myself with Alma's afghan. And shouldn't Alma's story enter the equation whenever assisted suicide is being considered?

I truly believe that it is incumbent on a physician never to take away hope from a patient. Not only is it cruel but occasionally our estimates of time left to live are grossly in error. To wit: the story of Morry who survived thirty months rather than the three months I had predicted. The case histories of two other patients give testimony to this pitfall that is never far from the practicing clinician.

John, a retired steelworker, came to my office because of abdominal pain. A pancreas isotope scan showed a tumor while endoscopic drainage from the duodenum demonstrated malignant cells, confirming a diagnosis (a death sentence) of cancer of the pancreas. John refused to undergo surgery. I told Mary, John's wife, that there was no other treatment and that his days were numbered in months, not years – these were the days before chemotherapy, fortunately for John as it turned out.

To my surprise (you might consider chagrin) John never returned to my office. Periodically I kept in touch by phone, hearing only that John was healthy. I remember one particular phone conversation with Mary. "Can I speak with John?"

"He's out in the garden."

"How's he feeling?"

"Fine."

"How's his pain?"

"He doesn't have any."

Desperately seeking to elicit one little symptom, I pleaded, "Does he burp?"

"No. He's just fine."

In disbelief I had eminent specialists review the tissue slides. Always the same answer: the diagnosis of cancer was reaffirmed. Five years after my prediction of an inevitably early demise, an ambulance brought John to my office parking lot for me to officially pronounce him dead. Mary gave authorization for an autopsy; I witnessed it from beginning to end. Knowing what the pathologist had to find, I prevailed upon him to be more meticulous than usual. The cause of death was an acute myocardial infarction. There was no cancer to be found. John's isotope scan was published in a textbook of nuclear medicine, before the autopsy, as a proven case of cancer of the pancreas! Whom can you trust these days?

In *Love, Medicine and Miracles* Bernie Siegel states that a proper attitude on the part of the patient can positively affect the course of his cancer. I now recommend gardening at the very least.

My last example of erroneous prognostication was Marie. Marie was a nurse at the Aliquippa Hospital and a personal friend. How smug I was, and yet wretched and a mite guilty, when I diagnosed colon cancer from a barium enema I performed in my office. I had to remind myself that I hadn't put the cancer there. On Thanksgiving Day a cancer surgeon operated on Marie. I watched as he deftly removed the cancer and one cancerous node. Three months later while attending a course in Cleveland, I received a phone call from Steve Zernich, a colleague at the Aliquippa Hospital. "Dave, I just opened Marie's belly. It was sprinkled with tiny metastases everywhere. Oh, yes, I did splash in some nitrogen mustard (the first chemotherapy drug) before I closed her but you know that can't do much good." Steve told Marie's husband that she had three to six months to live. I concurred.

M

As with my patient John, when Marie continued to live in good health defying our prediction, I sent tissue samples from both of her surgeries to two eminent Pittsburgh pathologists who confirmed the diagnosis of metastatic cancer. Not one of the many oncologists I consulted would credit the nitrogen mustard for her remission.

Marie lived thirteen years after the initial surgery until death came from a massive stroke. Autopsy showed no evidence of cancer. Chalk up one more case for Bernie Siegel.

Whatever the reason for these miracle patients, it is incumbent on me and all physicians to be humble and truthful and that includes taking precautions not to set rigid limits on the projected life span of any patient. I only wish that when I used to estimate the amount of time left, I could have been wrong an additional time or two or three . . . .

I have one other wish and that concerns all future Saras, that the day will come that cancer will either be prevented or curable and that these Saras will live healthily to an old age and die in their sleep. Then the only problem will be, what will doctors do with all their spare time?

GIANTS COME IN ALL SIZES

"Harry, other than you, are there any giants left at Harvard (Medical School)?"

This is a question that would interest many Harvard graduates who hold the medical school in high esteem. It did interest me, as a 1948 graduate and Harry Mellins, who spent the last twenty-seven years of his active career as professor of Radiology at Harvard's Peter Bent Brigham Hospital (PBBH). Harry happens to be Marcia's cousin.

I ask myself, "What constitutes a giant?" The answer is easy. A giant is a physician who, preeminent in his field, is idolized by his students. In the preclinical years, he is a scintillating lecturer who manages to demonstrate love and compassion for his students. These latter attributes abound also in the clinician, spilling over to the patient he examines while surrounded by his students at the bedside. His incisive history-taking and physical examination add to his luster. He looks each patient and student in the eye, sensitive to feelings while probing and conveying medical wisdom.

As you might expect, giants may be tall like William Castle, hematologist at Boston City Hospital (BCH), who with George Minot was the first to use Vitamin B12 in the management of pernicious anemia. And they may be short like Maxwell Finland, specialist in infectious diseases also at BCH. What comic relief they provided standing side by side at conferences, Finland a foot and a half shorter than Castle.

It is a given that all the clinician giants were brilliant diagnosticians. Take, for example, Mark Altschule, five feet two inches tall. With two hearing aids denying access to a stethoscope, he would place his hand lightly on the patient's chest and moments later announce, "There is a grade III systolic murmur of aortic stenosis and a grade II systolic murmur of mitral insufficiency." Astonishingly, he was seldom in error.

Paul Zoll, cardiologist at the Beth Israel Hospital (BI) was also a shorty. His groundbreaking research resulted in the development of external electric shock treatment of lethal disturbances of the heart rhythm and cardiac pacemakers. His work has saved hundreds of thousands of lives. Yet, initially, Zoll's critics considered his approach cruel, causing unwarranted interference with the process of dying. They accused him of playing God.

A giant might be a towering lung surgeon like Edward Churchill, Massachusetts General Hospital (MGH), about whom the following story is told. During an operation Churchill nicked an artery causing massive bleeding. He blamed it on the assistant professor. The latter in turn blamed the chief resident, who blamed the scrub nurse, and she, the retractor-holding medical student. The latter left the table and was seen gazing at the floor. "What are you doing?" roared the professor.

Came the timid reply, "I'm looking for an ant to step on."

Or Oliver Cope (MGH) who spoke like Lawrence Olivier. A pioneering surgeon, he advanced the care of burn patients. The catastrophic Coconut Grove Nightclub fire (492 perished) in 1942 was his laboratory. Following this tragedy public buildings were required to have exit doors open out.

S. Burt Wolbach, pathologist, five feet tall with a fresh, red rose in his lapel each morning, sparred with the much taller Merrill Sosman, radiologist at PBBH at weekly conferences. Sosman delighted in labeling symmetrical shadows on chest x-rays "Wolbach lines" which we all recognized as breast shadows. Above an x-ray viewing box in his office Sosman had hung a glass cabinet containing a stethoscope pinned to a blue velvet background. An inscription read, "This archaic instrument was used before the discovery of the roentgen."

A story has Sosman appearing in court as an expert witness. The opposing attorney put an x-ray of the abdomen on a viewing box. Trying to humiliate Sosman, he pointed to the air bubble normally seen in the stomach and sanctimoniously said, "Tell me, Doctor, is this benign or malignant?"

Sosman unhesitatingly replied, "It all depends which way it travels. Up, it's a burp; down — I'd rather not say."

Herrman Blumgart, chief of medicine at the BI, figures in several chapters already. Tall, austere but with a twinkle, he could raise you to the heights or lower you to the depths – I'd been dispatched in both directions. Every year he had the auspicious assignment of presenting a two-hour clinic on the opening day of medical school. His detailed patient presentations were awe inspiring. His enthusiasm for medicine endeared him to the entire class. Three years later on rounds at the BI he was presented a young man with unexplained fever. Dr. Blumgart asked for a glove and proceeded to perform a rectal exam. The patient screeched from pain. "The diagnosis is obvious – peri-rectal abscess." The admitting resident who had failed to perform a rectal exam was stunned and humiliated while the rest of us felt like applauding.

A. Stone Freedberg (Al) of the BI was my personal made-to-order giant. Al was Blumgart's assistant in charge of research laboratories. Around 1946 Dr. Blumgart called Al into his office. He told him to learn nuclear physics and all that was known in the field of nuclear medicine. "You'll soon be replacing Saul whose research is becoming increasingly erratic." Director of Nuclear Medicine Saul Hertz, a brilliant scientist, had been among the first to treat patients with radioactive iodine.

I had the good fortune to be Al's Fellow for the year 1949-50.

A. Stone Freedberg, M.D., my mentor, my friend.

He became a Dutch uncle while teaching me scientific methodology. Together we wrote and published a number of research papers. His advice in this matter remains with me to this day: "A worthwhile article goes through a minimum of eight drafts. When you think it's finished, have the cleaning woman read it. Only when she understands it, is the article ready for the medical community. However, at that point put the article in a drawer. After two years, reread it and if the article is still relevant, you may send it for publication." In this day of publish or perish, alas, the time frame has shortened.

Al's most precious gift was to introduce me to chamber music. I was hooked with the first hearing of Dvorak's *Dumky Trio.* And it was Al, who at the end of our year together, admonished me affectionately,

"Don't tease people until they get to know you. They won't know when you're kidding."

Henry Jackson taught the first course in medicine in our second year. As described in another chapter, it was Jackson who closed his last lecture at Harvard with, "It's not how can the students do without their teacher, but how can the teacher do without his students."

Three giant cardiologists come to mind: Louis Wolff (BI), Paul Dudley White (MGH), and Samuel Levine (PBBH). While a cardiology resident in White's department, Wolff first observed a strange electrocardiographic pattern in a group of patients with episodic, rapid, and occasionally fatal, heart rates. A dependable source relates that White summarily rejected Wolff's findings, adding himself as an author on the subsequent paper only after British Professor Parkinson concurred with Wolff. Not withstanding, Dr. White was world famous even before he became President Eisenhower's cardiologist. He was credited with having influenced Mayor Curley of Boston to designate bicycle lanes on Boston's busy streets thereby encouraging bicycling to prevent heart attacks. His biographer discusses the rumor that White had a problem with Jews. He did come to Israel on condition that a visit with Ben Gurion be arranged. A colleague of mine, (now over eighty himself) accompanied Dr. White to Sde Boker, Ben Gurion's retirement kibbutz. He sat with these two brilliant octogenarians and heard Ben Gurion query the professor, "Why can't man live beyond 100 years?"

"And what was the answer?" I asked my friend.

"I don't remember."

The third eminent cardiologist was Samuel Levine (PBBH), a great clinician and teacher, as Semitic appearing as White was Waspy. His 1958 textbook is a classic. When I retired, I could not assign it to a scrap heap as I did with so many of my outdated books; I kept it.

Fuller Albright (MGH) was an endocrinologist who clarified the gamut of low-calcium diseases. Afflicted with slowly progressive multiple sclerosis, he required that students, who were fortunate to obtain one of the treasured monthly rotations with him, act as his chauffeur. I can still hear the click of his long wooden pointer on the blackboard caused by the tremor with muscular effort that characterized his illness (as distinguished from the tremor at rest of Parkinson's disease). The tapping did not detract from his historic lectures.

Allan Butler (MGH) was chief of the Children's Service. He and I corresponded after I responded to his ad in a medical newspaper requesting support on behalf of Dr. Jeremiah Stamler. An eminent researcher, Stamler had been accused by the House Un-American Activities Committee of conspiring against the United States. Contributions from numerous sympathizers helped clear Stamler of all guilt and served instead to bring down that despicable, itself un-American, cabal of congressional tyrants.

White-mustached surgeon David Cheever (PBBH) resembled his Harvard Medical School progenitors whose portraits hung in the medical-school library. It was he who vented his spleen during a clinic on inguinal hernia which he presented during our second year. As a timid student nurse ushered a young male patient into the amphitheater seating 120 male students (ours was the last class not to accept women), Dr. Cheever ordered the patient to drop his pajama bottoms. Gazing at the blushing nurse and gesturing with open palm extending to the area under scrutiny, he exclaimed, "Gentlemen, this is the reason I fought having women at Harvard." (He said, "Haavahd.") Many years later, well after Dr. Cheever departed for that great operating room in the sky, I felt his presence and his discomfort as I guided a female medical student through the examination of a male patient's genitalia.

Harry Solomon was Chief of Psychiatry at Boston Psychopathic Hospital. I was one of eight male residents who attended Dr. Solomon's diagnostic interview of a gorgeous, dark-haired, young woman. After dismissing her, he requested our reactions. Mine was to feel sorry for this sad patient. "Gentlemen," he said, "this woman is obviously psychotic. I felt absolutely nothing during her story of woe. I use my penis as my indicator." Dr. Solomon doubtlessly would not have altered this statement if female doctors had been present, though my own naive discomfort would have been compounded.

Arthur Linenthal (BI) was one of my favorite bedside instructors. His father, once a famous clinician, was a has-been. One day, out of deference to the latter's advanced age and neglect by the house staff (BI) I asked to make rounds with him. And was I rewarded! He related the story of being at the bedside of an aged woman who would momentarily die. A grieving son pleaded, "Can't you do something?"

"I could give her a shot of adrenalin which might prolong her life a few seconds."

Again, pleading, "Do it. She just might smile one more time." This is a point of view to be remembered while we allow our patients to die in peace and in dignity.

Shields Warren, pathologist, whose forebears also grace the medical school's library walls, was part of the team studying victims of the atom bomb at Hiroshima and Nagasaki. I wondered if his somber countenance was a result of that experience.

Greta Bibring, psychoanalyst (BI), a student of Freud, rounded with us when I was a resident in medicine. By custom she would invite medical residents to her home in Cambridge for a concert of recorded music, printed program and all. Among the entire faculty in my graduation yearbook only one woman appears, Marion Ropes (MGH), a rheumatologist. Over the years the number of women on medical-school faculties has risen but not in proportion to their number as graduates.

Francis Moore (MGH), surgeon would perform the first successful kidney transplant from one identical twin to the other. It was predicted that only this kind of donor would result in a successful transplant. Years later (1997) because of the discovery of anti-rejection medications, my wife, despite being only a fair genetic match, was able to save her niece's life with a kidney donation (see chapter: "My kingdom for a kidney").

James Means (MGH), thyroidologist, on the first team to use radioactive iodine in the treatment of an overactive thyroid, made important inroads in patient care while reducing the income of surgeons. I didn't dream then that radioactive iodine would one day be my ticket to Israel.

I suppose that in every era giants have been glorified by their students. Is it possible that the student, bleary-eyed with awe, projects values not necessarily merited by his teacher? If this were true, some of these giants would have been unmasked with further consideration from a distance or with the passage of time. The ophthalmology professor, who said to me, "That was the dumbest question I ever heard," and two minutes later to my roommate, "Don't you ever read the literature?" hardly passed muster.

Maybe it is true that in all generations there have been giants at Harvard, giving it the worldwide reputation it has commanded. I return to my original question to Harry Mellins, "Other than you, Harry, are there any giants left at Harvard?" I was not being obsequious. Harry needed no validation from me. Even though from a base of radiology and not from the bedside, he had been chosen over the years as the students' favorite teacher.

Harry answered quizzically, "There must be. I'm sure there are, but I would not doubt that there are fewer. Maybe with the plethora of computerized diagnostic aids and the distancing of the professor from the bedside examination, there is less opportunity for demonstrating sagacity, diagnostic acumen, and humanism. The patient's disease rather than the patient now takes center stage.

"So, that's one element that is changing. The second is that the giants are being pushed 'upstairs' into managerial roles. Their concerns for the 'bottom line' remove them out of reach of the students and the patients."

I experienced this phenomenon in my cardiac care unit at Aliquippa Hospital in Pennsylvania. The two best bedside nurses were systematically promoted to head nurse, unit director, full-time teacher, and into administration. Each move brought higher pay, more prestige, and diminishing involvement with patient care; ultimately they lost all contact with patients.

Yet how can the giant resist the temptation of being a major player on the field of health care to the masses, of positively influencing health care of society as a whole. The giant knows that he can do a better job than some corporate officer with a Master's degree in Business Administration.

Maybe in the last analysis all these giants aren't needed. Maybe one occasional star like Harry Mellins or Herrman Blumgart will suffice to raise the student's vision as other giants are replaced by not-so-spectacular role model physicians like the Chamovitz brothers, my daughter Raina Chamovitz Rosenberg, and me.

M

MEDICAL SCHOOL ROOMMATES: MATCHES MADE IN HEAVEN

For the first eighteen years of my life brother Bob and I shared the same room. The word roommate was not in our lexicon. This relationship came to an end when I left for medical school in Boston. Bob would be replaced.

I arrived in Boston on July 1, 1944 and took a cab directly to Claverly Hall in Cambridge where I would be housed for the Harvard College summer session. Medical school wasn't to begin until October 1, but in order to comply with the U.S. Selective Service Agency's ruling that those men not in medical school by July 1 would be drafted into the army, Harvard called us in on that date.

I trudged up three flights of stairs to my room and found one of my two roommates, a dental student from New York, already settled in. Our relationship didn't continue past the summer.

Soon, in walked the third occupant of our suite. I never asked what anxiety he experienced as he anticipated my reaction. He was an Oriental who introduced himself as Nobuyuki Nakasone, Nobu, from Hawaii. "Japanese." Well, I swallowed hard. This was a highly charged moment. World War II was going full throttle. My brother Allen had been killed in the Air Force in June 1943, and as if that weren't enough, Americans were being bombarded with newsreel scenes of "Jap" subhuman behavior. Add to this my small town rearing where the only Oriental I knew was a laundryman, "the Chink" as we referred to him. While I was comfortable with Blacks (called Negroes in those days) and Christians, I was poorly prepared for a wider spectrum of cultures.

Along came Nobu who forced me to confront my prejudices. In the process he became my closest friend. We ate together and reveled in long walks in Harvard Yard and along the Charles River. At the end of the summer we decided to room together in Vanderbilt Hall, the medical school dormitory in Boston.

Nobu's was the prototypical family described by James Michener in the chapter about Japanese immigration in the book *Hawaii*. His parents and older sister, born in Japan, had moved to Maui, Hawaii around 1920. In the beginning the father and daughter worked in pineapple fields but once they had saved enough money, they opened a barbershop. That shop went on to finance university education for all the many other children.

Nobu, no more than five feet tall, had jet-black hair, twinkling eyes, and a cheerful disposition. At the University of Hawaii he had been a tennis champion. At Harvard, when he wasn't studying, he was performing favors for classmates, helping them move in and out of apartments. People took advantage of Nobu's good nature, abusing rather superficial friendships. At least, that was my perception. He, himself, was self-sufficient, never requesting favors from others. He was also an opera buff, attending many performances when the Met came to town.

During the Christmas vacation of 1944, Nobu came home with me. When we arrived at the Aliquippa train station, Mr. Mooney, a mill-worker who was meeting his daughter, offered us a ride home.

On the way Mr. Mooney turned around to Nobu and half-asked, half-announced, "You're Chinese, aren't you?"

Nobu accepted the challenge and with me cringing, countered, "No, I'm a Jap." I tried to extricate us by adding that he was a Japanese-American from Hawaii. Total silence the rest of the trip. Would I have been as self-conscious if Nobu had been a blond German?

When we arrived home, I remonstrated, "Come on, Nobu. We're at war with Japan. Would it hurt to just say you're Hawaiian?" As I posed the question, I knew the answer, for hadn't I so many times in my youth thwarted the racist question, "What are you?" by responding, "Romanian." In truth I wasn't as clever as I was purposely ambivalent, evading the issue of being Jewish.

Predictably, Nobu replied, "I have to let people know who I am at the outset." (Ironically in Israel "What are you?" equates to "Where are you from?")

When rooming arrangements at Vanderbilt Hall for the fall of 1945 had to be finalized, Nobu confessed a preference, for medical reasons, to live alone even though it meant taking a room on the sixth floor – and no elevator.

When Marcia and I returned to Boston where I had a fellowship in internal medicine at Lahey Clinic from 1954 to 1956, Nobu was a medical resident at the Peter Bent Brigham Hospital. Nobu visited often. As one of many presents, he gave us prints by the Japanese artist, Hokusai.

Nobu returned to Honolulu to practice internal medicine. In the fall of 1972 we visited him in Hawaii and met his wife Yoshino and two of what would be three daughters. Yoshino, a professional dancer from Okinawa, performed for us in her dance studio. I made rounds with Nobu in St. Francis Hospital where exotic flowers inundated every bed.

But the key moment of our trip took place during a conversation in Nobu's living room. I tried to describe to Yoshino how important Nobu had been to me in my adjustment to medical school. Nobu countered with a statement to Marcia, "David had been much more important to me." Somehow, my friendship had given him the self-confidence he, an outsider, needed. I was nonplused, but flattered.

We lost contact for years after, with not even a response to our annual letters. Nor had Nobu sent any messages for the every five-year alumni autobiographical compendium; I wrote tomes. Finally in 1994 we received a copy of a book describing his research on vitamin therapy. Enclosed were a photo of his handsome family and a warm greeting. The circle of our friendship was completed. If the *Reader's Digest* were to ask for my "Most Unforgettable Character," it would be Nobu.

Norman Boas, a senior, was the third roommate that first year. His grandfather Franz Boas, the father of modern anthropology, had died two years before. His father Ernst was a renowned New York City cardiologist. Norm called himself one-fourth Jewish. More accurately, he was a kind, intellectual Yankee.

Norm had a calming effect on his fledglings. Since Nobu had requested the suite's only single room, Norm and I shared the second bedroom, which was outfitted with a double-decker bed. He took the upper level. He introduced me to *Winnie the Pooh* and often would read a chapter aloud at bedtime. I'm pleased to report that neither my children nor my grandchildren had to wait until such an advanced age before appreciating Pooh, Eeyore, and Tigger.

Norm became a practicing internist in Wilton, Connecticut. Sometime in the seventies Marcia and I dropped in for a brief visit. This was the only contact since separating at our dormitory in 1945. Norm's hobby was collecting rare books and signatures of historically important people. I'm a little wistful that our relationship hadn't continued.

Norm did introduce me to two of his close friends, also seniors, who in turn became two of my closest friends, John Goldsmith and Cyrus Rubin.

John impressed me, first of all, by his brilliance. How could any medical student, even in the fourth year, begin to study the cello? How could he take time away from his studies and still pass? Well, he did. It was John who reminded me that I had organized a *seder* when I glibly mentioned one day that "I wasn't Jewish in those days." After John graduated we met at a couple of cocktail parties when I was at Lahey Clinic and he was picking up a Ph.D. at Harvard School of Public Health.

Twenty-seven years later during the planning period of our *aliyah* I was glancing through the Harvard Medical School Alumni Directory. To my surprise, listed in Israel were four names, one of which was

John's. I immediately wrote him a *megillah* (a long story) describing my life experiences; in return, there was a *megillah* from him. It was amazing how our lives had paralleled. John had been *shul* president in Berkeley. And two or three of his four kids (like my Raina and Danny) had gone to Young Judaea camps. He had made *aliyah* around 1978. John quoted an exchange with an American friend: "John, how can you tolerate a lower standard of living in Israel?"

His answer, "Just the opposite. My standard of living has risen. Where in any metropolitan area would you dare ride a bicycle to work or be able to walk to your swim club?" His reply affirmed my interest in *aliyah*.

When we visited his villa in Omer, a suburb of Beersheva, we saw concrete evidence of his appraisal; in his yard were a grapevine and fig and lemon trees. John continued as professor of epidemiology switching from Berkeley to the Soroka Medical School at Ben Gurion University.

As with so many late-life *olim* (immigrants to Israel) only Julie of John's four children lives in Israel. Julie, a social worker, was married to Bernie, a theoretical scientist. Along with three daughters they too lived in Omer. Marcia and I drove the one-and-a-half-hour trip for many of their celebrations and, alas, for Bernie's funeral.

While in California for a son's wedding, John, his wife Naomi, and Julie's family were in an automobile accident with John at the wheel. Bernie died instantly while the others escaped with only minor injuries. Julie eventually married a widower, also with three daughters. A year later we were guests at the circumcision of their seventh child.

John's wife Naomi treated us to an unusual day not long after our arrival in Israel. A Ph.D. paleontologist, she had acquired sole rights for digging a particular hill that she had spotted near Dimona. Imagine the scene: four of us sitting in the desert, sifting earth in search of tiny bones that Naomi would identify. This was the evidence she was seeking to prove her theory of a land connection between Africa and Eurasia hundreds of thousands of years ago. Marcia wanted to send a photo of John and me to the Medical School Alumni Bulletin, "Two Harvard graduates playing in the sand in Israel;" she never did.

One of the temptations of taking a position at Soroka Hospital in Beersheva was the possibility of singing in the Light Opera Group of the Negev. The latter put on a Gilbert and Sullivan Operetta every year. John sang in the bass section year after year. I was guaranteed only an audition.

John died after a long illness in 1999. He had been working feverishly to finish a monumental book encompassing his life work on environmental epidemiology with warnings of inadequate data on the safety of cellular phones and electromagnetic power stations and the danger of carbon monoxide fumes in bumper-to-bumper traffic.

Norm Boas's other friend was Cy Rubin. I loved Cy's swagger, his carefree gait, and his unabashed demeanor. It was Cy to whom I turned for assistance when I arranged a *seder* at Vanderbilt Hall. More important it was Cy who invited me for a walk when I received the life-sentence, "You've got a duodenal ulcer." How much more therapeutic he was than professor Chester Jones who flunked my test for empathy by saying, "Don't you know you're very ('too,' I interpreted) young to be in medical school!"

Cy and and his wife, Grace, had visited us twice in Israel. In 2000 we visited them in Seattle. We especially enjoyed seeing Cy's bonsai trees and his Japanese garden. Cy tried to teach me how to prune his grapevines. He was soon to return to full-time status as Chief of Gastrointestinal Pathology when his successor was murdered by a psychotic resident.

Cy was proud to have introduced Senator Henry "Scoop" Jackson to Yitzhak Rabin many years ago. Jackson became a strong supporter of Israel co-authoring the "Jackson-Vanik" bill which denied the Soviet Union most-favored-nation status (which would reduce trade tariffs) until she opened her doors to Jewish emigration.

After completion of the first school year, I moved into a five-room suite with Garry DeNeuville Hough III, Frank Bates, and Allen Crocker. In the fourth year Al moved back home to Cambridge; Modestino Criscitiello ("Cris") took his place.

Though fond of all of my roommates, it was with Garry that I bonded most strongly. He came from a prominent Longmeadow, Massachusetts family. His father was chief of surgery at Shriner's Orthopedic Hospital in Springfield. His mother was a Daughter of the American Revolution. How impressed and not a little envious I was during a visit with his family for Thanksgiving in 1946. Thanksgiving dinner consisted of more courses than I had ever consumed (I had never eaten boiled onions and squash). The dinner conversation was lively and confrontational. Garry's father was a Republican, his mother, a Democrat. I felt a little disloyal comparing Garry's family table talk with ours back home. Mom and Dad both read the *Forward*, a liberal Yiddish newspaper, but I can't recall discussions at dinner. Surely with Dad's interest in Norman Thomas, the perennial Socialist candidate for president in the '20s and early '30s, and in John L. Lewis, president of the United Mine Workers, there was much to talk about. Need I add Adolph Hitler and the plight of Jews in Europe?

All my roommates were serious, diligent students, each respectful of one another's privacy. Garry would make my English grammar more precise by blithely saying, "Yes," and continue walking by in response to my, "Could you please close my door?" He would return and add, "You didn't say, 'Would you?'"

After four hours of evening study, tired but needing more study time, we would go to the gym, only twenty feet from our suite, where we played squash. We worked up a sweat in a half-hour, showered, and then studied for another hour and a half. If that sounds luxurious, well, it was.

Garry was dating Nancy Greer, a proper Smith College student who, on being introduced, shook my hand with her arm fully extended. How shocked and pleased I was when Nan wrote me after the birth of the first of her four children, "I've become a great cow."

With time our relationship deepened. Once, Garry arranged to meet me when I was changing planes in Hartford, Connecticut. During that visit we opened up about problems with our children; the terrible sixties and seventies were also wreaking havoc with his brood. They attended our Amy's wedding in Amherst less than a year before she died in 1979.

Garry, who had retired early because of the threat of frivolous malpractice lawsuits, was a pioneer member of Orthopedics Overseas and later its international president. He volunteered for half a year in Malaysia, a month in South America, and in 1987, three months in Malawi. In the latter country he had a busy operating schedule and taught paramedics to set fractures and even to nail hips. "Where in America," he asked, "would I have had an opportunity to treat an infected fracture caused by a hippopotamus bite?"

Garry and Nan accepted an invitation to stay with us after his stint in Malawi. They spent the eight-day visit traveling with us. Despite torrential rains we covered much territory. Anxious for Garry and Nan to see Christian sites as well as ours, we went, for example, to the Garden of Gethsemane. The 2,000-year old olive trees were awesome. I suggested a visit to the adjacent church but Garry declined. "That's not my thing."

Our last get-together was in 1993 at the time of our forty-fifth reunion. We drove in tandem to Woods Hole where we caught a ferry to Martha's Vineyard. Garry's summer home there had been built by a sea captain named Hough four generations before, and was now one of a community of historic, preserved houses. We visited the Vineyard cemetery where his parents and three more generations of Houghs were buried. My memories of his parents had not faded.

The good-bye hugs at the harbor were warm and jovial but a bit hesitant. Would the four of us be around for our fiftieth?

Frank Bates was another sensitive soulmate. He was probably the most girl-shy of us all, but not after he met Hermie, a student nurse. Frank would get nasal congestion when he spoke on the phone with Hermie, an indication of excitement, I assumed. When they were married the year after our internships, I enjoyed being an usher, completely comfortable as the only Jew in the Protestant church.

It surprised me that Garry and Frank became orthopedic surgeons. True, they did their undergraduate work at M.I.T., at that time primarily noted for its engineering orientation, and, of course, Garry's father was an orthopedist. In contrast to Garry and Frank, orthopedists generally are not noted for their humanity or humility. These characteristics more typically are attributed to general practitioners and internists (like me).

Frank practiced in Boston, opting for early retirement like Garry, because of the constant threat of malpractice lawsuits. He moved to Center Sandwich, New Hampshire, where he began working half-time. This didn't last long when he realized that it wasn't financially feasible; malpractice insurance fees were the same as if he were working full-time.

Frank wasn't too unhappy about this turn of events. He loved tending his rustic wooden home and the acres of forests surrounding it. Marcia and I visited him and Hermie for lunch in 1988. Hermie was lovely as ever but failing in health. When Cris and his wife, also a Nancy, invited all the roommates and their spouses to dinner at their home in Newton, Massachusetts at the time of our forty-fifth reunion, Frank came alone. His sadness weighed heavily on him as he watched Hermie slipping away. She died in December 1995.

My memories of Al and Cris are fading. It seemed that Al was frequently in conflict with his mother. This led him to leave and live at home during our fourth year. I think it pleased Al to assert his independence when he married Marga, a beautiful young German he met while serving in the army. However Freudian this ploy might have been, it worked well for Al. Marga's affectionate nature complemented Al's more reserved disposition. Al, too, didn't come to Cris's dinner; he was at the Brigham recovering from hip surgery.

Cris took Al's place in the suite during our last year. His family was from Pittsfield, Massachusetts. His father was an Italian-born surgeon who graduated from Johns Hopkins Medical School. From him Cris got his ready wit and his unfettered worldly outlook. From his mother, a statuesque Scot, he got his formal nature. Commenting on my writing, Cris, noting the pervasiveness of my Jewishness, characterized himself simply as an Ivy Leaguer, detached from any religious or national dogma.

Al and Cris achieved high academic status. Al is Associate Professor of Maternal and Child Health at the Harvard School of Public

Health and Associate Professor of Pediatrics at the Medical School. Cris is Emeritus Professor of Medicine at Tufts.

Altogether, we were a cozy cluster of roommates free of rancor or conflicts. We were supportive of each other, and there was no dragging down due to depressive behavior or destructive habits. The worst we did was to goad Frank to defer urination to prove a bladder capacity in excess of one liter. He succeeded. All of us were puritanical. Each was careful with expenditures, mindful that none of us was working to help our parents pay for our expenses. Some of our classmates weren't so lucky, having to work at nighttime and weekend jobs.

I was flattered to find myself one of them. Puzzled by this happenstance, I wrote to Garry and Frank to ask how I got to live with them. I asked, "Was it affirmative action?" Garry wrote back that he and Frank had lived out of the dorm during the first year, moving in when this low-rental suite became available. Garry remembered that he had enjoyed playing squash with me during the first year. Frank denied affirmative action. "In fact I wouldn't have had any idea whether you were Jewish or not, nor would I have cared. In those days I was very naive about Jews – you taught me to understand them – remember you took me to hear Rabbi Joshua Liebman preach at Temple Israel? Growing up I had virtually no contact with Jews and didn't pay attention if I did." Frank further reminded me that I got the most desirable bedroom by lot and that at times I lent it to him and Hermie! He added, "I agree – it was a fortuitous matchup and I, too, am grateful for the friendship and support."

Addendum: Our fiftieth reunion took place in June 1998. We all made it! Well, not quite all. As already noted, Hermie had died in 1995. Frank had just married Lib, a minister's widow, and like Frank, a choral singer, nature lover, and grandparent. Lib fit into our group, speaking frequently of Hermie, who had been her friend as well.

Quite remarkably, there was not a divorce among the suite-mates or the others described in this chapter.

Bates, Criscitiello, Hough, Crocker, and me, 1998 reunion.

It was a pleasant surprise that Nobu and Yoshino came from Hawaii. In truth, they came to see one of their daughters perform in the Broadway musical *Rent* and to be at her wedding one week later. Nobu told Marcia the groom's name was Myers. Marcia asked, "Is he Jewish?"

The answer typified Nobu. "I don't know."

Nobu is well, convinced that megadoses of vitamin C are beneficial to health and longevity. (He has eighteen patients over the age of 100 years.) This subject consumed much of his conversation; personal topics were skirted. It did make me wonder how intimate our conversations had been as students.

Garry arrived with Nancy, having booked rooms at the same hotel as Frank and I. In an earlier transatlantic telephone conversation I had sensed that something was wrong with Garry when he had invited us to again visit him at Martha's Vineyard. "We'll find you lodgings." Had Garry been well, he would not have allowed us to stay anywhere but with him. When Garry turned me over to Nancy, I was crushed by hers news of his diagnosis: Alzheimer's. He was approximately a year down the road at our reunion. Sadly, conversation was superficial and hesitant. Yet just walking or sitting together during extended meals was gratifying. How wonderful it was to hear him sing barbershop music as in days gone by. For a few moments I forgot what was in store for him, and, especially for Nancy.

Cris and Nancy and Al and Marga were well and animated. At our dinners Al and Cris spoke in professorial modes of the historic nature of the occasion. During toasts, each of us contributed special memories, but the overriding theme was our good fortune to have found one another and for the success of having stayed connected.

Although I may not always be able to vouch for the facts in these memoirs, regarding my roommates, the fiftieth reunion validated the warm friendship and interdependence I've described. Here's to the fifty-fifth in 2003.

BETH ISRAEL ON THE OHIO

It was Nick DeSalle, an uneducated Italian immigrant, who fashioned the idea of a hospital for Aliquippa and who persevered until the day the hospital opened its doors in 1957. Aliquippa patients and physicians would no longer have to make the thirty-minute trip on congested roads and the long bridge spanning the Ohio River to Rochester General Hospital. Nor would these physicians feel any longer like second-class citizens, guests in someone else's home.

At least that's how I felt at Rochester General Hospital when I entered the practice of internal medicine in Aliquippa in 1956. True, I was given hospital privileges promptly enough but, wishing to implement innovations from my Boston ivory-tower training, I encountered a less than open-minded reception. At that time, for example, Rochester General Hospital patients suffering heart attacks were kept on complete bed rest for four weeks with two additional weeks of hospitalization for supervised ambulation. The routine at Boston's Beth Israel Hospital, one of Harvard Medical School's teaching hospitals where I had trained, was three weeks in bed and one more week ambulating in the hospital. (When I left the U.S.A. in 1984, the length of hospital stay after a heart attack fell to sixteen days and to less than half of that in 1999.)

Earlier ambulation as well as allowing the patient to sit in a chair at his bedside a day or two after a heart attack, reduced the number of deaths from blood clots in the lungs. These were relatively new concepts at the time. It should have been my pleasure to introduce them. Rather, it was my misfortune; I was met with derision. "You'll kill your patients. The exertion will rupture their hearts."

In 1956 there were no cardiologists in Rochester General Hospital. When I inquired about an electrocardiographic (ECG) service, I was rebuffed. "Each of us internists brings in his own ECG machine." This meant lugging a twenty-pound box from the office to the patient's bedside, recording the ECG, taking it back to our private offices to develop the then used photographic paper, and finally returning to the hospital to initiate the appropriate treatment as mandated by the ECG interpretation. For those doctors who lived near the hospital, this caused a delay in diagnosis of a minimum of a half hour. For me, it was over an hour. In truth, in those days before ECG monitoring and drugs for treating abnormal heart rhythms, this delay was more an inconvenience than a critical element in saving lives. When Aliquippa Hospital opened, an ECG service was immediately instituted; the use of private electrocardiographs was prohibited. I was delegated to order equipment and to train technicians. The responsibility for interpreting the ECGs was shared by two internists and me.

There were a number of deeply entrenched, unethical, possibly unlawful, practices at Rochester General Hospital which astounded me but, I should add, which were quite prevalent elsewhere in that era. There was no way that I, as a newcomer, could effect a change. The first outrage was fee splitting, especially practiced by surgeons. If a general practitioner sent a patient to a surgeon, the latter would kick back a significant percentage of his surgical fee to the referring doctor, which, of course, was without the patient's knowledge. Implied was the choice of a surgical consultant by the size of the kickback, not because of his superior skill. This practice fell into disrepute; surgeons could still express their gratitude to referrers with gifts such as *Fruit of the Month* and subscriptions to *Playboy* magazine.

Equally outrageous was "ghost surgery" which made a mockery of medical propriety. A patient's family doctor, dressed in surgical garb, would greet his patient in the operating room, remaining at her side until she was deeply anesthetized. He would then step aside while a surgeon, whose presence was unknown to the patient, would perform the operation, possibly allowing the referring doctor to "close up." The referring doctor would take all responsibility for post-surgical care and bill the patient as though he were the surgeon. Of course, the ghost surgeon received a sizable portion of the patient's payment and, needless to say, this income most likely wasn't reported to the Internal Revenue Service. This charade theoretically should not have caused injury to the patient except for the fact that it was usually the unscrupulous, poorly trained surgeon who participated in ghost surgery. This ruse was also banned at an early stage at the Aliquippa Hospital.

An example of ghost surgery at that time in an area hospital came to light within the medical community. An elderly woman was found to have a large tumor of the bowel. Her family doctor spoke to his "ghost surgeon" who was leaving for a ten-day vacation. "Set up the surgery for the day I get back." With the patient eating a normal diet, she developed intestinal obstruction three days before the scheduled operation. The doctor ordered a tube to decompress the stomach when he should have used a tube that enters the small intestine. When the ghost surgeon opened the abdomen, he found that the bowel had ruptured; the peritoneal cavity was filled with feces. The only surgery possible was a colostomy leaving the cancer untouched. After three days the patient died of overwhelming infection. The patient's doctor probably wrote "inoperable colon cancer" as the cause of death. In truth, the medical system had killed her.

A surgical practice harder to eliminate was the two-stage treatment of breast cancer. During an initial operation the patient's family doctor performed a breast biopsy, under general anesthesia, to be sure. No request was made for a frozen section that would expedite a decision for or against immediate breast removal. Rather, the patient was permitted to recover from anesthesia and two or three days later, if malignancy was confirmed, she would undergo a second operation by a surgeon and, more crical as for the risk to her, a second anesthesia. Since all physicians are licensed for "the practice of medicine and surgery," this was legally acceptable, medically, not. For a surgeon to fight this practice was to risk being called greedy, power hungry. More important, this surgeon chanced losing both the doctor as a referrer and considerable income.

It took one man, Steve Zernich, a surgeon, to call a halt to fee splitting, ghost surgery, and two-stage breast surgery at the Aliquippa Hospital. He, unlike surgical colleagues who as non-belligerents reaped the benefits, did not flinch from this volatile stance. He railroaded each corrective action into staff bylaws. Aware of the negative potential for himself, he remarked, "It takes a well-heeled bastard like me to do the job." Tough he was, but with scruples. The community owed him much.

It is no exaggeration to say, that as the doors of the Aliquippa Hospital were opening, my dream blossomed to make it the Beth Israel Hospital on the Ohio River. Well, maybe not akin to a Harvard Medical School affiliate but at least a high quality, teaching institution. All the antiquated practices of the surrounding hospitals would be forbidden from the outset; new doctors with specialty skills would be welcomed. A teaching program for doctors and nurses would be developed. Quality control practices would be instituted.

Within two years this latter program was put to a test. The same crusading surgeon who performed the already noted feats of bravery, noticed that one particular surgeon was removing appendix after appendix without significant disease being found. Poor Dr. Smith (not his real name) was a modest gentleman, well-liked by his colleagues. There was no maliciousness or intent on his part to increase his income. Acceptable medical practice had just passed him by. He would examine a youngster who complained of occasional stomachaches. Finding no explanation, Dr Smith, would advise an appendectomy. He would then choose a time for hospital admission convenient for the family. Naively, he would write in the operating room schedule book, "acute appendicitis." To repeat, if this diagnosis is suspected, immediate surgery is the appropriate course.

When the chief of surgery, again Dr. Zernich, and the pathologist completed a review of Dr. Smith's previous twelve operations for appendicitis, only one case of surgical need was documented. The surgical department deliberated on their report and decided that every patient admitted by Dr. Smith with the diagnosis of appendicitis would require a second surgical opinion. Dr. Smith did not contest the action; rather, he graciously discontinued all surgical aspects of his general practice. His colleagues breathed more easily.

The review of another surgeon, an ophthalmologist, whom I will call Dr. Black, was even less pleasant; the results of his surgery were such that close scrutiny was deemed essential. In this instance, the chief of that service was openly vituperative in all conversations regarding Dr. Black. Since it was important to have an unbiased assessment of Dr. Black's performance, Dr. Zernich invited a department chief from Pittsburgh Eye and Ear Hospital to come to our hospital one afternoon. As prearranged, Dr. Black presented a series of his patients. After each presentation, Dr. Black left the conference room; there followed a critique by the consultant.

At the end of the afternoon, the consultant recommended that Dr. Black's surgical privileges be discontinued for one year, during which he would be required to obtain a residency in a recognized teaching center. At the end of that year his reinstatement would be contingent on a satisfactory recommendation of the chief of that teaching service. The final result was that Dr. Black left town, never to return.

This is not to say that nonsurgical departments had less stringent standards. When it became apparent that the quality of service by the radiologist was not meeting adequate standards, the executive committee met to resolve the problem. The radiologist's advocates claimed that he gave service at every hour of the day and night. His detractors did not deny this but zeroed in on the issue of quality. Falling into the second group and being strongly biased against this radiologist because of his unethical obstructionist tactics toward my nuclear medicine department, I avoided joining a cabal to have him fired. The final decision was that he would acquire an assistant. The executive committee would, of course, have to approve his selection. To his credit, he hired a superb radiologist.

In still another instance, as nominal head of cardiology and with the concurrence of two other internists, I indicated to a fourth internist that in order to continue the responsibility of reading ECGs, he would be required to upgrade his skills. He accepted a suggestion to take a three-day ECG course in Indianapolis. He also redirected his study time and made satisfactory improvement.

My admiration for Dr. Zernich in his role of raising the standard of care at the Aliquippa Hospital was boundless. I used to characterize his nobility by saying "If the Nazis take over, Steve will hide my family in his attic." Nevertheless, when the Cardiac Care Unit nurses came to me as the unit's director to redress the hurt of public verbal abuse inflicted on a nurse by Dr. Zernich, there was no way I could avoid a confrontation. Normally an apology would have sufficed but Dr. Zernich refused this gesture, claiming that the nurse's refusal to follow his treatment order was detrimental to the patient's care. The incident was reported to the hospital administration. I was ambivalent when the Hospital Board of Directors considered suspending him for two weeks. I didn't doubt that one or two of the laymen welcomed the opportunity to bring a flamboyant surgeon to bay. In the end, the Board backed down; no action was taken.

A basic commitment to high standards was thus realized during the fledgling years of my hospital. But far more was required to give even a semblance of a teaching hospital. Several types of conferences were scheduled. Within both the medical and surgical departments, discussions leading from case presentations were the essential agenda items for monthly meetings. Another format was a monthly meeting at which a formal lecture was given by a staff member or by an invited guest from major hospitals in Pittsburgh.

A favorite conference was the bimonthly clinical-pathological conference (CPC). It became the responsibility of the pathologist to select a teaching case from the recent autopsies or as suggested by surgical specimens. He would summarize the pertinent clinical information including history and physical examination and laboratory, x-ray, and electrocardiographic findings. His summary was distributed to the members of the staff in sufficient time for their study. One staff member would volunteer to initiate the discussion, propose the diagnostic possibilities, and ultimately to offer his diagnosis. Also it was his prerogative to comment on the quality of the attending physician's management. After the discusssor had committed himself, others were invited to suggest differing opinions. At that point the pathologist presented his findings, dramatically keeping the suspense high until his last slide revealed the answer.

To discuss one CPC I invited the chief of pediatrics of a Pittsburgh hospital. While the summary of a nine-year-old child was being read, the pediatrician came over to me and whispered, "Dave, if I tell the truth, you will never invite me back again. The child was overloaded with intravenous fluids." It was sad that I had not anticipated the problem and thereby prevented the predicament in which I now found myself.

With no way to extricate myself I said, "Call it as you see it, but be as kind as you can."

He did conclude his assessment by adding, "It was an understandable error." The responsible doctor, true to form, blamed himself, not me.

I do take blame for the failure of a great teaching conference. This was called "Death Rounds." Every month or two I, along with an academically inclined radiologist and pathologist, would analyze the charts of two deceased patients who were of teaching interest. I would ask the attending physicians to present them to our medical department; the surgeons did likewise. It was agreed among the staff that every physician whose patient was to be presented would be required to attend. The first three conferences went beautifully. As a vehicle for learning it could not be excelled; colleagues learning from one another. And then came the day when without previous notification neither of two presenters attended. I felt this was especially inconsiderate. I was disappointed, even incensed that this failure would cause the conference to lose the momentum it was achieving. Acted impulsively and in a schoolmarm mode, I wrote letters to my two colleagues demanding excuses for their absence.

My righteous indignation was badly expressed. The responses were equally indignant. One attacked by telephone, "Who do you think you are to be judge and jury?"

The other came unannounced to my office, tearful. "Was it necessary to humiliate me?"

I knew I had blundered terribly. My excuse was that I so passionately wanted "Death Rounds" to succeed. In truth my action showed only my immature leadership skills. Asking forgiveness did little to assuage the intensity of my colleagues' anger and hurt. I presume that word of this incident got around for this conference soon fizzled out.

One of the criteria for hospital accreditation was that autopsies be performed on a minimum of ten percent of all patients dying in the hospital. Our staff had no trouble keeping the rate above fifteen percent. Competition among interns and residents in teaching hospitals for the best autopsy record in those days occasionally lead to unsavory, deceitful cajoling of vulnerable, bereaved family members. I wish I could say that I had an unblemished record. In the present day with CT, MRI, angiography, and needle biopsies, far fewer patients die without an accurate diagnosis. Accordingly the need for autopsies is decreasing.

One teaching program that was predictably doomed to failure despite an excellent faculty was an interactive closed-circuit television conference originating from Pittsburgh Medical School. The idea was exciting; attendance for the first screening was impressive. The following week two people showed up. Thereafter the TV set wasn't even turned on. I don't know what happened in the other participating hospitals. I reasoned that TV lulls the average viewer to sleep. Eye contact between teacher and student is an important factor in transmitting and absorbing new information.

The intensive teaching program for CCU nurses is described in a separate chapter.

In addition to the CCU, I instituted the Department of Nuclear Medicine. Having first placed the equipment in my private office, I soon realized that full utilization would come only in a hospital setting. As with the CCU I encountered strong resistance from the medical staff. I remember the admonition of William Beierwaltes, Professor of

Medicine at the University of Michigan School of Medicine when escorting him on his visit to Pittsburgh. I had expressed anxiety over a conflict of interest since the department would yield me a significant financial return. "Stop ruminating on your personal motives," he said. "If it's good for the hospital, go for it!" I did and proved its importance.

Over a twelve-year period, at the behest of University of Pittsburgh Medical School, I arranged six-week summer programs for post-first-year students. Members of the staff took each of the students in hand for a day or two. This meant tutoring them while seeing both hospital and office patients. All the ancillary services were included in the schedule, even time with home-health nurses on their home visits. The students, numbering one to four, accompanied me on scheduled days and whenever they had free time. I recall my discomfort during the first summer as I directed a female student through the routine physical examination of the male genitalia and prostate. Remember, my class at medical school was a last all-male stronghold; my contact with female medical students and doctors, after medical school, was limited.

One summer I was the host for a conference "On Death and Dying" arranged for fifteen post-first-year students studying in the area's hospitals. The moderator, a psychiatrist from the medical school faculty, asked me to begin the discussion by describing Jewish practices and concepts. I reveled in the opportunity to tout the wisdom of Jewish customs, to the point, perhaps of smugness, until confronted by a different point of view offered by a redheaded Irish oncology nurse. She described the coming of age of Irish youth when first permitted to attend a wake. She found the admixture of laughing and crying, as facilitated by imbibing of alcoholic drinks, therapeutic in the grieving process.

In the late 1970s there came a push for quality review. Insurance companies, in particular Blue Shield, helped develop formats for studying care by the hospital as a whole, and also as rendered by individual physicians. Length of hospitalization for specific diagnoses came under close scrutiny. There was no question that the doctor had a conflict of interest, for with each day of hospital care, the patient's bill rose. Gone were the days when a woman could ask for more prolonged hospital rest just because her mother was available to baby-sit, or because there would be nobody at home to take care of her. In the latter instance, when home health care nurses could provide care, discharge was mandated.

Brother Jerry recommended that I steer clear of this kind of committee activity – "You'll only make enemies." I ignored his advice; there was a job to be done. As the ancient Rabbi Hillel said, "Where there is no man, will you stand?" So I stood and often became the target. When I left any meeting where punitive measures were agreed upon, I mused that my Jewishness might have been an element in my colleagues' antipathy.

The hospital never strove for accreditation for teaching interns and residents. This would have necessitated establishing a position of a medical director. Should I not have pushed for this? For myself? For a specifically recruited outsider? Certainly the latter would have relieved me of many of my nonincome-yielding hospital activities. On the other hand it would have diminished the academic role I had fashioned for myself. I have no answers. The matter, as of 1999, is moot in that the Aliquippa Hospital has for economic reasons, become a satellite of the University of Pittsburgh Medical Center.

Aliquippa Hospital never became the Beth Israel on the Ohio. Possibly without interns and residents and without an affiliation with a medical school, it was a naive dream. Yet there were moments of near greatness, particularly when we physicians were teaching one another. The feeling of mutual responsibility, the spirit of professional camaraderie were heartwarming; learning together fit the expression in vogue in the 70s of replacing "teaching hospital" with "learning hospital."

At least, by adorning the walls of my Aliquippa office with photographs of my teachers at Beth Israel Hospital, I could keep the inspiration of that magnificent Boston institution alive within me.

A CARDIAC CARE UNIT: IT BEATS HAVING A MISTRESS

In 1966 I was invited to give the annual cardiac lecture in Steubenville, Ohio. Dr. Jack Scholnic, the program chairman, had heard of my cardiac care unit (CCU) at Aliquippa Hospital, the first in Beaver County and possibly the first in western Pennsylvania. I titled my talk, "The Cardiac Care Unit. It's Passé To Say, 'I Guess It Was Fate'." I'll explain this title in a moment.

As a resident in medicine at the Beth Israel Hospital in Boston in 1950, I had gleaned experience with the earliest electrocardiographic (ECG) monitors. This unique device had been developed by one of my teachers, Dr. Paul Zoll. Defibrillators and external cardiac pacemakers came on the scene soon after. Specific medicines did not catch up to these mechanical developments until the early sixties.

Prior to the availability of ECG monitors and specific medicines to prevent or abort life-threatening arrhythmias (disturbances of rhythm), countless doctors, included me, would be called to the hospital to the confirm the death of a patient who had succumbed to a myocardial infarction (heart attack). Customarily a nurse on her routine rounds would find the patient pulseless and not breathing. Arriving from home or my office five to ten minutes after being called, I would make a show of dashing into the patient's room closing the door behind me. I would ceremoniously check the various parameters of obvious death. After a few minutes' delay, during which the family would presume I was performing heroic efforts, I would walk to the family waiting room, pronouncing with finality, "Your husband passed away" and, by way of explanation, "I guess it was fate."

But attach the patient to a monitor viewed by a nurse who has been trained to inject lidocaine for ventricular arrhythmias and atropine for slow heart rates, to deliver electrical shocks for ventricular fibrillation, and to give other drugs such as adrenaline and sodium bicarbonate, the mortality rate in acute myocardial infarction drops from thirty percent to fifteen percent. With more recent developments, the death rate today is even lower.

Aliquippa Hospital's administrator must have heard of CCUs at national meetings, for he gave a sympathetic hearing to my proposal to establish one. It was 1964. (The first unit in America opened in 1962 in Kansas City, Kansas.) Together, over objections from the staff and with special hostility from the surgeons whose beds we were appropriating, we converted a four-bed ward into a three-bed CCU. The area of the fourth bed was outfitted as a nursing station. Five of our brightest medical nurses were assigned to me for training. Together we set up procedures and stocked the unit with three bedside monitors (the monitor screens then were about five cm. in diameter), a defibrillator, an external cardiac pacemaker (for the nonbeating heart), and all the other equipment and medications for cardiac resuscitation. We conducted mock exercises knowing that we could not simulate the anxiety our first admission would create.

It wasn't long before the first patients arrived, frequently the sickest of the hospital population and often unresponsive to any treatment. The optimal candidates for salvage were treated as usual in unmonitored beds because my colleagues feared that "the unit will frighten the patients to death." It was not surprising that one of the most vocal antagonists blasted me with, "Why is it that everyone you put into the CCU dies?" This was a low blow from an old friend of the family who was smart enough to realize, though not humble enough to admit, that medicine, in general, and I, in particular, had outdistanced him. Then one day, not long after, a young general practitioner admitted a forty-year-old man with an acute myocardial infarction to a general medical unit. A few hours later the patient abruptly died. His physician became an instant supporter of the CCU.

The CCU thereafter took command of my life. My cardiology skills, though commensurate with that of most board-certified specialists in internal medicine, were not equal to the task. Over subsequent years all my courses and extended visits to centers in New York, Indianapolis, Chicago, and Miami focused on either upgrading my cardiology skills or introducing me to new techniques required for the most up-to-date performance in the CCU. I especially zeroed in on detection and treatment of cardiac arrhythmias. Thereafter it became my responsibility (which I seized on my own) to teach what I had learned to the staff and, most important, to the CCU nurses.

One special learning experience for me occurred during two weeks in 1972 at the Krannert Institute in Indianapolis. It began with a three-day course in electrocardiography. I divided the remainder of the time improving my skills with echocardiography, exercise testing, and placement of plastic cannulas into arteries. The latter I learned from nurses during nightly visits to CCUs in the area.

But the pièce de résistance was a mind-boggling visit to the single cell laboratory, light miles from clinical medicine, I presumed. Not at all. Imagine my excitement as I watched a young pharmaco-physiologist insert an electrode into a single living cell floating in solution in a glass dish. He recorded changing electrical waveforms on an oscilloscope as he varied the concentration of potassium and cardiac medications in the solution. I had used diagrams of these waveforms while lecturing on ECG but as with my garage door opener, I never understood one iota. I couldn't wait to get back to my nurses' classroom in Aliquippa.

As with all CCUs there arose the dilemma of deciding which physicians would be permitted to manage patients in the unit. I could have insisted on total control which at that time would have been in the best interests of the patients but for me would have created a monster, a twenty-four-hour, seven-day-a-week responsibility. The staff would not have tolerated it even if the plan had merit. Or I could have insisted on automatic consultation with me or with either of the two other internists on the hospital staff. After considerable soul-searching, I made the popular decision that each doctor would be in control of his own patient. Any other solution would have met with strife and cries of "foul."

This system worked fine; no one could accuse me of stealing patients. Patients, whose doctors had not kept up-to-date, were protected by my standing orders and recommended treatment plans, which the nurses would tactfully suggest. Quality review was unofficially in my hands as Unit Director. In only one instance did the Medical Staff Executive Committee have to get involved after I blew the whistle on a particular doctor who happened to be black. It followed my recommendation requiring automatic consultation for three months on every patient this doctor admitted to the CCU. Punitive action had been slow in coming because of staff resistance to police itself and dread of incurring the wrath of the black community. If he had been white, the more appropriate action of withdrawal of all CCU privileges would have been taken. Predictably this did not improve my popularity with my colleagues ("Will I be next?") nor, of course, was I ever asked to be the mandatory consultant for any patient.

In time we moved to a remodeled fourteen-bed unit adjacent to the emergency room and, several years after that, to a newly built ten-bed circular acute care unit with a central nursing station permitting an unobstructed view of all beds. Next to this latter unit was a fourteen-bed step-down unit for recovering heart patients. Considering that the number of beds in the hospital was 200 and even fewer in 1984 when I left Aliquippa (hospital stays had shortened progressively), this showed not only the rise in the incidence of coronary heart disease but the importance the staff and administration attached to this endeavor. Four patient vignettes come to mind.

The first concerns Peter Roff, a close friend. Peter was admitted to the CCU and instantly developed ventricular fibrillation, a situation in which the heart has no effective pumping action. I immediately resuscitated him with an electric shock. He survived without health problems for twenty-two years during which time he courageously relinquished tenure as a university biology professor to study for and earn a rabbinic degree.

The second was sixty-year-old Alfred Pfeiffer of German extraction. His severe congestive heart failure required endotrachial intubation which delivered oxygen via a tube directly to his lungs and which, incidentally, prevented his speaking. On the third hospital morning, even before it was safe to remove the tube, he motioned me to open his bedside table drawer and to remove and open a medium-sized envelope. There was no disguising my shock as I flipped through a dozen black-and-white photographs of the Nazi death camp, Mauthausen. I subsequently learned a lot about Alfred. As an eighteen-year old U.S. infantryman in 1945 he had been among the first to enter this concentration camp. What prompted him to take the photographs I do not know, but he made commendable use of them as secretary-treasurer of his battalion and frequent contributor to the battalion magazine in confronting deniers of the Holocaust.

The next patient evoked a lighter mood. I was called to the emergency room to treat a fifty-five-year-old mill worker who, before I could obtain much information, went into shock. A day later I was able to ask questions regarding his past health. When I asked if he drank (one needn't add "alcohol"), he answered, "Only on Hoover's birthday."

I took the bait, "When's Hoover's birthday?"

"I'm not sure so I drink every day not to miss it."

Finally, George, who credited me for his recovery from two heart attacks. During an unscheduled office appointment he sat opposite me, staring at me and scowling. His fists were white-knuckled. Waiting minutes for him to initiate a dialogue, I finally took a leap, "George, are you angry at me?"

"You bet I am." He calmed a bit, "Well, in a way. Why don't you get a haircut?" In truth, as a symbol of alignment with the anti-Vietnam War movement, I had let my hair curl in back and my sideburns become bushy.

"Why is that so important to you?"

"My new son-in-law." Out poured his rage. His sweet little daughter had brought home "this shiftless hippie" who sat around all day slouching on the furniture, wearing no shoes, "eating my food," blasting the government, and, of course, his hair was long and unkempt except for "a "fairy pony-tail." My subsequent counseling helped somewhat to reduce his anger to a level of annoyance; this had no further abated when the young couple moved out. At least a third heart attack never materialized. In view of trends in history-taking in the late ninties I say to myself, "If I had spent the time of the interview gazing at the patient's data on a computer, I would have missed George's fury, his reason for seeking help."

Other than for patient care – and my cardiology practice soared – the greatest expenditure of time involved teaching the CCU nurses. With the small unit, tutorial sessions sufficed. Once the staff expanded to meet the needs of the larger units, formal courses were required. I gave a three-day course, followed by one-day courses every six months. In addition, every two weeks we met in the evening for a two-hour session. All of these teaching activities were well attended not only because of "work credit" they received, but also because of the nurses' zealousness. Certainly the prospect of having me parade a second time in front of a morning class for two hours with an unzipped fly (as two of my students sheepishly informed me between classes) was no inducement.

Can you imagine the nurses' satisfaction and pride, when a patient would be successfully resuscitated, especially when no doctor was available? It was difficult to be humble when one of my protégés would wake me in the middle of the night, "No need to hurry over. We just defibrillated Mr. X., gave him lidocaine and he's fine." We were a great team functioning smoothly together, handling the excitement of emergencies, while apologizing and hugging after the event if I had yelled unkindly. For the record, it was only in the final few years that I received any financial compensation from the hospital for my CCU supervision.

Early during our initial efforts, I was asked for a private interview by one of the CCU nurses. "Why is it," she asked, "that whenever you walk into the unit, you look disapproving, even mad, at us?" Wow! What a misreading! I virtually got down on my knees claiming the opposite to be true. I was proud of each of the nurses and thrilled by their enthusiastic participation. I could not extol their praises more highly. I tried to explain that my furrowed brow and inverted half-moon mouth were indications of my anxiety that we might not be doing all that was needed. Also, I confessed to the pressure created by the throng of jealous, nonbelievers waiting for me to fall flat on my face. I believe that rapport between me and "my gals" never again hit that low level. Over the years I gave out beautiful red-and-gold heart-shaped pins that were adapted from one I had seen worn by CCU nurses at the Peter Bent Brigham Hospital in Boston. The engraving included CCU Nurse and Aliquippa Hospital and on the back, the nurse's name. "My gals" wore them with pride.

My joy, my reward, as a teacher came one night when after a two-hour seminar, a practical nurse, in her sixties, complimented me for giving the "best lecture ever." It was obvious that she had grasped a very complex electrocardiographic rhythm disturbance. I told her that the compliment rightfully pertained to her. We both left the hospital elated, and friends forever.

I can see how a fragile marriage could shatter completely under an assault by the responsibility for a CCU. Before I entered medical school in 1944, Harvard's Peter Bent Brigham Hospital would not accept anyone for training who would marry before the age of forty years. "Medicine is a demanding mistress," we were admonished. A superb family doctor in Aliquippa, Dr. Basil Owens, repeatedly said to me, "Priests should marry; doctors should not." During much of his life he lived alone, separated from his wife. Constantly available to his patients, he spent the day in his office and his nights, making house calls.

Well, a CCU also required a similar twenty-four-hour commitment. Aliquippa Hospital was lucky. I loved "my" CCU and "my" staff. I spent many hours each day caring for my patients, teaching, and supervising the entire operation. I was the nurses' "big Daddy" helping at times even with personal problems. One nurse called her son "David" as his middle name.

It was fortuitous that in the early years this intense relationship between the CCU and me was highlighted in articles in Medical Economics entitled, "Doctors as Husbands" and "Doctors as Fathers." They taught me that wives and children, especially the latter, interpret the time not spent with them as desertion, even if spent saving lives. At least, I realized that I should eliminate the time spent kibitzing at the hospital. And when Amy, watching me put my golf clubs in the car, asked, "Aren't you going to spend any time with us today?" I was crushed. The following year I dropped my golf-club membership. Of course, that latter decision wasn't as noble as it sounds; I was becoming increasingly uncomfortable as CCU calls interrupted my foursome on the golf course. As to trips away from home, I had to weigh, for example, the benefits from spending two weeks at the Krannert Cardiac Institute in Indianapolis against the needs of family. Medicine won.

The CCU staff threw a good-by party for me in 1984 before I moved to Israel. We exchanged declarations of affection and warm hugs. Years of friendship and mutual respect were an incomparable legacy. (It gave me no pleasure to hear that no physician at Aliquippa Hospital ever again took on any teaching responsibility, not even one lecture.) As a tangible gift I received a driftwood framed photograph of the entire CCU staff posed in front of the hospital fountain. This photo adorned the wall of my office at Wolfson Hospital. As an introduction to lectures given in Israel, I would show a slide of this photo and follow with a slide of my solitary technician at Wolfson; "This is what I gave up and this is what I got in exchange."

In early 1999 while on a trip to America, I visited the CCU. Very few of my nursing staff remained. One nurse I had known only casually introduced me to a new staff physician, "This is Dr. Chamovitz. He used to work here." As I wrote about my brother, Irv, it is written in Exodus, "A Pharaoh arose that knew not Joseph."

I have elsewhere pondered the question, "Why did I leave Boston?" I know this: my twenty-year love affair with Aliquippa Hospital's CCU could not have been equaled elsewhere. I accomplished much for my town while fulfilling a rich medical career for myself. As I once said, by way of encouraging a friend to agree to his wife's becoming actively involved in Hadassah, "It's better than for her to take a lover." For me the CCU was a healthy equivalent.

MY THREE G. P.s

"I'm sorry but I don't make house calls," I said. The conversation ended with a slammed receiver, like a bombshell exploding in my ear. Reverberations of the noise have yet to stop. Let me exonerate myself.

When I began my practice of internal medicine in Aliquippa in 1956, I aspired to introduce Boston-quality medicine to my town. High sounding? Of course. Arrogant? Well, if so, my attitude did not turn away three of Aliquippa's most senior general practitioners (G. P.).

Not long after I opened my office, I visited these three to introduce myself formally. Each had known me as a youngster. I visited a number of other G.P.s as well. One of the latter was a longtime friend of the family. His advice to me was, "Aliquippa doesn't need an internist." For the next twenty years he rarely referred patients to me and only then, when it was demanded by the patient. Surely he was threatened by me as a medical specialist.

Drs. McMillen, Miller, Owens, and me at 1963 presentation.

Dr. Howard McMillen, in his 80s, was the oldest of the three G.P.s. His medical practice, once flourishing, was small and therefore I was consulted for only an occasional patient. When he did send a patient to me, in good conscience I could not always return the patient to him after I had completed the acute care; I was fearful of putting the patient's life in jeopardy. Dr. McMillen was no longer the excellent doctor he had once been. Nevertheless, he was great for my ego. He would call on the phone for advice on the management of one of his patients. During those moments I was this senior doctor's teacher. That felt good.

Eventually Dr. McMillen became my patient. He had diagnosed his chest pains as angina pectoris (insufficient blood flow to the heart muscle). And when did this late octogenarian develop pain? During sexual intimacy, of course. Wiping the foolish grin off my face, I recommended that he place a nitroglycerine tablet under his tongue five minutes before initiating the act. "Ol' Doc McMillen" was well into his eighties when he retired and over ninty when he taught sex education in an Ohio college.

Similarly Dr. John Miller, "Ol' Doc Miller," the second G.P., a fine doctor past his prime, would humbly call for medical advice. He, too, had few patients to refer. Doctor Miller was a gentle man. My earliest memory of him was of the days when he was our school doctor. I can still see him running onto the football field to assess the injury of one of the players. How vivid also is the memory of his physical examinations in the gymnasium, most especially my shame as I took off my shoes revealing holes in my socks. Financial success to me meant not having to wear darned socks ever again.

Basil T. Owens was the youngest and most important of my three G.P.s. His colleagues referred to him as B.T. Just as I could never call Harvard Professor Blumgart, Herrman, even though we worked intimately together for a year, I could never call Dr. Owens anything but Dr. Owens, even when he became my patient. He quickly made it apparent that he wanted only office and house call patients; the hospital patients would be referred to me. This was manna from heaven, exactly the form of practice I envisaged.

Dr. Owens treated me like an esteemed medical consultant. More than that, he gave me full control of his hospital patients. In return, I scrupulously adhered to the ground rules that his patients would be referred back to him for post-hospital care – except as dictated by special situations and with his consent. Furthermore, I reciprocated by avoiding any semblance of competition by steering clear of all aspects of general practice. I could not be credited with altruism since the modus vivendi that Dr. Owens and I established was the best of all possible worlds for us both. Yet it was not always smooth sailing. Adhering to this fairly rigid arrangement that we had adopted, led to disturbing confrontations.

Late one night, not long after I had established my office, I received the frantic phone call, which started this chapter. It was from Mrs. Berte Neiman, an old family friend. Her sister, visiting from New York, had become very short of breath. "Please come quickly." I recommended that she call an ambulance to take her sister to the Rochester General Hospital. (Aliquippa Hospital was still under construction.) "No, I want you to treat her here at home," she demanded. Knowing that Mrs. Neiman, herself, was a patient of Dr. Owens, I told her to get in touch with him. I explained that I didn't make house calls except as a consultant. I added before she hung up, "I'll be here by the phone if you can't reach Dr. Owens." There was no return call and it took hours before I was able to fall asleep; I was so upset for rejecting a sick patient. Did the poor lady have to suffer because of my principles?

Hoping to make peace, I called Mrs. Neiman the next morning to inquire about her sister. She struck me with, "I got hold of Dr. Owens and he came and treated my sister. He's a wonderful doctor and I'll never call you again!" The noise of her slammed telephone receiver may have assuaged her anger; it crushed me. I can't imagine why I would have anticipated any other reaction. And yet while suffering from humiliation for days, I came to realize that it had been made eminently clear, at least within the Jewish community, that I was not a G.P. and that my pact with Dr. Owens was confirmed.

The strength of my relationship with Dr. Owens was exemplified by our comanagement of Rose Costanza. Rose, recently married, was not satisfied with Dr. Owens's recommendation to "avoid becoming pregnant and if by mistake you do become pregnant, don't nurse the baby." Her medical problem was mitral valve disease caused by childhood rheumatic fever. Dr. Owens's advice was obsolete, which was unusual for him.

After two weeks to complete Rose's study, she and I sat together to discuss my findings and recommendations. Satisfied that her medical condition was excellent, I quoted one of my medical school teachers, Sam Levine, who wrote in his cardiology textbook about patients like Rose, "I urge the first pregnancy, I encourage the second, and I consent to the third." I was triumphant until Rose announced that her menstrual period was late: as I was telling her that she could get pregnant, she was. Rose went on to give birth successfully three times and to nurse each child. Years later Rose attended both our moving-to-Israel party and another several years later, with her entire family, a reception Marcia and I gave for our Aliquippa friends. Forty-three years after our first meeting Rose called me in Israel, not for my opinion, but rather, for my blessing regarding scheduled repeat heart surgery. I gave it. She never made it off the table.

I do believe that Dr. Owens knew how much I admired him. Here is an example that commanded my respect. Very late one night I was called to the emergency room to treat a young black male. Dr. Owens had admitted him to my service with the diagnosis of diabetic coma. Knowing the diagnosis from the outset, I had a simple task; standard treatment was quickly effective. And how did Dr. Owens make the diagnosis without the backup of a modern laboratory? First of all, he had been called by a neighbor to treat this man who was unknown to him. There in a rooming house in the worst part of town, Dr. Owens climbed three flights of stairs – he was about sixty-two at the time. He found the patient lying comatose on the floor on urine-soaked sheets. The man's breathing was fast and deep. Dr. Owens took a "Dip-Stick" (chemically treated paper that measures the amount of sugar in urine), placed it on the wet sheet, and confirmed his diagnosis of diabetic coma. As an aside, the patient's lapse into coma was triggered by meningitis. I mention this because the hospital administrator chided me, informing me of his concern for the large amount of money the care of this black, nonpaying patient was costing the hospital – an element of racism could not be denied. These days, Managed Care organizations would reward this administrator by appointing him their senior executive director.

Dr. Owens's practice suited his life style. He, more than once, commented that "priests should marry, but doctors should not." In fact, he was separated from his wife and lived alone out in the country in a ranch-style home designed by a student of Frank Lloyd Wright. He was also estranged from his daughter and son who lived significant distances from Aliquippa. Separation was total; Dr. Owens had no other life but medicine.

Ultimately I became Dr. Owens's doctor and enjoyed that role. He developed congestive heart failure from aortic valve insufficiency. Fortunately this responded to conservative medical treatment; aortic valve replacement was in an experimental stage at the time. As his medical situation deteriorated, I staged a reconciliation with his children.

Late one night Dr. Owens called to request an urgent visit. I found him in a panic. He had returned from a house call to find his house ransacked. Approximately $300,000 in municipal bonds had been taken from his closets. This became public knowledge and an embarrassment when the police recovered many of the bonds from a creek near the house. Dr. Owens's breathlessness responded to sedation. The next day's newspapers treated him worse than did the thieves; they stripped him of his honor. They emphasized tax evasion possibilities, while giving only passing mention to Dr. Owens as the epitome of the ideal doctor and no mention of the thousands of patients he had treated, many of whom were unable to pay.

The final call came several months later. I could hear noisy wheezing over the phone. I called an ambulance and then a cardiac care unit nurse, requesting that she meet me at the hospital entrance with relevant supplies. Together we sped to Dr. Owens's home and administered emergency treatment – oxygen, morphine, a mercurial diuretic, and extremity tourniquets, all in vogue at the time. He was more comfortable by the time the ambulance arrived. (Our inflexible Director of Nursing later chastised the nurse for leaving the hospital even though her unit was adequately staffed.)

Dr. Owens died several days later. Our seventeen-year friendship was over. His family and many colleagues, but shockingly few patients, attended the morbidly cold church service. I can understand the children's reticence to speak publicly about their father but many of us physicians would have eulogized him, giving him the honor he deserved. And where were the thousands of families who should rightly have been mourning him? I didn't doubt that they were busy worrying, "Whom will I find to take Dr. Owens's place?" They never did and never would. And the papers' obituaries? Of course, they referred back to the break-in and the municipal bonds. Was there no shame?

The Aliquippa Chamber of Commerce arranged a special banquet to honor these three doctors in April 1963. To my delight and great honor I was asked to present a certificate of appreciation to each of them. I don't remember the words of my presentation but the three doctors represented a style of medical care that is sadly missing in today's increasingly impersonal health care delivery systems. I expressed my personal gratitude privately and individually.

Here is a final vignette in contrast to the lovely relationship with my three noble G.P.s.

One of the tragedies to which doctors are prone is narcotic addiction. I became involved with a case, when one afternoon I was phoned to hurry to an old G.P.'s office. To my shock I found him slumped in a chair in dire need of a "fix." After obtaining a bottle of morphine to handle the acute situation, I called Dr. Tom McCreary, Sr., who was the pathologist at Rochester General Hospital and, more important, president of the Pennsylvania Medical Society. "What do I do?"

His advice was as swift as it was competent. "Yes, write morphine prescriptions for him but quickly report his addiction to the Beaver County Medical Society. They, in turn, will revoke his medical license so that he can no longer treat – or harm – patients." I complied. My subsequent involvement was short-lived for, soon after, the addicted doctor moved from Aliquippa. I knew Dr. McCreary's advice was correct but I was sad to be the one to bring a long career to a close. I was to have the same ambivalent feelings years later when, after my eighty-three-year-old mother drove into a truck, I took away her driver's license. In both instances lives were saved, but at such a price for me!

M

ORGANIZED MEDICINE: WITH FRIENDS LIKE THESE

In 1956 when I first entered private practice, it did not occur to me to question the legality of hospital staff privileges being contingent on membership in county and national medical societies. The benefits of this membership were quite imposing: I received the *Journal of the American Medical Association* (AMA) and was eligible for inexpensive medical disability insurance; I had the opportunity to attend local, statewide, and national educational sessions. Also, in an appearance of propriety, I joined with fellow physicians to improve health care. Doubtlessly, the larger the AMA membership, the stronger its voice in Washington. All well and good.

In the beginning my Beaver County Medical Society membership was comfortable and pleasant. I enjoyed new friendships with several internists and the educational programs were of high quality. In those days nationally known physicians would travel great distances to give a one-hour lecture for reimbursement of expenses only. Within a couple of years I was appointed program chairman. With an almost unlimited expense account, and fresh out of "Mecca" (Boston), I captained a stellar year. I brought Sara Jordan, Chief of Gastroenterology and Sam Marshall, Chief of Surgery, both at Lahey Clinic, for a panel program.

Al Freedberg (much more about him in other chapters) and Paul Zoll, developer of the field of monitors and pacemakers, came from the Beth Israel Hospital. Bob Bradley came from the famed Joslin Diabetes Clinic. I had the pleasure of being their chauffeur and, for some, an overnight host.

But there were incidents, rumblings of trouble ahead. As program chairman I had the assignment of sitting next to AMA president Dr. Orr at the annual County Medical Society banquet. At that time socialized medicine was first being considered as an answer to the America's health crisis. Not consciously meaning to provoke him, I quoted to Dr. Orr from an article dealing with a survey of British doctors. I related the first question of the survey, "How do you feel about the National Health Service?"

The answer was overwhelmingly, "I hate it!"

The second question was, "Would you like to return to the prior system?"

The answer, an equally overwhelming, "No!"

"Well," said Dr. Orr, "you know the survey was supported by the Commonwealth Fund and you know that's a Communist organization." I was dumbfounded.

Frequently I would receive letters lobbying against the income tax. The letterhead included names of several past presidents of the AMA, identified as such. I found it highly improper that there was no disclaimer that the opinions were not those of the AMA itself.

During these same years I was appointed to serve on a county committee to implement a national AMA effort to improve rapport between physicians and clergymen. The goals of the Physician-Ministerial committee were open-ended. We were asked to discuss with one another precepts and priorities that had a bearing on patient care and how we might better share information about the patients' physical and emotional status. I remember that long before cardiac arrest teams were instituted, whenever a Catholic patient collapsed, the Director of Nursing at Aliquippa Hospital would take upon herself the responsibility of contacting the priest and the attending physician, in that order. The nurse was a graduate of Mercy Hospital (Catholic) in Pittsburgh.

This practice came to a halt on instructions from my friend, a priest from Aliquippa's St. Titus Church, to call the doctor first and then the priest.

Prompted by my appointed role I organized an evening get-together of Aliquippa's clergy and our staff doctors. My agenda for this first meeting was merely to raise issues worthy of subsequent in-depth discussion. I described my discomfort when a clergyman would leave a patient's room as soon as he saw me walking in. I suggested that, unless the doctor's visit was urgent, if possible, he, the doctor, should excuse himself, saying, "I have other patients I can see first." The clergy praised me. The doctors? They felt that I was pandering to a foolish cause. No one expressed interest in a follow-up meeting.

So what did the county physician-ministerial committee do? Either I was out of town or I wasn't invited to the planning meeting, but the one and only function was a banquet with representatives of the various faiths as speakers. I remember only two of the speakers. The first was a Christian Missionary Alliance or Baptist minister. He gave a "hell-fire and damnation" call to Christianity. "I can't wait to die to get to sit with my Lord, Jesus!" I couldn't wait till *he* would sit down, at least, so that we could eat. There was still to be a last speaker, Rabbi David Shapiro. He was so upset that he spoke less than three minutes, touching on the ruling that all Jewish religious observance should be brushed aside in order to save a life. Most disturbing to me, the medical leadership registered no dissatisfaction with the committee's corruption of a worthy pursuit.

How well I remember a Society dinner dance, sitting at a table with a fellow Aliquippa internist and his friend, Norman. The discussion got around to a banking problem. Norman, whose tongue had been loosened by alcohol, blurted out, "Ask Dave. All Jews know about banking." Please don't ask why I didn't throw the rest of his drink into his face or at least change tables.

Then there was the meeting open to the public in the evening after Professor Jack Myers had earlier addressed the County Medical Society. During the dinner between the two events Dr. Myers and his companions plied one another with drink after drink even as I kept pointing to my watch. Dr. Myers's entourage arrived to a packed auditorium forty-five minutes late. The other panelists, including my friend George Kurland from the Beth Israel in Boston, were angry but patient. Don Gressley, an internist from Beaver, who was to chair the meeting, met me at the door and tore into me. Without sensing my frustration at having no control of the drinking hour, he stalked out of the building saying, "It's *your* baby. *You* be the moderator!" Would he have acted in that manner if, rather than me, it had been another colleague? I'm not certain. It gets worse.

A year or so later, as a member of the education committee, I urged a debate on the government proposed Medicare Program which would provide payment for health care for those sixty-five years of age and older. I suggested a protagonist from the government and an antagonist from the AMA. The committee's sentiments were mixed. No decision was reached.

Just a word first about our Medical Society president, Dick Crain. Dick was an associate radiologist at my hospital. One morning he expressed terrible anxiety to and for me that I, the anti-Christ, would "perish three years hence." It was so ordained.

Well, the day after the program committee had met, Dr. Crain phoned me to say that that there would be no program on Medicare. "Dave," he said, "I know that you're a communist and you know that communists are close to socialists and, of course, the socialists of Germany became Nazis."

In the days after Dr. Crain's phone call, I contemplated various immediate responses: I hung up; I debated Medicare with him; I thanked him for all his compliments, asking if he were calling from hell; I recommended a return visit to his psychiatrist or his keeper; I threatened to sue him for slander. What I actually did was say, "Why, you son of a bitch! You can call me a communist or a socialist but don't you dare call me a Nazi!" I thereupon reported this conversation by letter to the secretary of the Beaver County Medical Society and asked for President Crain's immediate resignation. I received no written reply, only a long delayed oral request to "drop it." Of course, I didn't. I sent a copy to the AMA; that was in 1964. I'm still waiting for a reply.

This was the last straw. I now joined with kindred spirits who had parted company with the AMA many years before. I mailed a letter of resignation listing the numerous points of contention between us, including their bitter opposition to Blue Cross-Blue Shield – a prepaid health insurance program. I ended by saying that I had no desire to give support to their political objectives. Done. There was no response asking me to reconsider. That the letter was received was evident; I got no further dues statements.

That leaves one more traumatic event to relate, ending any illusion that the Beaver County Medical Society and I had something to offer one another. Around 1980 the nominating committee of the Society asked if I would be a candidate for its Board of Directors. "Who are the other nominees?", I asked.

"Ken Carlson as president." I could not have had a finer gentleman for a friend. "Other board members will include Tom McCreary and Bill Coglan." I considered Tom, a nuclear-medicine physician, a kindred spirit. Bill, a surgeon, though almost always on the opposite side of most issues, was bright and kind; disagreeing with him was an enjoyable exercise. As we would constitute a significant number on the Board, I felt my voice would be heard, and that the meetings would be worthwhile and fun. I consented to run on this slate.

The election came after our monthly dinner. All went well until the call for nominations from the floor? Someone stood up and nominated a popular anesthesiologist. Three others rose to second his nomination or to endorse it. The oft-repeated message was clear, "He's one of us," which I felt was directed only against me. That might have meant that I had stopped being a member of the parent organization, the AMA, that I was a liberal Democrat in favor of governmental health insurance, or that I was a Jew. Now instead of a straightforward election of the entire slate, there would be a secret ballot, a contest. Someone had to lose and I reasoned that I would be that someone.

My heart and respiratory rates accelerated. I felt flushed and weak-kneed as I rose and exclaimed something resembling, "To avoid any conflict I withdraw my candidacy."

The election proceeded by voice vote, accepting the revised slate of officers. Finish. Well, not quite. As I hastily exited the room – I had to get out – Andy Culley, a pathologist, a sensitive friend, stopped me to pay me the highest possible compliment he could imagine, "My, David, that was a mighty Christian thing you did." I knew he meant well but . . . .

I rushed home. Before I could ventilate to Marcia, the phone rang. It was Tom McCreary who wasn't at the debacle. He had already heard what had happened. "But, Dave, they were gunning for me."

"No, Tom, I can't believe that, but even if so, if you weren't on the Board, my serving would have less appeal." The following day he resigned.

Early the next morning Ken Carlson appeared at my door and with tears in his eyes, apologized for the previous night's insult to me – further proof that Tom was wrong. He indicated that he, too, would resign. This he did but ultimately was persuaded to serve.

I could have – should have – resigned posthaste from the County Medical Society but didn't. Inexpensive medical disability insurance was reason enough to remain a member. I never attended another Society function. I doubt if I was missed.

I had been criticized for backing away from a fight. "Work within the organization to improve it." True, I agree, if the organization is a proper vehicle for making the changes I envisioned. Obviously I didn't have the stomach or the political aspiration to deal with the characters I would need to influence. I heeded the advice given during my involvement with Senator George McGovern in his battle to oust President Richard Nixon in 1972. "Better not try to convert people to your way of thinking, but rather to join with those who agree with you and, thusly, avoid insanity."

To my delight, by court action the requirement of AMA membership for a hospital staff appointment was declared unlawful. A stressful chapter in my life had come to an end.

POTPOURRI

PSYCHIATRIST PAR EXCELLENCE: A TRIBUTE

I cry out in pain, in disbelief that Karl should have died a broken spirit and by his own hand; that he, who brought solace to so many in torment, should have met death at such an early age, deprived of dignity, dishonored by colleagues and friends.

Karl and I first met in Pittsburgh during our internships in 1948, he at Montefiore and I, at Presbyterian Hospital. After entering private practice of internal medicine, I began referring patients to various psychiatrists. I derived only mild satisfaction from their consultations. It wasn't until brother Bob heaped praise on Karl for his success with Bob's patients that I decided to give Karl a try.

And I couldn't have been happier! Every patient was helped and every referral yielded a twenty-minute tutorial session as Karl would phone me after his initial consultation to give a summation of his thinking and treatment plan. (For professional reasons he would never again discuss the patient with me.) His call always came in the middle of my busy afternoon office hours. I could not have cared less; his insights were sterling beyond measure. And he was eminently quotable. About a pediatrician he said, "You know he really despises children." To a very immature mother of two equally neurotic children he said, pointing to an empty chair, "You know your mother (deceased) is sitting in that chair next to you." This patient initially berated him to me for such "idiocy." She reversed herself during therapy, when she finally got the impact of that revelation.

To another he said, "You have three choices: continue having Dave treat your neurotic symptoms: spend five years, five days a week on my couch at the end of which you'll be no better; or 'sit *shiva*' (week of bereavement) for your mother now." The patient chose the third option, never again being in the same room with his mother, that is, until years later just prior to her death. The patient and his wife frequently thanked me for the referral to Karl. The patient's brother on the other hand, was decimated by this family upheaval. Too bad he wasn't included in a family therapy session. Possibly Karl should have anticipated that complication.

To cousin Evie, Karl was a life saver; she doesn't mind me identifying her. Evie's depression had been treated by an excellent psychiatrist in Philadelphia (300 miles away) with two back-to-back hours every two weeks. Her father couldn't accept her need for therapy. He suggested that he would take her out for lunch from time to time "and you can tell me your troubles," hardly a viable solution. And when Evie couldn't handle the long trips from Pittsburgh to Philadelphia, at my suggestion she switched to Karl and made excellent progress. After a year of therapy Evie's business went bankrupt. Karl continued to treat her free-of-charge for another year until Evie could function alone. This lays to rest the oft-repeated adage that without paying, the patient doesn't benefit.

Imagine our shock (Bob's and mine) when a newspaper article described a lawsuit brought against Karl by a female patient claiming sexual abuse. Soon after, another patient joined the action against him. Visiting in Pittsburgh at that time, I called Karl to ask if I could tape a deposition on his behalf before returning to Israel. He was moved by my gesture, stating that, of the entire medical community, only Bob had offered help. Evie called Karl from California also to offer testimony on his behalf. One psychiatric colleague testified against Karl. Soon after, we heard that this colleague was accused of drug trafficking and that one of Karl's "victims" was proved to have lied. Of two other members of my family, one, Karl's patient, extolled his praises while another, not his patient, claimed that Karl "ruined" one of her friends. Neither the former nor Evie expressed any sexual discomfort when in Karl's presence.

Whatever the truth, Karl lost his license to practice medicine; it had been suspended at the onset of the legal proceeding. When I spoke to him about an appeal, he indicated that the first trial cost him over $100,000, and that he could not afford another. Thus, in addition to his license, he lost his livelihood and his purpose for living. A year later Karl ended his life, his shame, his depression, and his deprivation.

Please note I did not say guilt. I once described Karl's story to a psychiatrist who stopped me after a couple of sentences with, "Guilty." He started to cite similar cases, which just didn't interest me. I was aware of the seductive potential of the psychiatric encounter and I was sensitive to the risk in the bonding that took place between me and my own patients, especially those with cancer. Any physician hungry for validation of his or her sexuality could easily corrupt the sacred doctor-patient relationship, but theoretically much less so the psychiatrist who is protected by a training analysis.

It was doubly sad if there had been no one around to discuss other options with Karl or if he could not find someone to love him unconditionally. In his book, *The Heritage of Illusions*, Karl wrote that people are obsessed with the search for unconditional love they experienced from Mother until one day she said, "Not in your diaper, in the toilet." Ironically his next book was *Sexual Self-Destruct.*

I am sad also for myself. I was hoping that Karl would be around should my own coping systems fail. And I'm heartbroken for my patient and friend, a middle-aged woman who was helped so much by Karl; deprived of his support, she hanged herself in her cellar.

INHERITED VALUES, NOT INHERITED PROFESSIONS

"But you always wanted me to be a doctor!" Thus Raina initiated unending discussions of her projection, and, as it turned out, Danny's as well, of what she assumed was her parents' career choice for her. It is not difficult for me to fathom the multitude of factors that may have contributed to this misconception. The truth is that it was never my intention to steer my children on a course toward medicine. With both children now fully grown any discussion is academic; their perception has already had its full impact, whether negative or positive. It is my hope that this exposition will give some insight to Raina and Danny and, at the same time, clear me of guilt.

At the time that I was manning the first-aid station in fourth grade, brother Jerry was starting medical school or was soon to enter; I can recall no other influence on my decision to be a doctor. This was a far cry from the reality of my children's formative years. They were surrounded, possibly inundated, by a family of doctors – my three brothers, two cousins, and me. Certainly, the excitement of medicine was transmitted daily at the dinner table and if my brothers were present, this excitement was compounded. I assume that Raina and Danny had to be impressed with the the sense of fulfillment that I constantly exuded. Though not discussed, the financial reward must also have been apparent.

With my office attached to the house, the children were frequently near me. In the evenings when I would be doing patient chart work, writing letters, or tending financial matters, they would either read in a chair opposite me or play with my dictaphone. Or, if they had friends visiting, "Daddy, take us for a ride on the x-ray table." Two or three youngsters would climb on the table, which I would rotate to an upright position or to a head-down position. How much more fun when I repeated this in the dark. This should have been enough to convince anyone to be a radiologist.

The hospital, only a three-minute walk away, was visible from our house. Though the children didn't often visit patients with me, more than once they helped distribute Christmas presents to the hospital staff. A couple of times Danny dressed as Santa Claus.

In terms of career selection there was little indeed to balance the scales away from medicine. The family didn't breed lawyers or rabbis. True, their closest cousin Evie Sherman enjoyed managing her shoe business; Danny worked for her if only briefly. Schoolteachers included Marcia, who organized our synagogue kindergarten, which our children attended and cousin Rose Eger, a teacher who gushed over her students. For Danny there were two handymen, Red Marcus and Mike Zvalchek who could fix anything, an attraction for any red-blooded American boy.

One summer when Raina was about seventeen, she was hired by our hospital administrator to conduct a door-to-door marketing survey of the health care received by residents living within a five-mile radius of the hospital. During her visits she heard many negative comments about the medical profession. This did not deter Raina from entering Brandeis University as a premedical student. But after one semester, sickened by the competitiveness of other premeds, she switched to clinical psychology. She became a competent sex counselor and teacher of Re-evaluation Counseling. After receiving a Bachelor of Arts degree, she worked for a year as a nurse's aide in a psychiatric hospital in Boston. Finding this depressing, she resigned.

Motivation for *aliyah* is complex and personal; suffice it to report that Raina arrived in Jerusalem in August 1977. She began as a volunteer for *Shilo*, a counseling service for women with problems related to pregnancy and abortion and soon became its executive director. Being the first of its kind in Israel, *Shilo* had to prove itself and the need for more health services for women. Abortion was then still a whispered word. Raina had to fight with Hadassah Hospital gynecologists who might finally agree to perform an abortion on a teenage client but with a delay beyond the twelfth week of pregnancy. Not intimidated, Raina would successfully argue for a medically reasonable date.

In 1980 Raina attended an International Women's Conference in Paris. There was an all-night confrontation with friends that brought her to the realization that she, herself, wanted to be a doctor. The following day she phoned me. The conversation was as follows: "Daddy, I've decided to apply to medical school."

"That's nice, Raina."

With consternation she replied, "Is that all?"

"Raina, I'm very pleased if that's what you want."

Again Raina, "Aren't you excited by the idea?"

"Raina, I'm already thrilled with your life, your living in Israel, your pioneer work with *Shilo*. I couldn't be more proud of you."

And then the accusation that started this chapter, "But you always wanted me to be a doctor!"

Raina successfully completed medical school and specialty training. By mid-1997 Raina had already achieved a reputation as a respected specialist in Family Medicine while Danny was receiving accolades as Ph.D. director of a molecular biology laboratory at Tel Aviv University. One day we received a clipping from the *Beaver County Times*, our Aliquippa newspaper. The writer credited the Chamovitz family with having one more doctor than another prominent Aliquippa family, the Zernichs. The latter included three colleagues of mine plus four in the next generation. For us, they cited us four brothers, Raina, nephews Bruce and Allen, and Danny. I composed a letter declining the competition, saying that Danny wasn't an M.D. and secondly, wanting to defuse the pressure of academic achievement, that there probably were other Ph.D.s and masters degrees and fine youngsters without degrees in both families. Danny read my letter and took umbrage with it and with me, accusing me of downgrading his Ph.D. Wow! I never mailed the letter.

Again I'm in the dock! I had to prove my satisfaction, this time, with Danny's career choice and I had to reaffirm my admiration for his academic accomplishments. "No, I'm not disappointed that you're not an M.D." Oh, yes, there is one drawback to his not being an M.D; for me the language of molecular biology is as difficult as Hebrew.

Of course Raina and Danny knew that I wanted them to be happy with whatever field they chose. They knew I respected scholarship but they, at least Danny, knew that I also envied skilled workmen. "Just be good at whatever you do and do whatever will give you satisfaction" is such a hackneyed phrase.

Danny told me that he felt I would have been happy if he had studied for the rabbinate. Twenty-five years ago this wouldn't have been an option for Raina as a woman.

I conclude that except for the environment we created, Marcia and I did not direct our children's educational and career choices. We hope that the perceived pressures have played a positive role and maybe the confrontations enlightened them about parenting. And don't they think they will do a better job with their own children?

FUND-RAISING HAS ITS REWARDS

Frequently in the early thirties during the Great Depression, there would be a knock on our back door. Invariably, it would be a hobo, a destitute male on the road, looking for work so that he could buy food and, when possible, send money to his family. Without hesitation, Mom would invite the usually disheveled supplicant into the kitchen for a meal of hot soup and buttered bread. Despite the fact that we were in debt to the dairyman, no one went away hungry and without a few coins. In those days one of the main staples in our own diet was soup made from cattle bones the kosher butcher gave my Mother. Hot dogs and baked beans were infrequent delicacies, possible whenever Dad would make a few extra dollars peddling.

On our kitchen windowsill was the famous *pushkie* or blue box. From time to time my parents would give us pennies, rarely nickels, to place in the box. We knew that the money would go to Palestine via the Jewish National Fund. Jews there were "worse off than we were." It was strange that I never felt "worse off."

Giving to needy individuals and to worthy causes was a way of life in my family. Not to give was unconscionable.

Sometime in my childhood I learned that Dad and Uncle Harry Jackson had an arrangement with Mr. Adam, the Greek owner of the Liberty Restaurant. The deal was this: whenever a hobo would come into the restaurant, Mr. Adam would feed him soup, bread, and coffee. Each Monday morning, either Dad or Uncle Harry would come to Mr. Adam to settle the bill for the previous week's handouts. One particular bill seemed unusually small for the number of meals served. Dad expressed disbelief to which Mr. Adam replied, "What's the matter? Can't I be a partner?"

Black-hatted, usually unkempt rabbis who came into the store never went out empty-handed. I never knew when they were soliciting for themselves or for Jewish organizations; I doubt if it mattered to Dad. Years later as Dad's successor, I could not deny entreaties from similarly clad *shnorrer's* (beggars) who came to my office. I got demerits for hurrying them away. Had I remained in Aliquippa, I might still be ill at ease to be seen associating with this Jewish foreign element.

Dad's generous discounts or giving shoes away free were hardly good for business; his needy customers seldom became less needy. A note from black Reverend Clark always gave the bearer a sizable discount. Call him an easy touch or a *freier* (some one who is easily taken advantage of), Dad never felt abused. I don't believe his partner in the shoe store, Uncle Harry, was always comfortable with Dad's practices but he did nothing to discourage him.

It was only after I completed my formal medical training and moved back to Aliquippa that I became involved with United Jewish Appeal (UJA) and Israel Bonds. (The latter qualifies as "charity" since the return from the purchase of a Bond was four percent at a time when eight percent was easily obtained from saving accounts in banks and with no risk.) Marcia and I accompanied Mom and Dad to banquets for both organizations in Pittsburgh and were inspired by such speakers as Golda Meir, Pinchas Sapir, Senator Wayne Morse, James Roosevelt, and Robert Briscoe. The latter introduced himself thusly. "My name is Robert Briscoe. I am Jewish. I am the mayor of Dublin, Ireland." Then using the oft-repeated American boast, he ended with, "Only in America . . ." We have a photo of Dad handing Briscoe a check for Aliquippa's total donation. This honor frequently fell to Dad or Uncle Harry as the top givers, though hardly the richest, of the community.

Attending these dinners was a rite of passage, of entering into the world of supporters both of Israel and of distressed Jews. It was also a statement to my parents that I wanted to emulate them. It was heartwarming to be in the company of fellow lovers of Zion from each community in the tri-state area of Western Pennsylvania, contiguous Ohio, and West Virginia. No one was ashamed to respond with tears to the plaintive pitches by our UJA executive director Meyer Mintz for increased giving. Many were sparked to stand up a second time to announce an increase in their pledge. I won't deny an occasional plant who started the ball rolling.

I knew I would join the contributors but the question was how much to give. Compared with most doctors and other professionals, I would have seemed magnanimous by giving very little. Businessmen were generally the annual stalwarts. It was Louis Jacobson, a clothing store merchant, who wouldn't accept a several hundred-dollar pledge from me. My medical practice and my income were just beginning to build. Foolishly, I said to Lou, "I don't even have enough money to pay my quarterly taxes." Lou taught me financial planning and not to think of available cash. He extracted a $1,000 pledge while giving me my first lesson as a fund-raiser. Increases thereafter came easily.

Becoming involved in fund raising was educational, ennobling, humbling, and frustrating. Several unrelated experiences come to mind – and as usual, feelings of guilt keep them accurately available in my memory bank. The first concerns Alex Fisher, a pediatrician from East Liverpool, Ohio, a lovely human being who devoted himself to leadership roles in Israel Bonds. Every morning before office hours he was on the phone either with the Bond office or with one of us serving on his various committees or with a potential bond buyer. Unfortunately, his pace when chairing a meeting was narcotizing. At the close of one particular meeting Alex stormed to my end of the table and accosted me with, "What are you so angry about?" This was the first time that I realized that in repose, the corners of my mouth turn down. Alex saw anger rather than boredom. When, as president, I would sit on the *bima* (dais) during services at our synagogue, Marcia would grimace to remind me to smile.

For years before I arrived in Aliquippa, it had been a practice at UJA banquets to place at each setting a list of the previous year's givers to UJA along with the dollar amount. It wasn't long before I topped the list. I did feel embarrassed but rationalized that this would present others with a yardstick by which to measure their own level of giving. (This antedated the days of the "fair share" concept – giving related to one's income.) I was further consoled by the fact that Hadassah Women's Zionist Organization of America had been doing this for years, giving names to dollar categories, such as "Sponsor, Builder, Pioneer, etc.;" the dollar range of each code word was known to all. While I might claim that I had no intention of hurting anyone, in truth, I did intend to prod a few individuals who were giving far below their ability.

Well, the custom or should I confess, this ploy, finally blew up in our collective faces at a UJA affair when two couples, seeing the lists, proclaimed their indignation and stormed out of the banquet hall. It is unimportant that these dissidents were among those whose giving fell short of our expectations. The death knell of the list had been sounded; it never appeared again. Hadassah, hearing no complaint, continued its categories.

What a memorable day June 5th, 1967 was for Israel, UJA, and me personally. This was the onset of the Six-Day War. By chance it coincided with Aliquippa's annual UJA pledge night. Cecil B. DeMille couldn't have orchestrated a more fortuitous concurrence. The visiting speaker was Hy Kalus, an American-Israeli theater director. His Israeli wife and two small children were home in Jerusalem.

There we sat, secure, in a restaurant in Aliquippa having lunch while planning our strategy for the evening and Hy's personal solicitation of potential big givers that afternoon. Imagine the scene, Sid and Milt Eger (my cousins), Moishe Selkovits, Lou Jacobson, Uncle Harry, and Marcia and I watching Hy's facial expression as he listened to a portable radio for news flashes from Israel. He was terrified and helpless being so far from his family. One of us emphasized the need to get people to give at levels never before achieved. Another urged, "Let's not push the panic button"; doubtless, he knew he would be a prime target that afternoon. No one responded but I'm sure Hy wanted to strangle him.

The evening began with a cocktail party for potential big givers. Bernie Fuchs, a radiologist with a history of token giving, handed me a check for $1,000 saying, "It's money down the drain. Israel will lose the war." Feeling as he did, he deserved a doubled *mitzvah*.

Emotions ran high at the meeting. We were happy to have Raina and Amy witness the community's response. Hy spoke emotionally transmitting his own personal dread. Youngster Nancy Moidel, without asking her parents' permission, pledged her *bat mitzvah* money. Phil Cohen, another teenager, gave his savings – some odd figure like $78.61. Almost everyone voiced a pledge, some even raising his or her initial pledge as the evening progressed. As was true across America, Aliquippa did itself proud that night. Our community ranked first among those of comparable size in the country as to funds raised and to the percentage of givers. Even before knowing that Arab forces had been thrashed, Israel made us proud to be Jews and Zionists. Equally impressive, no one reneged on a pledge even once the crisis had past. Hy Kalus's family was unscathed.

Our biggest donations went to UJA and Hadassah, topped only during building fund drives for Aliquippa Hospital. One year I deducted $1,000 from my UJA pledge, sending this sum directly to the Conservative Movement in Israel. I registered my protest against the Jewish Agency, distributor of a major portion of UJA money, because they allocated large amounts to Orthodox institutions but nothing to Conservative or Reform Movements in Israel. I got a hasty call from the executive director of UJA in Pittsburgh saying, "Dave, you're one of our role models. You can't reduce your level of giving. New York is very upset."

"Good," I replied, "that's exactly what I want." (I did compromise by adding another $500 to my UJA pledge.) Many years later this type of gesture mushroomed. With the manipulation of Israeli politics by the extreme Orthodox and their refusal to acknowledge Conservative and Reform Jews as legitimate Jews, the response of American Jews has been to siphon UJA moneys to non-Orthodox movements. Again, good.

Being involved with Israel Bonds broadened our awareness of Israel's needs. From the time of our first visit to Israel in 1961, when we saw the initial pile of rocks forming a quay in Ashdod, we have taken pride in the fact that Israel Bond money was instrumental in building what would become Israel's largest seaport. And so often on trips north, we crossed over Israel's National Water Carrier, a system of trenches transporting water southward from Lake Kinneret (the Sea of Galilee). This water flows even to the Negev sustaining agriculture east and west on the way.

As part of his pitch to encourage purchases of Israel bonds, cousin Sid Eger used to say, "four percent interest and four percent *nachas*" (joy). For many Jews in the early days, purchase of an Israel bond required a leap of faith; the risk of default was on everyone's mind. As my medical practice grew I began buying higher denomination bonds for my pension plan and for that of my office staff. Not all my friends were so inclined. I had Jewish colleagues whom I approached on behalf of Bonds, who considered Israel bonds a bad investment. I must say I felt wistful and guilty when I cashed in some of my bonds when I needed the money in Israel. It was as though I were reclaiming a loan from a still needy friend.

Fund-raising is an acquired skill. At a UJA physicians' training seminar for potential solicitors I volunteered to play the role of the solicitee. I expressed expertise since I had so much experience having people say "No" to me when I solicited Jews on behalf of Israel or doctors on behalf of the Aliquippa Hospital or United Fund. I knew all the negative answers. For example, I had volunteered to go after doctors with a record of zero giving to UJA. My first prospect was a successful gynecologist who knew of me and my brothers. He claimed concern for Israel but couldn't contribute. I asked for $25, just so his name would be among the contributors. "Sorry," he said, "I have three *bat mitzvahs* coming up." I swallowed hard, wished him "*mazel tov,*" and hung up.

At this training seminar pair after pair of colleague-solicitors were teamed up against me. I was indomitable. "Who are you to tell me what to give?" "Whose business is it how expensive a car I drive or where I vacation?" "You don't know how much I give to my poor relations." "I'll give what I want, when I want. I don't need to be solicited." All of these confrontations were videoed. Each replay showed me aggressively leaning forward with arms folded across my chest.

At that point Stan Hirsch was pitted against me. At last I met my match. Stan was a volunteer surgeon during Israel's 1967 and 1973 wars, a known big giver, and a veteran solicitor. He began with compliments. "David, we're both successful doctors and we both care strongly for Israel. We visit often and work for her security. To our sorrow we both have very large psychiatric bills for our kids. Somehow we both manage to go skiing out West. Remember when we divided a two-week ski vacation? I really think you ought to consider approximating my level of giving . . ." When Stan finished with me, there was no way I could deny him his trophy. And what did the video reveal? At the outset there, for all to see, was my pugnacious demeanor. It showed me gradually backing away against my chair, lowering my hands until they covered my crotch. He figuratively had me by the "short hairs." The laughing was at my expense. Blushing, I joined in.

I subsequently used these techniques for building fund campaigns at the Aliquippa Hospital. First I would indicate my pledge and suggest at least no less from the other internists and even higher figures from surgeons. I made no friends but the campaign was a success. For the United Fund I indicated in a letter intended just for doctors the results of the previous year's drive. I listed the number, not names, of givers at various levels of contributions. This, too, was a successful ploy, enlightening some and shaming others.

During the thirteen years of working at Wolfson Hospital in Israel, I raised over $100,000 for the Department of Nuclear Medicine. This doesn't seem like much when you consider that my purchases amounted to well over $800,000. While Marcia was packing our household goods for shipment to Israel in July 1985, I was on the phone calling UJA and Bond friends. Gifts varied from $25 to $4,000 totaling $15,000. Some were one-time pledges as a gesture, probably to compliment Marcia and me for making *aliyah*. One particularly interesting pledge came from Bill Lippy, an ear surgeon from Warren, Ohio. Bill had given a fund-raising seminar in my house some years before. I subsequently learned that he had visited Israel numerous times to teach and to perform the stapes operation. More important to me, Bill was Israel Tennis Center's most important organizer, fund-raiser, and contributor. I spoke to him at a tournament and indicated that I would no longer seek to divert any of his largesse from the Tennis Center.

Every year thereafter before Rosh Hashanah I wrote solicitation letters, each with a personal note. A rich correspondence ensued with many friends and family. I added a comment to each letter that I would appreciate the correspondence even without a pledge. I affirmed this when I sent letters – without requesting money – after I retired.

My favorite fund-raising story concerns Lou Borsani. Born of Italian immigrant parents, Lou learned the grocery business and Yiddish under the tutelage of the Farkas brothers in Beaver Falls, Pennsylvania. He opened his own store in Aliquippa, years later expanding to the largest supermarket in town. Not only were his prices competitive but every encounter with him was a delight. Always cheerful, he conversed with his customers in their native languages, Serbian, Italian, and Polish. He was charitable to all organizations, not the least to his Catholic church. Lou was one of only two Aliquippians to receive both the Man of the Year and the Brotherhood Awards from the Chamber of Commerce.

Lou enjoyed the friendship of many of Aliquippa's Jews. He was frequently invited to *bar* and *bat mitzvahs* and was very much at home wearing a *yarmulke*. His only child David was in Marcia's nursery school at the Synagogue. Lou and his wife Angie frequently attended Israel Bond dinners, always buying a Bond, probably a larger one at the banquet at which Marcia and I were honorees. One year our committee convinced Lou to serve as campaign chairman. You can imagine his success, a Catholic asking Jews to buy Bonds for Israel. It was beautiful.

Lou became my patient one Rosh Hashanah morning when I was called from the synagogue (five miles away) to the Aliquippa Hospital to treat his heart attack. The heart damage was extensive. Without interns and residents in the hospital there was no way I could comfortably return to the synagogue. I remained with him during the critical hours of that first day and night. Lou recognized how important the holiday was to me and was immensely grateful. He made an uneventful recovery and saw me periodically over the years for office checkups.

In 1991 during one of our trips "back home," Lou asked to see Marcia and me. We visited him in his tiny retirement office. "Dave," he opened, "I hear you're raising money for your isotope department in Israel. I want to give you my Israel Bonds." What a pleasant surprise. Lou didn't indicate what their value was. He asked that I make arrangements through the Bond office and stipulated that there was to be no public acknowledgment. Months later the bonds began to arrive at Wolfson Hospital. With the last, the total contribution came to $19,500!

Despite Lou's insistence on keeping his gesture quiet, on behalf of good public relations for Wolfson Hospital, I took the liberty of sending the story to the Israeli Hebrew newspaper *Maariv.* The headline read, "Doctor, Called from his Prayers to Care for Heart Patient, Receives Donation." Fortunately, the item didn't come to the attention of international news services.

The Wolfson Hospital administrator offered Lou $1,000 for a plane ticket to Israel for a recognition ceremony. Unfortunately Lou's traveling days were over. He was approaching his eightieth birthday. Danny's mother-in-law, Yardana, who works in the Bond office in Jerusalem, obtained a beautiful Israel Bond plaque, an engraved metal relief of Jerusalem. I added an engraved inscription. Instead of a ceremony at Wolfson, Lou and Angie received the plaque at a restaurant in Aliquippa. Modest and selfless, he accepted this token as though it were the trip to Israel. Lou died several years later. Angie wrote to tell me that she had put Wolfson Hospital into her will.

There are many who have no stomach for fund-raising. It either embarrasses or offends them. I see it as a noble pursuit as long as it is conducted with tact, sensitivity, and humility. I'll never know whom I may have offended or made uncomfortable (other than as admitted earlier). I like to think that I educated while offering opportunities for my solicitees to perform *mitzvot.*

I can pose but not answer the question whether or not American charity has been good for Israel. Surely there can be no doubt that Hadassah's provision of health services beginning in 1912 was critical to the health of a growing community. Nor is there any doubt that UJA funds allocated to the Joint Distribution Committee enabled care for destitute communities all over the world and transportation to Israel of Jews especially from Europe and Moslem countries. There is no question that philanthropy built universities, hospitals, and sport centers and eased the rigors of absorption of masses of Jewish immigrants.

For many Jews in America, Israel served as their only connection to Judaism. Through *divrei Torah* (words of Torah) at organizational meetings, they were introduced to brief Bible lessons. Through the melodies of the *birchat ha'mazon* (blessing after meals) they were reminded of the sanctity of food. Thus, while raising money for Israel, Jews learned history and Bible and tasted the joy of ritual.

Were there any adverse effects on the State of Israel? It is said that we spoiled Israel's citizens as only a rich uncle can do. On that I have no expertise. The amount of money raised compared to the budgetary needs over the years could not have been that significant.

Independent of its value to the recipients, fund-raising of itself was infinitely important to those engaged in the process. For me, this process was the reward.

TAKING ROY FOR A SWIM

My hometown, Aliquippa, should have been a true example of the melting pot which characterized the American dream. Though numerous ethnic groups settled the town, the Jones and Laughlin Steel Corporation (J&L) which enticed them from Europe and from the USA's deep south, segregated them by nationality and color by selling each group houses on the various hills. The inhabitants did come together somewhat as mill workers: mid-Europeans were laborers while office and foreman jobs generally were assigned to Anglo-Saxons. Mixing of cultures was more complete in the public schools though a small number of students went to Catholic schools. By 1956, when I returned with my family to live in Aliquippa, most neighborhoods had become integrated except for the continued exclusion of Blacks. It took more than a decade for that particular wall to come down.

From the days of my childhood to the year of my return to Aliquippa, three public swimming pools existed in the town. The largest was in Plan 12, a predominantly Anglo-Saxon neighborhood, serving several other Plans within a mile or two – for me, about a mile. There was a second pool across the railroad tracks in West Aliquippa, which housed predominantly Poles and Italians. The third pool in Plan 11 Extension, was exclusively for Blacks. The latter were not to be found in the other two pools, at least not until the seventies. There was also a small private pool for more affluent residents of Hillcrest.

Private neighborhood pools were becoming fashionable in the fifties. Soon after we moved into our house on Hospital Drive in 1958, my neighbor, Ed Nanasi, and I approached the DiMattias, builders of all the houses in the neighborhood, to request a parcel of ground for the purpose of building a pool. They made the gift on condition that the pool be named for their son, Daniel, who was killed in an accident not long before. We promised; the honor was ours.

Ed and I invited neighbors to my house one evening. From this meeting grew an organization with elected officers and committees. Membership grew to include first-and-second-generation Italians, Poles, Ukranians, Greeks, Serbians, Croatians, Germans, and Irish – all Caucasian. There were also Jews, Roman and Eastern Orthodox Catholics, and Protestants. Knowledge of democratic process was well-known since many of those involved were active in the steelworkers' and teachers' unions. At one meeting I had my comeuppance after making what I thought was a suggestion to streamline our proceedings. A coarse-looking steelworker shouted, "I don't know who you are (what an insult!) but you're out of order;" he was correct.

The organizational details escape my memory except for several significant incidents. Mother's Day in 1960 was never to be forgotten. Volunteers assembled to construct the pool clubhouse. The foundation had been laid; it was now a bricklaying job. There were Ed, a paint chemist, and I, a Harvard internist, making cement (mud) – my only relatives who did this were delivered from Egypt by Moses – carrying it in hods to five professional bricklayers.

We had considerable difficulty keeping up with the demands of "More mud! Get a move on!" After about forty-five minutes of me being pilloried with expletives, one of the bricklayers, an elderly, old-school Italian gentleman, discovered that I was "Dr. Chamovitz." His embarrassment, his mortification (no pun intended), were touching. To him I was the Professor Doctor equal to a priest in stature. It took a while for me to reassure him that I loved the anonymity and the sharing of this venture, like homesteaders of bygone days raising a neighbor's barn on the wild prairie. After this dramatic interlude, construction progressed, though at a slower pace out of respect for the doctor.

Marcia served on the bylaws committee. As to membership she suggested the phrase, "regardless of race, creed, or color." Resistance was heated. "Why bother with 'color' since no Blacks live in our area?" Residing within walking distance of the pool was a substitute precondition. Marcia kept pushing but to no avail. The committee decided, "We'll handle the matter when a problem arises." Marcia was not reassured.

When the Roy Harts, a Black family with two sons, moved within a stone's throw of the pool, they applied for membership. Their application was summarily rejected. The father Roy was a steelworker as were most of the pool members. "You know he was accused of using J&L telephones for personal calls," hardly a capital offense among speeding ticket fixers, numbers writers, and God knows what else. It seemed to Marcia and me that our dream of neighborliness was being vandalized.

These were the dreadful years of the sixties when Detroit was burning from race riots. During an annual Brotherhood meeting I rose to confront the political leaders and clergy who were spewing forth platitudes that had characterized so many fatuous showpiece gatherings.

The following day I was confronted by phone by a Black steelworker, James Downing. "Did you mean what you said last night or are you just another smooth talking White liberal?" That was the moment "to put up or shut up." I could hear Dad saying, "Just be a good doctor," as James and I planned our first interracial meeting. It was to be held in my living room. "You bring six Whites and I'll bring six Blacks."

One of my six was Eric Garing, my high-school teacher of American Civics. To me he was the epitome of morality, a preacher of excellence in scholarship and justice in human behavior. All that had been twenty years earlier. He was dumbfounded at the opening meeting when he heard angry Blacks attacking the City Council, the schools, and white society in general. His naiveté reminded me of my own childhood acceptance of Negroes sitting upstairs in the theater balcony. Mr. Garing's reaction paralleled that of visitors to the Holocaust Museum in Washington. They shake their heads from side-to-side in disbelief and say, "I didn't know." He was humiliated by these same Blacks who had been his admiring students or so I had assumed.

The most enlightened member of my group was Father Phil Schaffer, a young pastor of the Episcopalian Church. Shortly after we began our deliberations, Father Phil was inspired to remove his clerical garb and go to live for two weeks in a Chicago slum. The experience for him was earth-shattering; he now had a new calling. And for these efforts his congregation ran him out of town. "We want a minister who will devote himself to religion," was their excuse. I wish I could say I never heard such a remark in a synagogue.

I don't recall that our group accomplished anything of significance other than meeting alternately in White-and-Black homes. Many Whites had never been in a Black home, let alone been to Plan 11 or Plan 11 Extension, a mix of low-to-middle-class homes bordering the town's garbage dump. If Blacks had been in a White home, it would have been only with mop and pail in hand. But one of our group's Blacks was Roy Hart who, as previously mentioned, had moved into a house near the pool.

One morning without any advanced planning, without consulting either the American Civil Liberties Union (ACLU) or any other civil rights group, I called Roy to ask if he felt like taking a swim. Without hesitation he accepted an invitation to be my guest at the Daniel DiMattia Swimming Pool.

Accompanied by Marcia and Danny and attired in bathing suits, Roy and I drove to the pool, walked through the gate, and within minutes, were in the water. Little did I realize that for us it was hot water. But why should that be? Wasn't I Dr. Chamovitz, physician to many of the members? Wasn't I one of the pool's founding fathers? How vindicated I felt not seeing any bather jump out of the water. Nor did any mother haul her child from infested waters. Surely my action would be universally approved. Hardly! It and we were universally denounced.

That afternoon with only Amy at home, I was visited by three members of the pool board. Poor Amy, sitting on the stairs outside the living room, heard them threaten me ". . . if you ever to do this again." The threat to do what was open-ended. I dared not ask.

When they left, Amy rushed into my arms sobbing, "Daddy, can't you do something?" Like call the police? How could I explain to my daughter that most of the police were friends and relatives of my attackers? I was paralyzed with the shock, the embarrassment at my naiveté about how far my patients' goodwill would carry me. It really was sheer arrogance that I hadn't done my homework to prepare a plan of action, or to consult with the ACLU, for example.

That same afternoon the pool board canceled all guest privileges. Soon after, they were restored, though to blood relatives only.

Almost everyone was scornful in varying degrees of my blatant move to integrate the pool. Marvin Neft, a member of our Jewish congregation, called to offer endorsement. It was only Steve Plodinec, an older Serbian friend and businessman, who called, saying, "Call me if there's trouble."

I remember having visions of burning crosses in the yard. Poor Amy must have suffered even worse fantasies. Raina remembers only being proud of her parents. We had anonymous threatening phone calls but there were no dirty tricks. We did feel isolated from our neighbors. For months I could not escape the feeling that my family and I were in physical jeopardy.

A few days after the event my sister-in-law Irma was having her hair trimmed in Sewickley by a former Aliquippian. He asked Irma if she had heard what her brother-in-law had done. "Yes," she knew.

He continued. "Can you imagine the kind of Negro he took to the pool, a real shady character?"

Irma replied, with tongue in cheek, "He tried inviting Ralph Bunche, (a famous American United Nations diplomat and Nobel Peace Prize laureate, a light-skinned Negro) but he was busy."

The hairdresser asked, "Who's Ralph Bunche?"

Did we accomplish anything worthwhile? One teenager, a stranger to us, related some years later that she got into an argument with her parents when she expressed admiration of us. Did we liberate her? Are Roy Hart's sons less prone to be racists because of one white family's courage? Did we delay integration that might have come from more considered action? The Plan 12 pool did become integrated several years later when economics forced the closure of the Black pool on Plan 11. By this time there were a number of neighborhood pools that presumably siphoned off a significant number of politically strong opponents of integration.

Our standing at the Pool had hardly been enhanced by a poolside discussion regarding intermarriage with Marcia participating. This was prompted by the elopement of our baby-sitter, Donna. She had run off with an Aliquippa Black after prolonged and futile attempts to have her family accept him. Her father was a devoted cardiac patient of mine, an Italian immigrant whose self-image was already marred by a congenital clubfoot. Marcia posited that a shared philosophy of life was more important as a basic ingredient to a happy marriage than was matching skin color. A Catholic worrying about his soul burning in hell would find little solace from a Jewish spouse for whom the concept had no meaning. Similarly, a couple harboring strong but opposing political opinions might tangle over them. Marcia's conclusion: "Better for a white Jew to marry a black Jew than a white Christian." So much for intellectual pursuit of the good life. Word went around town that the Chamovitzes were "nigger lovers" and Christian haters.

I did have the shallow satisfaction of confronting my neighbors at a dinner in 1980 when I received the Aliquippa Chamber of Commerce Brotherhood Award. Dad had been the recipient in 1960. (Dad's fourth-grade English bested many of the college-educated speakers on the program.) He and I were the only Jewish Brotherhood awardees since its inception in 1958.

After introducing my family and giving the perfunctory "Thank Yous," I lashed out: "And where were you when I needed you, when I ran for Democratic delegate in the presidential year meant to bring down Richard Nixon (I came in ninth in a field of twelve aspirants beating one Governor Wallace and my two fellow Senator McGovern candidates) and where were you when Roy Hart and my family went for a swim in the Daniel DiMattia Pool?" By then Roy was a county detective; I had him stand up. Dad used to quote a Harry Truman supporter who shouted, "Give 'em hell, Harry!" That's what I was doing, but for whose benefit? Surprisingly the award wasn't rescinded. Only Racheal, Marcia, and Danny acknowledged my remarks.

Soon after, we resigned from the pool, but only after Danny stopped using it. We are still awaiting the refund of our building assessment fee as mandated in the bylaws.

In January 2000 I wrote a letter to Roy to remind him of that epical moment in our lives. In return I received a video cassette, a promotional message advocating Roy's candidacy for the United States Congress. He presented the image of an elder statesman. I doubt that it would have helped his case for membership in the DiMattia Pool.

MY LIFE'S REFRAIN

Presumably, love of music was transmitted through my genes. Dad had a strong baritone voice. He excelled as a cantor for prayer services in *shul.* If we happened to secure the services of a professional cantor for the High Holy Days, it was Dad's pleasure to complete phrases with his own unique harmonies. His *Shabbat* evening *kiddush* was incomparable. His Passover seder was a musical masterpiece.

We sons have questioned Dad's belief in God but never his delight in communicating with Him. Much of the joy I find in *davening* (praying) comes from my remembering Dad's melodies. As a child accompanying Dad "on the road," I would hear him sing *Shabbat* or holiday prayers.

Mom was gifted with a melodious alto voice. Though shy and modest, she was enthusiastic when asked to sing at *shul* banquets. Her favorite song was the poignant, "*Eli, Eli*" (God, God, why have you forsaken us?) or in the same mournful mood, "*Al Tashlichenu*" (God, don't cast us out in our old age). Mom would often make us boys cry when she sang, "*Just For the Sake of Society.*" The song describes the death by fire of children when their mother leaves them to play cards with friends.

Neither Mom nor Dad could read a note of music.

As long as I can remember, in our home in Aliquippa there was an upright piano, initially for Jerry. At about the same time that Allen started trumpet lessons, at age 11 I began studying piano with Margery Selkovits. This was in 1936 with the Depression in full force. It may be more apocryphal than true, but to finance the fifty-cent-an-hour weekly lesson, Mom removed the telephone. Cousin Dan Jackson remembers running up the steep hill to our house to give us messages.

I was always in awe of Margery, and though she wore dowdy, sensible shoes and no makeup, she was a magnificent woman. At the first lesson she clipped my fingernails. I was humiliated but not scarred. She made me feel that I was her favorite pupil, as she probably did with all her students. In truth her favorite must have been Henry Mancini. A few years earlier Henry had mastered all she had to teach; she passed him on to a teacher in Pittsburgh. Henry went on to become world famous, writing many popular songs such as "Moon River" and the musical score for numerous Hollywood movies like *The Pink Panther* series.

How guilty I would feel if I hadn't practiced enough and, on the other hand, how elated I would be, when Margery, satisfied with my playing, would affix a gold star to the top of that music page. My biggest thrill came when we played duets, she at the upright piano in her dining room (used for lessons) and I, sitting at the concert grand piano in her living room. I was permitted to play this magnificent instrument also at Margery's annual recitals. At the recital her students performed in sequence beginning with the novice and proceeding according to ability to the most accomplished; I never was in the latter category.

Margie was much more than my piano teacher; she was my guide through the world of music. She saw to it that I had a ticket to the monthly Sunday symphony concert series at the Syria Mosque in Pittsburgh. Margie and I sat in the second balcony – how much better to see every instrument with an unobstructed view. Among the many great conductors I saw: Fritz Reiner with the Pittsburgh Symphony, John Barbirolli with the New York Philharmonic, the Boston Symphony under Serge Koussevitsky, Frederick Stock with the Chicago Symphony, and the Cleveland Symphony under Artur Rodzinski. Unforgettable was the gaunt pianist, Rachmaninoff.

I worried and fantasized about Margie. I thought, "What is this lovely, amazingly talented graduate of the Boston Conservatory of Music doing married to a butcher, living in a mill town? Why doesn't she have a concert career in New York?" To me, Sam, Margie's husband, didn't exist, that is, until many years later. When his family sold their corporation, leaving Sammy without a job, he went to work as a door-to-door Fuller Brush salesman. Through Marcia, and later for myself, I learned what Margie knew; he was a bright and cheerful human being. Later he became the ultimate caregiver when Margie became ill and died from amyotropic lateral sclerosis, "Lou Gehrig's Disease." We still treasure a table-crumb sweeper Sammy gave Marcia in 1970 as a Fuller Brush bonus.

Marcia had her own special relationship with Margie. Together they worked on many Hadassah shows. Marcia rewrote Broadway scripts to conform with Hadassah plots while Margie accompanied the singing, changing key to match the vocal range of us amateurs.

Piano lessons were terminated abruptly in my sophomore year in high school. Looking for ways to be accepted by classmates and hardly built for football, I sought out Dr. A. D. Davenport, the school's legendary musical director. He had played the tuba in John Philip Sousa's U.S. Marine Band. Davvy, as he was affectionately known, needed a bassoonist and an oboist. Being "the man," I took the bassoon while Margie's older daughter took the oboe. Davvy could teach every instrument except strings; he left that to Miss Erla Coleman. He taught brother Allen the trumpet and Bob, the flute. He, too, was one of Henry Mancini's mentors.

The school lent me a new bassoon and in a short time I played it well enough to join the band and orchestra. I also played in the Presbyterian Church Orchestra, which included some fine older musicians, several from the Musical Political Italian Club.

In my junior year after one and a half years of lessons, I was selected to participate in the Midwestern Pennsylvania Band. This took place in Millvale near Pittsburgh. All I remember of that weekend is that I experienced my first nonfamily kiss; since my date played the

French horn, our differing embouchures must have made it interesting.

As first chair at Midwestern, I was selected for All-State band in Meadville. When I arrived late for the opening rehearsal, only the first chair was vacant. With great trepidation I sat down, ultimately earning the position after tryouts. The conductor was Professor Rivelli from the University of Michigan. To my chagrin he included the "William Tell Overture" in the program; this work requires a bassoon to play the part written for the cello in the orchestral rendition. The piece began with a two-measure bassoon solo arpeggio (the ascending notes of a chord) which was repeated after six measures by the band. This was frightfully difficult for me. After my first failed attempt, Rivelli announced, "I want to meet privately with you after rehearsal."

"Uh, oh," I thought. "I'm out!"

Not at all. He gave me a few pointers and to my amazement I wasn't bad. "Now," he ordered, "no more rehearsing before our concerts."

On Friday night there was a recorded concert. Bob brought Mom. I played my solos well and was pleased with myself. Then came the main Saturday night concert. Rivelli waved me in for my solo; blow as I would, no sound ventured forth. The audience was unaware of the lapse hearing only the band begin with their six measures. Rivelli waved his baton for my repeat solo. On the second go-around I wasn't so lucky. Out came unmistakable, readily audible gurgles. I wanted to die or at least disappear through the floor. I became flushed; my heart raced. After the overture ended, Rivelli turned to the audience. "The bassoonist performed beautifully at last night's concert. What occurred tonight happens at times to the most experienced professional reed instrument players. He shouldn't feel bad." I saw Davvy standing in the wings, making a gesture as though wiping tears from his eyes, smiling at me. He tried to lighten the situation but nothing could then or during the long ride home with him. Fifty-seven years later the pain is gone but the memory remains vivid.

Singing in the high school Bach Choir was an enjoyable part of those growing-up days, especially being in the a cappella choir. Mrs.

Grace Mansell, our director was a marvelous coach. She sent me to the Midwestern Pennsylvania Regional Chorus where I was selected for All-State Chorus at Coatsville. I had what might be called a solo at this latter event. I jumped the gun, coming in one note earlier than the other hundred singers. Did the audience or the conductor hear me? It was humiliating enough that I did.

In Geneva College I sang in a barbershop quartet which entertained at college banquets, but my brief experience with the Harvard Glee Club in Cambridge during the summer of 1944 was incomparable. I auditioned and was accepted. I can only describe my feeling as the sound I produced merged with scores of rich, resonant, male voices by referring to a movie called *You Light up my Life*. In it a young woman composes and sings a song with that same title. After much effort, she manages to perform it with a full orchestra. Her excitement is so overwhelming as she sings that she places a hand on her head as if to keep it from exploding.

Christmas caroling in the hallways of Magee Woman's Hospital in Pittsburgh during my internship provided an annual exposure to lovely harmonies. Entertaining hospitalized patients seemed like a good deed for this nice Jewish boy.

During the sixties I was the bass section of our Aliquippa *shul* choir; Norman Thomashefsky was the tenor section. Four women completed the group. At times Hy Gorman, who couldn't read a note, would add depth and resonance to my section. Occasionally Marcia would draft me into her Hadassah shows; I enjoyed the limelight.

I came to opera late. A movie version of Verdi's opera, *La Forza Del Destino* that I saw in Boston in 1945 opened the door. Somehow this experience made it easier for me to enjoy future operas.

My love of chamber music, which later superseded all other forms, developed in 1949 in Boston under the tutelage of my mentor, Al Freedberg. I became hooked on hearing Dvorak's *Dumky Trio* and Schubert's quartet, *Death and the Maiden*. Chamber music now constitutes two-thirds of my CD collection.

Remain in Boston with me for another moment and imagine my first Boston Pops concert at Symphony Hall. How excited I was to anticipate hearing again the Boston Symphony under Serge Koussevitzky. But how far off the mark was my expectation. First of all, the perennial conductor of the Pops was Arthur Fiedler, not Koussevitsky. Second, the program consisted of light classical and popular music, not the three B's. Third and most upsetting of all, sitting in the balcony, I was thoroughly distracted by the informality, the din of people talking and laughing, the clatter of dishes, and the movement of waiters scurrying about. How could this behavior be tolerated? I later learned that the musicians themselves also hated these concerts "but the money was good." I was less critical of similar concerts that took place along the Charles River.

Serving in the U.S.Army bore unexpected musical fruit. With a recommendation from Milt Hamolsky, who preceded me in the residency program at the Beth Israel Hospital, I succeeded him in an assignment at the Army Medical Research Laboratories in Fort Knox, Kentucky. That I had this position seemed unfair, when married doctors were being shipped to Korea.

Of several Fort Knox scientists who had fled Nazi Germany in the midthirties, two were accomplished musicians; one a pianist, the other, a violinist. Every Friday evening they played chamber music, recruiting a third instrumentalist whenever they could. When they learned that I had played both the piano and bassoon, they launched into a campaign to have me learn to play the cello – music for the bassoon and the cello are interchangeable.

They contacted Grace Whitney, first-chair cellist of the Louisville Symphony under the direction of her brother Robert. She agreed to take me on. During our first conversation Grace recommended a music store for purchasing a cello. For $300 and another fifty dollars for a bow, I was fully equipped. I bowed increasingly expensive instruments but heard no difference until I tried one selling for $1,500. "That will be my next one," I vowed.

Grace, in her midforties, reminded me of Margie, warm and supportive. Through her I obtained a magnificent beginner's book by Diran Alexanian, a student of Pablo Casals – more on Casals later. I practiced an hour a day in my lab beginning at three o'clock, the time that everyone else vacated (read fled) the building. Being alone, I didn't have to worry about the searing, abrasive sound produced by beginners on string instruments. Once when I was practicing at Irv and Helen's apartment in Chicago, the Australian maid remarked, "My, but it does sound like a cow."

After six months Grace let me study easy, slow movements from trios and quartets by Haydn and Mozart. In an additional month or two I entered the magical world of chamber-music players. Three or four of us would play almost every Friday evening. I played pitifully, at least at the outset. My colleagues didn't complain – actually they plied me with praise and encouragement – since my contribution afforded them a wider repertoire.

After moving to New Haven, I took a few uninspiring lessons but once I met Marcia, courting took up all my spare time.

One day Marcia will have to tell her own story but several comments are germane to my story line. From an early age she studied violin with a distinguished teacher, Mrs. Suzanne Gussow. Marcia attended Music and Art High School in New York City where she also learned to play the viola. Among her many claims to fame, she relates being in the second violin section when a visiting conductor stood before the orchestra. He was young and enormously handsome. She swooned, when looking in her direction, he said, "Don't be nervous, second violins." His name? Leonard Bernstein. Marcia adds, "Don't ever tell me that the conductor doesn't make a difference. We never played better than on that day."

Now visualize this scene two weeks after we met. It was Sunday morning in Marcia's parents' apartment in Brooklyn. Modestly attired in pajamas and bathrobes in Marcia's bedroom, we were playing duets – violin and cello to be sure. My future mother-in-law walked in and, astounded by this intimacy, exclaimed, "*Mishigas*! (craziness). It's not even normal." (This latter expression is etched on her tombstone.) Sad to say, we didn't play much after that. It wasn't because of my mother-in-law; it was just that medicine dominated my life. We do have movies of Raina in Boston at nine months standing in her playpen howling as I practiced my cello close by. When we tried playing trios with

Margie Selkovits in Aliquippa, she suggested that I practice before our next session, which never came.

Here in Israel my cello gathers dust under the piano. Once several years ago I took it out to show my granddaughter Maia. I could have cried from shame – all the bow hairs, like a patient receiving chemotherapy, had fallen off. When I next made a serious attempt to practice, with bow rehaired, within minutes pain developed in my left shoulder and right wrist. I did not persevere.

Our piano itself has an interesting story. As soon as Marcia and I moved into our new home in Aliquippa, our first priority was a piano. Margie found just what we wanted in the want ads – a Steinway grand. It had been sitting in the owner's basement in Pittsburgh. Margie, who went with us, tried out the piano and, despite a cracked sounding board, the instrument was deemed satisfactory. We paid all of $600! Within days it sat in all its splendor in our carpeted but furnitureless living room.

Let me list the various inscriptions inside the piano: Steinway and Sons. Manufacturers by appointment to His Majesty George William II, German Emperor and King of Prussia; His Majesty George V, King of Great Britain and Emperor of India; His Majesty Nicholas, Czar of Russia, etc. Engraved around twelve names are ten crests. Marcia guesses the date of manufacture to be between 1908 and 1914.

When the piano arrived in Tel Aviv in 1985, we lived in an eighth-floor apartment. The typically small Israeli elevator could manage the stool and the piano legs. Movers detached the metal stringboard and slowly maneuvered all the parts up the narrow stairwell. They literally collapsed on the floor after their third and final trip. A year later they reversed this agonizing trek, transferring the piano to our new first-floor apartment.

I am ashamed to write that I rarely play the piano. Shira, our daughter-in-law, has played it, as has our granddaughter Tamar. Shlomo Gronich, one of Israel's most famous and loved musicians, who used to live in the apartment above ours, has played it. Our friend, Maggie Engel, when a student at Rubin Academy of Music, gave her first recital in our living room for an audience of fifteen guests.

I will mention my daughter Amy at this point only to note the power of music in relation to grief. For many months after her death I found it impossible to sing even the simplest melodies in *shul*. In the attempt I would simply choke up. Marcia and I should have known better but two months after Amy died we went to hear the Pittsburgh Symphony. Tears flowed down our cheeks as the music played. The romantic program compounded our fragility.

Let's now return to Pablo Casals, the greatest cellist ever. That he performed all over the world and taught generations of virtuosos was to be expected. But what made him a step above other artists was his massive effort to bring music into the lives – into every school – of the youth of his beloved Spain. I first heard of Casals when I acquired recordings of his playing the magnificent Bach *Unaccompanied Cello Suites* and, soon after, recordings of Bach's *Brandenburg Concertos* conducted by him at the Prades Festival in the Pyrenees across the Spanish border in France. The festival had been organized to honor Casals in the town of his self-imposed exile, his way at age sixty of protesting the dictator Franco. Many of the world's great performers came to Prades to pay homage to this great man and to publicize his political campaign. (I must add that the above recordings are the ones I would take to my desert island if I could take no others.) And as I mentioned earlier, a student of Casals wrote my most important study book.

While still in the army I wanted to express my indebtedness to Casals and did so by writing him a letter. I received a reply, an autographed photograph. Two weeks later there came a short, form letter requesting a contribution on Casals' behalf to "The Spanish Refugee Organization (S.R.O.)." This is known as "put up or shut up" time. I knew that the Attorney General had blacklisted the S.R.O. as a Communist front organization. What was I to do? Friends, though sympathetic, advised, "Stay clear" but somehow I felt ashamed for being prudent. I took my friends' advice and made a contribution in Casals' name to Hadassah Hospital in Jerusalem and so informed him. Casals, himself, was a supporter of Israel. His recital in the sixties inaugurated the restored Caesarea Roman amphitheater. There was no acknowledgment. I have always regretted this timorous decision. I would have considered it a badge of honor to have made the Attorney General's list. But who knows if the Veterans' Administration would have rescinded my subsequent residency appointment under that cloud.

I am a little wistful about how much more of an appreciation of music Marcia and I might have imparted to our children and even our grandchildren. If Marcia and I had continued playing chamber music with friends in our home, would not the children have seen string instruments and classical music as important ingredients for a rich life? Raina studied piano with Jim Green and then Margery Selkovits, stopping short of a significant level of expertise. Amy's piano career was even shorter; she switched to the flute for a brief period, primarily as a means for spiritual communication. In her junior-high-school years she gave more energy to cheerleading. Later she constructed and taught herself to play a zither.

Danny chose the guitar as did so many of his generation who wanted quick musical results and camaraderie. He became accomplished enough to earn money on the street and in a café in Jerusalem. In high-school he studied the saxophone and was a soloist in the high school band. Danny also had a major singing and dancing role in his sophomore year at Columbia in the production of *Godspell.* As we watched him completing a jumping split, I exclaimed to Marcia, "Why, he can't do that!"

. So why am I beating my breast? It sounds as though they had enough exposure to be able to decide on the importance of music in their own lives. My thought is that more important than suggesting lessons is a musical ambiance that stimulates a youngster to choose to play an instrument.

When I fantasized the girl I would marry, along with having the build of my mother, being Jewish, and having a sense of humor, she would have to love music. Well, with Marcia I got it all. With the music we experience together, her enjoyment serves to intensify my own. Is that sentiment not the refrain of my life?

ALIYAH

GOING UP IN THE WORLD

Part A: Background

The Hebrew word *aliyah* means ascent, going up. In synagogue an *aliyah* is a call to come up to the Torah. As used exclusively in these reminiscences it refers to emigration from any country for purposes of settling in Israel. As with approaching the Torah, there is both a physical and spiritual component in moving to Israel, "making *aliyah.*" When interviewed on her own radio talk show sponsored by the Pittsburgh Jewish Federation prior to our *aliyah,* Marcia explained that making *aliyah*, going up, occurred independent of altitude; a Jew moving to Israel from the Himalayas was still "going up." Our rabbis attached so much importance to living in Israel that a person could be granted an immediate divorce if the spouse chose to leave Israel. How consistent it is that the word for emigration from Israel is *yerida,* going down.

The word *aliyah* is specific for Jews. God told Abraham, "Get thee out of thy country . . . to the land I will show you." Though Christians may live in Israel, for them there is no biblical injunction to do so.

There are as many answers as there are questioners as to why Marcia and I made *aliyah*. The depth of our reply is determined by how we read the inquirer. One example was Marcia's reply in a theater while waiting for the movie to start. We had been practicing our Hebrew by reading a newspaper published for beginners. A young male snob asked, "You're Americans? Why would you want to come here?"

"I heard you were leaving so I came to take your place." To those whose interest is casual, we say that we are Zionists. To those who ask with sincere amazement, we share parts of the following.

We verbalized our desire to live in Israel after our first trip in 1961 but there were numerous factors, conscious and unconscious, that influenced each of us. Marcia remembers being influenced by Meyer Levin's, *My Father's House* and Arthur Koestler's *Thieves in the Night* in her freshman year at Sarah Lawrence College. It was the fall of 1948 when Israel was struggling to consolidate its independence. Later she was impressed by the experiences of a classmate who had lived in Israel in 1949.

What about the blue boxes (known also as *pushkies*) that sat on our kitchen sinks in the early thirties? We would insert pennies and nickels knowing that the money would be used by the Jewish National Fund to plant trees in barren Palestine. And "Next year in Jerusalem?" These words are shouted after the blast from the *shofar* (ram's horn) at the close of Yom Kippur and at the conclusion of our Passover seder year after year. Abhorring hypocrisy, Marcia and I felt a stirring as we mouthed them.

My mother helped organize Aliquippa's first Hadassah (Women's Zionist Organization of America) chapter in the forties. Meetings were held in our living room. United Jewish Appeal (UJA) and, later, Israel Bond drives were spearheaded by Dad and Uncle Harry Jackson.

I can't say that I was politically awake as a youngster. A startling lapse of memory concerns my *bar mitzvah* which took place on *Shabbat,* the twelfth of November 1938. I say startling because on my birthday, two days before, *Kristallnacht* had occurred. This was the night when Germans went on a rampage randomly murdering Jews, burning synagogues, and vandalizing and looting Jewish stores. What *bar mitzvah* wouldn't gleefully have welcomed the opportunity to scrap his "Today I am a man" speech to pronounce his commitment to the survival of the Jewish people! And yet, my mind is a blank. Well, I do have a vision of a luncheon in our dining room and more vividly, Uncle David Eger giving me his standard gift, a ring with my Hebrew initials and a tiny diamond.

I attended Geneva College, a small western Pennsylvania Reformed Presbyterian college, where daily chapel attendance was required. I never considered raising an objection and even took a rotation reading from the pulpit. I usually read one of our Psalms.

I didn't remember being very Jewish at Harvard Medical School, that is, until John Goldsmith, a senior when I was a freshman, reminded me that I had organized a Passover *seder* in my room. Attending were John, two other seniors, Norm Boas and Cy Rubin, and my Hawaiian roommate Nobu. I had gone to South Boston to buy matzoh and wine but it was John who bought the chickens. Fifty-four years later John told me that, because of rationing and because Canada's chickens were infected, it was almost impossible to locate one. He did succeed, and why? Because the chickens he bought were filled with bread stuffing, rendering them religiously unfit for the Passover holiday.

In 1948 at the close of my fourth year, brother Jerry who was completing a two-year fellowship at Lahey Clinic, took me to an Israel rally at Boston Gardens. Moshe Shertok (later, Sharret) Israel's first foreign minister, was the main speaker. Alas, there was no follow-up.

During the next couple of years at the Beth Israel Hospital (BI) in Boston, while many of my present American-Israeli friends were active in Zionist organizations and while my Romanian cousins, in Israel unbeknown to me, were languishing in *mabarot* (camps of tents and huts made of tin and wood), I was uninvolved with Israel's concerns. My interests were limited to medicine, chamber music, and the Boston Red Sox.

When Marcia and I married in 1954, our Jewish concerns centered on creating a traditional home. A couple of months before our wedding we met with New Haven Rabbi Klein. Primarily, we discussed *kashrut* (the laws of keeping *kosher*). Rabbi Klein emphasized the moral principles (such as not eating the meat of an animal killed for sport) and ended with a practical reason: "If your home is *kosher*, everyone of your friends will be able to eat at your table." We elected in its favor.

In 1956 we moved back to Aliquippa. While I built my medical practice, Marcia quickly ascended to the presidency of the local chapter of Hadassah as well as the Western Pennsylvania Region. Marcia's Zionist knowledge grew exponentially; some of it rubbed off on me. I soon took Dad's place on committees for United Jewish Appeal and Israel Bond campaigns while becoming increasingly involved in leadership roles with the synagogue and the Conservative Movement. I too, rose to the presidency of the latter's Western Pennsylvania Region. Over the years we heard such notables as Moshe Dayan, Menachem Begin, Chaim Herzog, Eleanor Roosevelt, and consecutively on the same program, Louis Pincus and Abba Eban. I remarked to Marcia in regard to the latter two, "How I love Israeli accents;" both sounded like Cambridge dons. Imagine the surge of our commitment at a closing convention banquet of the United Synagogue of America, the organization of the Conservative Movement, when Abba Eban roared, "Will you stand with us?" We were ready to catch the next plane.

At the time of that banquet as one of fourteen national vice-presidents, I took my rotation on the dais. Since two weeks earlier Eban had collapsed during a banquet in New Orleans, I was requested to be prepared in the event of a repeat occurrence. Accordingly, in one pocket of my tux there was a stethoscope while in another were drugs used to treat a heart attack. Nothing happened to warrant my resuscitative services but had it been otherwise, what a story my heroic treatment of Eban would have made for my children. When I related the event to my adoring cousin, Evie, that I was asked to be prepared if something happened to Eban, she inquired, "What would you have talked about?"

One evening in June 1961, I came from the office into our family room and proposed to Marcia, "How would you like to take a trip to Israel?" Her immediate response was approximately, "Great! When?" Uncle Harry and cousin Milt Eger had gone the previous year with Israel Bonds and brother Jerry and his wife Irma had gone a few months before. (Jerry witnessed one day of the Eichmann trial.) Our trip would take place in six weeks under the sponsorship of the American Physicians Fellowship for the Israel Medical Association. I immediately applied for membership while Marcia and I obtained passports, vaccinations, and cholera shots.

The tour traveled back in history with three days each in London, Paris, and Rome, ending with eleven days in Israel. Of all our thirteen trips to Israel before *aliyah*, this one stands out only because it was the first; the organizers wasted many valuable hours for cocktail parties with Israeli doctors. We were impressed with the apparent peace. As we gazed from King David's tomb on a smiling Jordanian soldier sitting in a church window with a weapon on his lap, our guide discussed with enthusiasm the possibilities of a permanent peace settlement.

In Paris we had seen the Chagall windows on display prior to shipment to their destination in the chapel at Hadassah Hospital in Ein Kerem. What a thrill to come upon the chapel and find the empty window frames, naked among the otherwise completed walls. We later visited the chapel many times to see the wondrous, sunlit, stained-glass representations of the twelve tribes of Israel. Marcia *shept nachas* (was overjoyed) to visit Hadassah's Community Health Center at Kiriyat Hayovel, a pioneer model for Israel's medical program. It continues to thrive at the time of this writing thirty-nine years later.

Meeting Mom's cousin Nachman Liebovitz for the first time was highly emotional. His family – wife Bertha and two sons Kobi and Yossi – lived in a tent during their first two years in Israel. Nachman was a laborer at the outset but rose to be a factory foreman. This contrasted with the increasingly luxurious life Marcia and I were achieving in Aliquippa. Upon our departure from Lod Airport they came with flowers and gifts.

Everywhere we went, the same question, "When are you moving to Israel?" Many American tourists are annoyed, to say the least, by this seemingly aggressive confrontation. In reality, it's similar to the query about our moving to Israel, depending on who and how it is asked. It could simply be an invitation to join their struggle to build the land or, more emotionally, "It's time your children replace ours on the firing line" or the warning, "Don't you realize how much your

Jewish lives are in jeopardy in America?" For Marcia and me these were clarion calls for *aliyah*.

In December 1967 we returned on a commercial tour with Mom and our three children. Danny was just over four. Mom had gone with Dad on a disheartening tour sponsored by Religious Zionists of America several years before. She was exasperated by the time spent *davening* and stopping to recite prayers at numerous gravesites of rabbis at the side of the road.

This trip took all of us from one high to an endless flow of others, literally gooseflesh experiences. On the first night we checked into the Shulamit Hotel in Haifa and, while Mom went to sleep, the rest of us took a walk. Our feet followed the sound of Israeli dance music to a school building. Raina and Amy, twelve and eleven, respectively, peeked through a window and saw young teenagers having a Hanukah party. They were spotted and were invited inside. Imagine. Within hours of their arrival in Israel, our girls were dancing the *hora*, competently from summer camp experience, with Israelis. Raina wrote in her diary that night, "I'm coming back to live in Israel" and in 1977 she did. Don't tell me that parents don't influence their children's destinies. Where would we all be today if we had spent that vacation in Acapulco?

I have no doubt that our guide Matanya Siegal was crucial to the impact of those two glorious weeks, to the strengthening of our children's positive attitude toward Israel. His cheerful mix of Zionist fervor and knowledge of history and Bible kept us attentive and receptive every moment of our protracted days of touring. He lectured us before we approached the Western Wall, fine-tuning us for a maximally emotional experience. It should be remembered that our visit came six months after the Six-Day War. How triumphant, how invincible, how optimistic, how validated we felt as God's Chosen People! I had no faith in the notes-in-the-Wall tradition but who could resist inserting one or two?

Mom cried at least twice, once at King David's Tomb and again at Rachel's tomb on the Bethlehem Road. These were her first tears since my brother Allen's death. Over the centuries infertile women would come to Mother Rachel beseeching her to intervene on their behalf.

Twenty-three years later when Marcia's brother Bob came to Israel for Danny's wedding, Marcia suggested that he go to Rachel's tomb on behalf of his daughter Elizabeth; he did and four months later she conceived for the first time. Twins were born. Also at Marcia's counsel, her friend Audrey Lasday did likewise and, lo and behold, soon after, her daughter conceived. As the retarded GI prisoner said in the movie, *Stalag 17*, on reading the news that his wife bore *his* child fifteen months after his capture by the Germans, "I believe it. I believe it."

How proud Danny was when Matanya handed him the bus microphone letting him remind us, "Any of you who need to use the facilities, go now." Danny repeatedly asked Matanya where David had killed Goliath. After a few days, though still in the Galilee and realizing that Danny might not have the patience to wait until we would travel south to the likely area, we gave Matanya license to choose any roadside spot. "Here, Danny," he pointed. Danny thereupon picked up a stone and tossed it into the shrubs; that satisfied him. No trip to Israel would ever equal this one.

An Israel Bonds representative arranged a private trip to Masada while Mom took that opportunity to visit with a school chum from Romania she hadn't seen in sixty-eight years. Our driver let us off on the western side affording us an easy climb up the ramp that the Roman army had built during the three-year siege of the fortress. How well I recall on another tour being asked at the base of Masada to read Josephus's rendition of Eleazer Ben Yair's final address to the faithful 900. "Shall we live to see our wives and daughters raped and marched off as slaves or shall we die here as free men?" I started reading in a detached manner but gradually, empathizing with Ben Yair's call to mass suicide, I waxed more and more melodramatic as if, indeed, I were Ben Yair and the tour group, my followers.

Our Israel Bond driver met us at the base of the eastern side of Masada. This mandated our descending the steep snake path – no cable car until around 1970. I was in a temper with my children on the descent, fearful that they would slip and go careening down the mountainside.

As Mom's doctor I had considerable anxiety about her taking the trip, since she was eighty years old with a history of difficulty walking stairs. This reminds me of Marcia's mother Madge when we were planning a trip to Israel in 1978. We were visiting her sister-in-law Aunt Eve Hoffman, when Madge expressed anxiety over the trip. Eve reassured Madge by saying, "But, Madge dear, even if the worst should happen, every Jew wants to be buried in Israel!"

Back to my mother. In Israel she had no physical limitations. Call it mystical or surges of adrenalin, steroids, or endorphins. Mom kept up with the group, even climbing the numerous steps leading to the Caves of Machpelah where our patriarchs and matriarchs (excepting Rachel) are buried. It was incredible standing there knowing that our biblical father Abraham had purchased this property from Ephron, the Hittite.

In Jerusalem we were invited to a gathering at the apartment of Nathan Rabinovitz, Hadassah Professor of Surgery and his wife Batya. We had met at the Boston Beth Israel Hospital in 1950 when he was a Fellow in Surgery. Without hesitation Mom climbed the four flights of stairs to the apartment without shortness of breath. How youthful she felt to be among Israeli intelligentsia.

And how delightful to be at the home of Dr. Kalman Mann, Director of the Hadassah Medical Organization. It was the last night of Hanukah. We had the honor of being driven to the party with Rabbi David DeSola Pool and his wife Tamar. He was a renowned scholar and the rabbi of the Portuguese Synagogue on West Side, New York City and she, a beloved former National President of Hadassah. The chauffeur, Mr. Adin, had written a book on his experiences as a Hadassah driver during the blockade and massacre on the road to Hadassah Hospital on Mt. Scopus in 1948.

The scene at Dr. Mann's apartment defies description. It was a heady time, six months after the Six-Day War. Each family unit was supplied its own *menorah* (candelabrum) with eight candles and the *shama*sh (the candle that lights all the others). We sang the *bruchot* (blessings), "Rock of Ages," and, lastly, "Hatikvah" (The Hope, Israel's national anthem). All those candles! It was the crowning moment of our Zionist journey. On subsequent Hanukah holidays Marcia and I tried to duplicate that wondrous evening by providing *menorahs* for each visiting family.

Part B: The Planning Stage

In Dec. 1967 in Haifa we met Jack and Gila Abrahamson from South Africa. Marcia's parents had met them the previous May while their cruise ship *Shalom* was docked in Haifa Port. As was the custom, there was a gala onboard party; each family could invite a local couple. Knowing no one, they passed on the selection to the ship's nurse who chose a struggling young surgeon and his wife. Jack discussed his own *aliyah*. In Capetown at age sixteen he lived in a *Shomer Hatzair garin*, a clubhouse whose members were preparing for *aliyah*. Jack was given the assignment to learn shoemaking. "But I want to be a doctor."

"Follow group discipline or you're out," he was admonished.

"But Israel will need doctors too."

"Be that as it may, you will be our shoemaker."

"In that case I'm out." He went on to study medicine in England and soon after made *aliyah* with Gila. And the rest of the *garin*? Not one moved to Israel!

Thus, Jack and Gila entered our family circle. Over the years they hosted Raina, later Danny, and then us. Jack became the first of my two personal *shlichim* (*aliyah* facilitators). We discussed private versus government medicine, cardiology versus nuclear medicine, Hebrew language requirements, and money. When I knew that I would be spending two months in Israel in 1979, Jack arranged for me to work with an Israeli-Arab cardiologist to learn echocardiography, a conspicuous gap in my diagnostic capability.

Yet something warned me that, although I was equal to the task of supervising a cardiac care unit in a community hospital, without further training, my cardiology skills were hardly transferable for a position in Israel. Besides, my relationship with patients and nurses required communication skills, which I was certain would never to be achieved in Hebrew. How accurately I predicted that failing!

I wrote to Professor Henri Atlan at Hadassah Hospital and subsequently received a two-month appointment in his Department of Nuclear Medicine. (Nuclear medicine, a specialty involving the use of radioactive materials in the study of internal organs, was a secondary activity in my practice in Aliquippa.) My family's involvement with Hadassah was profound – how could I have thought of working anywhere else in Israel?

It was June 30, 1979. There we were with Irving, my father-in-law, living in a furnished apartment on David Marcus Street in Talbiah, Jerusalem. (Amy had died in April and Madge, my mother-in-law, the previous September.) On my first day at work I wore a seersucker suit and tie. The next day I removed my jacket and the following day, my tie. I never joined the masses by wearing sandals, or God forgive, going without socks; my self-image would never tolerate such a hippie mode. How could any patient respect me if I were so sloppily attired? In 2000, how I have changed!

I arrived in the Nuclear Medicine Department where the secretary Esther, handed me a note from Professor Atlan. "Welcome. I'm sorry I'm not there to greet you. I'll see you on my return in two weeks." I was being shown around the lab when in ambled the only other senior doctor, Lawrence David Samuels. Suffice it to say that Larry briefed me for less than two hours, which included time for an extended snack and a prayer session (Christian) with his wife. I was flabbergasted! He then took off for the rest of the summer, the entire time of my tour of duty. I subsequently learned the word *freier*, someone who lets others take advantage of him. True, the word fit my situation, but I enjoyed the new status. I did, however, think it was irresponsible of Dr. Atlan to allow me to be in charge of his department without knowing more about me. Presumably seeing Harvard on my curriculum vitae was enough for him.

Waiting for me on Larry's desk were more than forty nuclear scans, some unreported for well over a week. I waded in, completing most and arriving home at eight P.M. I had written Atlan indicating that "I want to work and not be an observer in the 'third row'." I reported to Marcia that not only was I not in the third row, rather, I was the department! Esther was astonished, asking Marcia, "What kind of a man is your husband, working so late?" The truth is that though I had been a pioneer in nuclear medicine, I was really not prepared to handle a university department and the complex problems not encountered at Aliquippa Hospital.

The saga of Dr. Samuels would make interesting copy. Larry had made a name for himself in academic nuclear medicine in America. He told me of a fire in which he lost his first wife. Soon after the tragedy, while he was traveling to Greece, he received a "calling" that "Hadassah Hospital is waiting for me." I also heard him repeat this on TV on "The 700 Club" in 1980 or so. How did I happen to tune in? My office typist, a devotee of the Club, alerted me. Despite what his name would suggest, Larry was a Missionary Baptist. In truth Dr. Atlan never heard of him but was in need of help – half a credit for Larry – and he had a very respectable curriculum vitae. On TV he claimed to have prayed with Golda Meir when she was being treated for lymphoma at Hadassah Hospital and to have danced with Menachem Begin during the latter's hospitalization for heart trouble. He didn't confess his failure to convert anyone in the lab, not even a terribly intimidated Moslem technician. I'm sure I wasn't the only one to blow the whistle to Hadassah in New York for his missionary activities.

There was another confrontation, this time head-to-head. Once a week I would present nuclear scans at various department conferences. One morning at an oncology meeting, Professor Izak, a powerful member of the staff, started berating the Nuclear Medicine Department, "not you personally," saying how incompetent Dr. Atlan was. This took place in front of a dozen senior doctors, residents, interns, and medical students. I was outraged. (Sinclair Lewis wrote in his novel, *Arrowsmith*, "It was tradition that faculty members did not discuss their colleagues with students . . .") On returning to my office I phoned Dr. Izak's secretary to arrange an appointment.

So there I was, little David from Aliquippa, entering Goliath's fortress. I let him know, as diplomatically as I could, that his behavior in reference to Atlan was unacceptable. I even quoted Dad, "If you can't say something nice about a person, don't say anything."

"But he is awful!" he replied.

I countered to the effect, "I don't believe it's true but if you are correct, use your position to remove him. Don't plead your case in front of the house staff." The next morning "Old Stone Face," as he was called by the staff, shocked Esther by a once-in-a-lifetime appearance in our department – ostensibly to discuss a scan. I knew better; it was a peace offering!

Was there any other result? All I know is that Dr. Izak died within a year or two while Dr. Atlan remains in a respected position at Hadassah twenty years later.

The 1979 stay in Israel was a therapeutic break in our lives albeit when first considered, we did not know that we would be grieving Amy's death. Circumstances put us all together; Danny was on an Israel summer Young Judaea program; Raina was already an Israeli citizen living in Jerusalem and working for a pregnancy counseling service. We entertained and were entertained as though all Israel awaited our *aliyah*. I even had the honor of sitting next to the wife of Rabbi Mordecai Kaplan at an Israel Philharmonic Symphony concert featuring Pavarotti. At age eighty or so Mrs. Kaplan was an engaging companion. How timid and shortsighted I was not to accept her invitation to visit on *Shabbat* afternoon. "What would I say to such a great scholar?" I thought. We later learned that in their old age the Kaplans were frequently alone on *Shabbat*. We missed both an opportunity and a *mitzvah*.

My return visit in 1980 coincided with the month that Prime Minister Menachim Begin collapsed on the floor of the Knesset. He was rushed to the cardiac care unit (CCU) at Hadassah Hospital under the care of Professor Mervyn Gotesman. (Quite ironically many years earlier, having already founded the CCU at Aliquippa Hospital, I asked Prof. Braun, Gotesman's predecessor, why Hadassah Hospital didn't have a CCU. "We reject the premise of the CCU and prefer to care for heart patients in the general medical units.")

There are several vignettes related to Begin's hospital stay. The CCU was an eight-bed unit, four beds against the wall on each side of the room. Begin's privacy consisted of closed curtains and an unoccupied bed on both sides. Two beds away was a truck driver recovering from a heart attack. On the morning after Begin's admission this roommate blurted out, "Hey, Begin, I hear on the radio that Ezer Weizman (a political opponent) is ready to take your place."

Another story concerns Begin's request for a glass of tea. No problem. Then he asked, "Could I have saccharin?"

Replies the nurse, "Saccharin he wants! Ever since the government lowered the subsidy to the hospital, we have none."

"Well, could I have some lemon?"

"Lemon he wants! Ever since . . ." Ten minutes later Begin's tea appeared and, as might be expected, with saccharin and lemon. Obviously the nurse reconsidered her options.

And there I was at his bedside performing a portable thallium heart scan looking for proof for or against a myocardial infarction. Begin asked, "Are you making *aliyah*?"

I replied, "Not yet. Isn't it enough that I've given you my daughter?"

There was no answer to this, but continuing, he asked, "What does she do here?"

"She's the Executive Director of Shilo."

"Oh, Shilo from the Bible!" How could I tell this traditional Jew, a fighter against England's restrictive immigration policy and the leader of the conservative party, that Shilo was an organization, the first of its kind in Israel, that provided family planning and sex education and, important in its early years, helped terminate unwanted teenage pregnancies? I said a simple, "Yes" and closed the subject.

I couldn't resist name-dropping, and mentioned that Ivan Novick was my cousin. Ivan was a strong supporter of Begin, especially later as national president of the Zionist Organization of America (ZOA). "A fine young man." (Years later Marcia and I resigned from our life membership in ZOA when it became clear that ZOA was an active partner of Likud and not with the government in power as I had believed.)

It was Gotesman who admonished me, "No samples." He meant that I wasn't to make copies of Begin's scans for my personal use. "And do not discuss the results with anyone because this information could have tremendous political implications." So much for my need to boast – and fabricate – to one and all that, "I, Doodie, from Aliquippa had been crucial in the treatment of Menachem Begin and that my testing confirmed . . . ." An article in my hometown newspaper erroneously reported my fantasy as fact.

I did take one sample. In the step-down unit several days later Moshe Dayan was sitting at Begin's bedside. I just could not resist pushing the button giving me a recording of Begin's ECG. I can report that despite a conversation with one of his opposition's leaders, there was no indication of any strain on Begin's heart.

Another encounter again involved Professor Gotesman. I requested and received a thirty-minute appointment with him to discuss my *aliyah*. When I had talked to Professor Braun years before about a job at Hadassah Hospital, he bluntly asked if I could bring $100,000. Gotesman was no less inconsiderate. After twenty-five minutes of respectfully listening to him describe his long workday at three different jobs in order to make ends meet, I asked that the last five minutes be about me. It was obvious that he had no need for me at Hadassah Hospital nor had he any interest in addressing my quandary. In all fairness to Dr. Gotesman, many Israelis are bored with tourists for whom toying with *aliyah* is an academic exercise. Time has shown that my intentions were serious; he should have sensed it.

Over the next three years I volunteered for a month on two other occasions. These working months were crucial for they were later credited to me for Israel's specialty requirements. It was also important that I met Professor Ernesto Lubin, Director of Nuclear Medicine at Beilinson Hospital. I believe that he subsequently facilitated my receiving board certification in nuclear medicine, without which I would have had no future in this specialty in Israel. The road to a significant job was being paved.

In 1983 I cancelled reservations for my thirty-fifth reunion at Harvard Medical School, electing instead to go to St. Louis for the annual meeting of the Society of Nuclear Medicine. What a fateful decision! First I encountered Dr. Atlan who offered me a position at Hadassah Hospital starting September '84. I said that that was great but I wanted to start my life in Israel with an *ulpan* (a school for the intensive study of Hebrew). Dr. Atlan didn't appreciate my discomfort working only in English at Hadassah Hospital. His answer deeply disappointed me. "Come work for me for a year and after that you can begin *ulpan*." Neither of us understood the other's needs; his probably being the need for a second senior physician in order to meet the requirements for a residency training program.

The next encounter, arranged by Elscint, Israeli manufacturer of nuclear medicine equipment, was with Lionel Lieberman, Director of Nuclear Medicine at Tel Hashomer Hospital.

Lionel, two years younger than I, studied nuclear medicine under William Beierwaltes at Ann Arbor. He collected a masters degree at Harvard's School of Public Health and, before making *aliyah*, was Professor of Nuclear Medicine at the University School of Medicine in Madison, Wisconsin. Married to Mara, an Israeli Ph.D. biochemist, he came to Israel in 1973, before the Yom Kippur war. He remained for two years, serving as nuclear medicine chief at Kaplan Hospital in Rehovot. Lionel returned in 1982 to replace Israel's most senior nuclear medicine physician, Professor Czerniak, chief at Tel Hashomer – my entry into the field of nuclear medicine antedated them all.

Lionel and I went out for a five-hour spaghetti dinner near the Arch in downtown St. Louis. After patiently listening to a summary of my past life and aspirations for making *aliyah*, he took over the conversation. "OK. I see you've got the fever. Now, let me tell you exactly what to do. First enroll in a *mercaz klita*, an absorption center, where you will live and devote yourself to the study of Hebrew. Go to the *ulpan* and stay there as long as you can afford it. (Lionel's own frustration with Hebrew made him the right adviser for me.) When you're ready, you'll come to Tel Hashomer and work with me. We'll upgrade your nuclear medicine expertise. The Ministry of Absorption will pay you $200 a month. You won't cost the hospital anything and, besides, you'll be able to help us with nuclear cardiology. When you're ready, we'll find you a job somewhere in Israel."

I could have kissed him, both because he listened to me and understood my plight and also because he presented me with a tailor-made outline designed for a successful *aliyah* – with no hidden agenda on his part. A $35 tax-deductible dinner and look what I gained!

Freeing myself from Aliquippa was far easier than adjusting to Israel. I was fortunate to hire Dr. William (Bill) Slemenda to take over my practice during the trial year in Israel. Knowing Bill's high quality, I never felt that I was abandoning my patients. Marcia and I returned after that first year, sold my practice and home-office to Bill, and packed up our household goods for shipment to Israel. At a dinner arranged for close friends, Libby Elbaum, one of Marcia's Hadassah confidantes, gave tribute to Marcia: "How can I remain chairman of the *aliyah* committee when I'm losing Marcia to Israel?" Nor was I oblivious to the upheaval in the lives of key people in our life: cousin Evie, our housekeeper Racheal, and Elaine, my secretary for twenty-seven years. We arranged an open-house farewell reception for family, friends, and patients. The hugs and kisses seemed endless but did close the circle of this phase of our life.

Part C: The Realization

How fortuitous for us that Danny's *aliyah* program coincided with ours. He had planned to transfer to Hebrew University upon completion of his second year at Columbia University and arrived in Israel one month before us.

With help from Moshe Yakir, an official in the Aliyah Department of the Jewish Agency and father of Raina's medical school classmate, we were accepted into the *mercaz klita* in Raanana. It wasn't the practice to admit *olim* of our age – I was soon to be fifty-nine – but my plan to work put us into an acceptable category.

The absorption center provided mini-apartments, schoolrooms, and personnel to facilitate entrance into Israeli life: job counselors, social workers, and financial advisors. Having come only with clothes, we were pleased to be provided with bedding and kitchen utensils. An immediate problem was learning how to deal with the 400% inflation rate during our first year in Israel. One reason that a pharmacist-friend returned to England, was that his job in a drug store was to change price labels every second day.

It was an education in Zionism that we had to learn to deal with multiple nationalities. Group characteristics emerged. The Romanians played canasta every night; the Russians learned Hebrew quickly and garnered all the available jobs at the Center; the South Africans were cheerful, and along with the English, cleaned up after parties; the French were late for bus trips and were generally undisciplined; the South Americans brought soup to the sick and were jovial, while the Americans formed a committee to go to the director to complain that the telephones were out of order.

As in retirement communities, newcomers are eager to form close relationships to replace those left behind in their native countries. One South African couple remains among our closest friends while another couple from Cardiff, Wales who needed our parental support and remained in Israel only five years, left to live in Birmingham, England. Another couple, Saul and Ruth Rothschild, old timers from Raanana, picked our name from a list of new residents and visited us with cake and wine on the second day of our *aliyah*. They later volunteered to be guarantors of potential indebtedness to our first landlord. This carries considerable risk, since sudden departures from Israel were not rare. Saul once took me on a search for my new Volvo, stolen outside the Center; five days later it was found on the Egyptian border waiting to cross with two Peugeots.

A Brazilian family arrived with a huge German shepherd dog despite explicit directives against animals at the *mercaz klita*. In fear of being caught – knowing their children's dependency on the dog – they took the dog out only at night. Imagine their anxiety when they were requested to meet with the director. "This is it," they feared. "So, how are things going?" was the essence of the interview. Not a word about the dog. Most of us had little to do with the director, who merited the job because he was a retired army officer. At a Hanukah party four months after we arrived, one of the residents asked while the director was speaking, "Who's that?"

There were two influential visitors during those months. One was former general Rafael Eitan, member of Knesset, who spoke slowly enough that even I could almost understand him. The other was Rabbi Yitzchak Peretz, also a member of Knesset, who enraged us when it was reported that he blamed the death of seventeen youngsters in a train-bus collision on their parents for permitting a film screening on *Shabbat*.

The transition from life in Aliquippa was highlighted by Marcia and me having so much time together. We felt like our own children away at summer camp. To compare it to a second honeymoon wouldn't be far off the mark. Sleeping the whole night through without hospital calls was an unexpected plus. And seeing our six-week-old granddaughter Maia lying on our bed on the day of our arrival, was reason enough for moving to Israel. Except for the constant cloud of my depression, quickly incurred as I fumbled through the early days of *ulpan*, the first few months would have been an exciting adventure. Unlike most around us, we didn't have to worry about money, and I had a job waiting for me whenever I chose to leave the absorption center.

In *ulpan* we learned, and subsequently saw for ourselves, that two dates are written on the gravestone of David Ben Gurion. These are the dates of his birth and his *aliyah*. We weren't as *farbrent* (fired up) as he but we did appreciate the feeling of entering a new life.

It's to be expected that Marcia's family blamed me for our *aliyah* while my family credited her. Marcia's sister Elaine presented a scenario that could have fictionalized a third of this memoir. "If Raina would have married in or soon after college like any normal girl, by the time that they might be planning *aliyah*, they would have had three grandchildren and that would have kept them planted in America." I can't disagree with Elaine but I choose to believe that Raina could only have married a Zionist or that, under her influence, her husband would have become one. Nor do I doubt that Raina's *aliyah* and Danny's Zionist zeal accelerated the process for us.

Another scenario concerns Amy. If she had not died, it is most unlikely that we could have put the Atlantic Ocean between us. Her last five-year history was one of increasing emotional and financial dependence on us, albeit intermittent,. As for the latter, I would not have been able to stop working; her therapy costs were escalating. In addition I would have had to amass an estate of enormous proportions to provide for her unpredictable future. Suffice it to say, Amy's leap into eternity freed us to follow our hearts' bidding.

Why me and not my brothers? Why Marcia and not her brother or sister? First and foremost we encouraged each other. We know of American couples who have come with unequal measures of enthusiasm and commitment. For some, *aliyah* didn't succeed; couples either settled for a disgruntled existence, divorced, or left Israel. And, if the latter, the more Zionist partner experienced guilt of abandoning Israel and a dream.

Possibly living in a small Jewish community like Aliquippa cast Marcia and me into the role of "super-Jew." We were called upon for *yahrzeit minyans*, for positions on the boards of the *shul*, Sisterhood, Sunday School, Hadassah, UJA, Israel Bonds, United Synagogue, etc. Though our siblings were involved in Jewish community life, their participation was to a lesser degree and less crucial than ours – we were more needed. Maybe living in a small town as isolated Jews within a Christian milieu required us to be constant and vigorous as role models for our children. I must confess that once we moved to Israel, our *shul* attendance was down by ninety percent. *Kashrut* continues to be important; *Shabbat* and holidays are built into the work calendar.

Would Freud say that being babies of our respective families, we had to break out of the mold, to be different? My Mom and Dad had died in 1974 and my mother-in-law in 1978, six months before Amy's death. My father-in-law was bedridden, dying in Bridgeport five days after our arrival in Israel. We can't be accused of separating ourselves from them. And certainly we weren't running away from our siblings.

If, indeed, we were running away from anything, it would be *shul* boards, hospital watchdog committees (from which I could have more easily just resigned) and, maybe, from a capitalistic Christian society. But let there be no mistake: I love the United States, and often here in Israel, speak of her greatness. Nor have I forgotten that this was the country that provided us the financial means to make our move to Israel.

I firmly believe that anti-Semitism did not enter into the equation notwithstanding the few anti-Semitic encounters I have described in these memoirs; most of these occurred in the decade preceding the Six-Day war. Overt anti-Semitism seemed to decline after that event. Generally we felt none from our neighbors, although it did become evident when we took a black friend for a swim in our neighborhood pool. Infrequently I would sense it when as chairman of a quality review committee, I would spearhead a review against an errant staff physician.

As of 2000, although we've helped tourism, no one in our families has emulated us. We might feel validated if scores were to follow in our wake, but we are hardly glib about what *aliyah* entails.

When Bob was visiting for Danny's wedding in 1990 with his wife Sheila and teenage children, Julia and Max, we were all invited to travel north with good friends Chaim and Chana Adar. Chana had lost her first husband and her older son in the Israel Armed Forces. Together we visited the British Acre prison where Chaim had been one of forty-one prisoners who broke out in 1947. We also visited Tel Hai and the cemetery at Kfar Giladi. While sitting in a shady area near the graves of young soldiers, I thanked Chana for being so inspirational to Bob's children. I added, "All this despite its being a bit heavy."

In an effort to lighten the emotional load the youngsters were experiencing, Chana said, "Listen. I don't expect you to make *aliyah.* I don't even expect you to give money to Israel. I do expect that wherever you are, you will speak up for us (Israel)." These are my sentiments as well.

My brothers each reacted characteristically when we phoned to announce our decision to remain in Israel. We called during their *seder* on the first night of *Pesach.* Jerry's response was, "Well, you've always been more Zionistic than the rest of us."

Bob's turn. "There's nothing left for you in Aliquippa. You've been president of the medical staff and of the *shul.*"

Irv was no help; explicitly honest he said, "Oh, shit."

Marcia loves to quote Judith Epstein, a national president of Hadassah who explained her lifelong devotion to Hadassah by quoting the leader of a wagon train that took her grandfather west: "Choose your rut well because you'll be in it for the next 1,500 miles." Well, we have chosen our rut and it has suited us just fine.

WHAT'S IN A NAME?

I was born David Chaimovitz. Seventy-four years later I am Dah-veed Haimovitz, the "H" pronounced gutturally. In between I was David Chamovitz, the "Ch" pronounced as in champagne.

Chaimovitz was how Dad's last name was spelled at Ellis Island in 1903 as was that of his half brother Berish who preceded him to America. For me the name was not an encumbrance, rather a badge of honor and an admission ticket through so many doors at Aliquippa High School and Geneva College. After all, I was the son of Morris Chaimovitz and the brother of four Chaimovitzes before me. The only problem presented to me was having strangers spelling the name with an "s" at the beginning and leaving out the first "i."

Maybe my attitude toward the name was more complex than I have admitted. I remembered hearing stories that Dad's name in Romania was Adler. "If true," I ruminated, "why not adopt such an elegant name as that?" Was "not so Jewish" a consideration? As I later learned from cousin Bernie Haimovitz, my grandfather, unable to obtain his own passport, left Romania for Palestine with a passport purchased from a man named Adler. It was under this name that he was registered with the ruling Turkish authorities. So much for that fantasy; an Adler lineage was ruled out.

On the first day in my dorm in Harvard in 1944 someone answering the phone on a floor below, shouted, "Is there a Dave son-of-a-bitch here?" Obviously Mom and Dad were checking to see if their last-born had arrived intact. This highlighted that I was starting out with a clean slate, removed from my past, from my name. As far as new friends would be concerned, I could very easily have been David Smith.

After World War II ended in Europe, brother Jerry was shipped to California to await transfer to the Pacific Theater. Fortunately, during this time, Japan surrendered and Jerry was discharged. In the ensuing days he experimented with several substitutions for Chaimovitz: Chandler, Shelbourne, and Champagne. We never discussed his motivation, but to my relief, by the time this exercise became known to me, Jerry had already settled for eliminating the initial letter "i." The Aliquippa newspaper featured a front-page story: "Local doctor performs surgery on his name, removing the i." I can't imagine myself as David Shelbourne.

Irv helped me recall that we three other remaining sons went to Dad in 1948 to ask his approval for changing the spelling of our name and for him to do likewise. I don't remember Mom's entering into the discussion; I doubt that she disapproved. Dad expressed no discomfort with the name's modification but he halted further discussion by adamantly declaring that he would remain "Chaimovitz." Thus, approval was granted.

None of us thought of adopting the spelling "Haimovitz" as had our New York cousin Bernard; this would have necessitated a change in pronunciation.

Bob and I met with John Stern, Dad's lawyer and good friend, who made all the arrangements through the Beaver County Courthouse. On April 23, 1948 two months before graduating from medical school, I became David Chamovitz.

The name issue hibernated until it cropped up at Amy's behest twenty-five years later. In her quest for roots she sought permission to return the "i" while at the same time making her legal name Chana (her Hebrew name) in place of Amy. We offered no resistance although she had to accept the fact that I could never call her anything but Amy. John Stern, who had removed our "I," put hers back.

A serious dilemma surfaced when we made *aliyah*. What should our name be in Israel? And, if it remained Chamovitz, how should it be spelled or pronounced in Hebrew? It had never seemed imperative to Hebraize our name, as Ben Gurion, whose name in Poland had been Green, required of his functionaries if their jobs took them out of the country. Shertok became Sharett, Israel's first Foreign Minister and second Prime Minister. Not aspiring to any government position, I was under no such pressure. Had I been, I probably would have considered Ben (son of) Haim or Ben Moshe, Dad's Hebrew name.

A perplexing question was how to spell it in Hebrew, with a *shin* or a *het*; with the former, the pronunciation would not be changed but with the latter, it would be pronounced gutturally as in the toast *l'chaim* (to life). In truth Raina, living in Israel seven years before our arrival, had already resolved the problem by opting for Chamovitz and spelling it with a guttural *het*. That was fine with Marcia and me.

I do believe Danny gave more thought to the possibility of Ben David and Ben Haim. Hadn't his future father-in-law gone from Schechter to Yalon? For Danny a major factor for not making a change was having already published scientific articles under Chamovitz. He knew that we would have approved any decision he made. Danny's wife Shira elected to keep her maiden name by hyphenating it, Yalon-Chamovitz.

Raina only briefly contemplated keeping her name when she married Zvika Rosenberg. And Zvika, himself, had earlier wanted to change his name but, knowing the trauma it would inflict on his father, chose not to raise the subject.

Thus, at age fifty-nine in 1984, I became Dah-veed Haimovitz. I won't say that it didn't give me conflicts. It's just that when I wouldn't be feeling very good about myself (such as during a hospital staff conference conducted entirely in Hebrew), this name change added to my identity crisis. I must confess to feeling a bit schizoid when answering the phone, especially at the hospital where I began by giving my Hebrew name. It would have been so easy to slip back to, "Dr. Chamovitz speaking."

The pronunciation created problems for tourists looking for us. In 1979 when I was a volunteer at Hadassah Hospital in Jerusalem, a friend of mine, Fred Ross, a Baptist Minister from Aliquippa, came to the hospital leading a tour group. "Information," looking under "Shamovitz," told him that they had no record of me. Similarly, when our name became listed in the Tel Aviv phone book, it was no help to non-Hebrew speakers asking information using the "sh" sound.

I'll close this subject by relating a short story, a lesson in an early *ulpan* book. Mr. Jacob Goldstein, formerly president of a large corporation in Argentina, is sitting in an *ulpan* class as a new immigrant. He's daydreaming: "Can I get you coffee and a croissant, Mr. Goldstein? New York is on the line, Mr. Goldstein. Your broker called to say that your stock shares rose ten points, Mr. Goldstein. Your tee-off time is arranged for two PM, Mr. Goldstein." His reverie is interrupted when the teacher directs a question to him, "Yaakov, make a sentence with a noun and a verb." He stammers an answer.

Returning to his reverie, he pleads, "When will I be Mr. Goldstein again?" Fifteen years later this no longer characterizes me. Well, maybe just a little.

MY BATTLE WITH HEBREW

This portends to be a humorless chapter, at least for me. My struggle to learn Hebrew has been no laughing matter. Quite the opposite. My despair was comparable to that of the first year in medical school and, I'm ashamed to add, to the years of my daughter Amy's illness. In the first instance I wasn't certain I would survive to be a doctor while in the second, I feared for Amy's survival. In all three situations I was out of control. With Amy's problems I never feared for my marriage, but in my struggle with Hebrew, I did.

As I look back, there was little reason for me to anticipate any problem. Did I not get A's in high school Latin and in college French? And didn't I have an advantage over immigrants who couldn't read Hebrew? I had been *davening*, albeit without comprehension, for forty-five years.

Because I knew the Hebrew alphabet and could read, I was placed in the advanced beginner's class. Yet, I knew I was in trouble on the first morning of *ulpan*. Immediately I was confronted with scores of gender connected words, a concept totally foreign to me, despite my French studies years before. And, of course, the teacher spoke only in Hebrew, which made absolutely no sense to me. I would break into a cold sweat when she would ask for a sentence, "Two words will suffice." I'm no genius but I couldn't stoop to composing such a simple sentence and therefore came up with none. Everyone around me appeared to be at ease. Within a few days Marcia, who had started in my class, was promoted. This was no surprise to me.

Classes were from eight AM to one PM, six days a week. Add to that at least five hours a day of homework. Marcia spent a minimum of time on the latter using her time to make friends while I had little energy for matters beyond my *ulpan* textbooks. As the first few days passed I descended more deeply into depression – frustration is too weak a word.

I was sorely tested on the fifth day of our *aliyah*. We were attending a wedding when our son-in-law Zvika brought us the news that Marcia's father had died. We were not surprised since he had been in heart failure when we said good-bye the day we departed for Israel. Though I dearly loved my father-in-law – God knows I wanted to be with Marcia – there was no way I could leave Israel. There was no way that I could miss one hour of class. If I did, surely I would never learn Hebrew. I felt that without Hebrew skills, my *aliyah* would not be successful and that I would flunk out of Israel. My ego would never have permitted me to be one of those Hebrew illiterate American-Israelis. Marcia took off by cab to the airport, leaving a dejected husband on the sidewalk of the absorption center. During the week of her absence I don't remember speaking to a soul outside of class.

How badly I wanted to accept the invitation posted on the bulletin board, "Feel like crying? Come to room No. 8 at 4 PM." It was a co-counselor offering help. Though I was familiar with the merits of this support process – Raina was a teacher of co-counseling – my reaction was snobbish. "Am I not a graduate of Harvard Medical School? Was I not one of Aliquippa's finest doctors, a teacher of scores of doctors and nurses? Surely I can survive this nightmare."

I rigorously attacked my homework, completing every exercise but soon realized that reading and writing came much easier to me than did speaking or comprehending the spoken word. "Why, oh God, can't my mouth release or my ear unscramble two consecutive words?" I must admit that the rules of grammar did fascinate me as did the concept of the three letter root of most words but this intellectual stimulation did little to open either my mouth or my ears.

When the class progressed to listening to a taping of the early morning's news, my anxiety level mounted; it abated only minimally if I had heard the news in English earlier that morning. How I welcomed the melody that introduced the news on BBC at breakfast.

Occasionally, banishing Marcia from our apartment in the absorption center, I added an hour's private conversation with the Israeli wife of one of the students. That didn't help. Nothing seemed to.

On January 1, 1985 after four months of living in the absorption center, Marcia and I moved out. This was contrary to the advice from Lionel Lieberman (see chapter, *Going Up in the World*) that thus far I had followed. He had achieved an inadequate level of expertise and wanted me to be more successful. "Remain in the center (and *ulpan*) as long as you can afford it." I felt compelled to get on with my new career in nuclear medicine, not at all because of the few dollars I would be earning. Maybe not having worked as a doctor for four months was also wreaking havoc with my self-image.

I certainly wasn't giving up my quest to master Hebrew. Moving from the absorption center in Raanana to an apartment in Kfar Saba to remain near my job at Tel Hashomer, I started studying in an evening *ulpan*. This was a most disappointing trial lasting no more than two months; I had been spoiled by the superb quality of the *ulpan* teachers at the absorption center. More upsetting was the carpool I joined. Even though two of the four participants were Anglo-Saxons (from English-speaking countries), everyone spoke rapid-fire Hebrew. Not even once in the four months of this carpooling did anyone take note of my frustration, my desire to make use of the time to speak simple Hebrew. I rode in isolation. When I did offer a complaint, the response was always, "Speak only Hebrew." Invariably after that, people would assess my failure, "You must speak only Hebrew," saying it in English. Very few had the patience to take the extra moments to have a Hebrew dialogue with me.

On May 1, 1985 I became Director of Nuclear Medicine at Wolfson Hospital in Holon. Two months later, primarily in order to shorten the bumper-to-bumper ride to work, we moved to Tel Aviv. In September Marcia and I began evening classes at *Ulpan Meir*, a five-minute walk from our apartment. The teachers were excellent; I had no complaint on that score. The first year our class met for three hours four evenings a week, the following two years, three times a week. On my final year in *ulpan* I tried an advanced class two evenings a week but was lost much of the time.

No one should deny me an A for effort, for concurrently I arranged private tutoring. The directress of the *ulpan* (Shoshana Tane) even met with me in her home for two consecutive hours once a week. With her, time flew. More than once it was three hours before either of us looked at a watch. With Shoshana I did progress, at least improving my conversational skills. Unfortunately these lessons ended when she took a sabbatical. Then for a couple of years I met once a week with a widowed, retired educator who let me devise my own program. My goal with her was to be able to fathom the radio news. I didn't get very far.

I did make considerable progress also under the tutelage of Liora, secretary in Lionel's office in Herzliya. After working one night a week for six months, I was writing reports in Hebrew and was more competent at lecturing to the medical staff at Wolfson Hospital and to new immigrant physicians from Russia. Often with the latter I would take detours to avoid words or expressions I couldn't recall in Hebrew. To my chagrin the Russians would supply me with the proper Hebrew word whenever I floundered.

My vocabulary was increased by reading newspaper articles and equally so by corresponding with my Pittsburgh cousins Lew and Ruth Gumerman and with Mort Johan, a psychiatrist, who was studying Hebrew at my level at the University of Pittsburgh. I once composed a satirical love letter – strictly as an exercise – to Marcia's friend who was also studying with my elderly teacher. The latter, reviewing it for me and having no sense of humor, was mortified.

In summary, regarding my Hebrew skills, I can say on the plus side that after four or five years of study I could engage in a one-on-one conversation, shop, pay bills, and write isotope scan reports. I could lecture on nuclear medicine or present isotope scans at conferences but I understand only twenty-five percent of what I heard on the radio or TV. Similarly I couldn't follow a discussion in a room full of people, especially when more than one person was talking at a time. I must confess that one of the benefits of retirement is that I no longer have to submit myself to the torture of staff or nuclear society board meetings. In contrast to my participation in meetings and conferences in America, where I was often in charge of the proceedings, in Israel I would sit in mortal embarrassment in anticipation of being asked for an opinion without knowing what had already transpired. Or, wanting to speak, I would be uncertain if the matter had already been raised. More than once I felt perfectly silly when I did venture a comment. And damned few colleagues gave any consideration to my language deficiencies.

Libby Elbaum, a wise friend of Marcia's, once said to her during Amy's depression, "If your marriage can handle this, it can handle anything." Well, Libby never heard of Hebrew. I must say that if Marcia didn't leave me during the first three years of our *aliyah*, she never will. I was constantly depressed, relieved only by working or when distracted by eating, seeing a movie, or being with the kids. I was totally self-absorbed, giving Marcia minimal support or attention. When we would study together or practice speaking in the car or read *Gateway for the Beginner* (the easy Hebrew newspaper), I would shout at her if she gave me a word sooner than I wanted or if she took too long to give me the word. Either way she couldn't win. I was pitifully out of control. Yet it was rare that I drove her to tears or that she rebuked me. How she tolerated me, I'll never know. Anybody else would have left me or taken a lover. It was all unbelievable; I was so miserable and cruel to her.

Wherever we went, I was a broken record, bemoaning my fate, my failure to learn Hebrew. One *Shabbat* evening during dinner at Raina's with all of Zvika's family present, true to form I was boring every one with my familiar refrain. Raina finally brought me to bay. Thinking in Hebrew but speaking in English, meaning to say, "Daddy, stop putting yourself down," she said, "Oh, Daddy, stop going down on yourself." As soon as the words were out of her mouth, Raina broke into one of her marvelous bursts of uncontrollable laughter, followed by Marcia, Zvika, and, reminiscent of my old self, by me. Translations around the table caused further laughter from Zvika's family. I was fleetingly in remission.

There were few other light moments those days. One stands out involving a blooper on my part. It took place during a telephone discussion with Malka, Dr. Lieberman's Orthodox secretary at Tel Hashomer Hospital. In my early years at Wolfson Hospital I had no budget for buying radioactive gallium, an expensive isotope used in the study of patients with lymphoma. Dr. Lieberman frequently had extra quantities, which he would give to me. Three weeks in a row Malka informed me that all their gallium had been used up; none was available. Jesting, I suggested to Malka that Dr. Lieberman should enlarge his standing order of gallium. Speaking in Hebrew, I added, "You're not supplying my needs." Having used the wrong preposition, what I really said was, "You're not satisfying me sexually." Humorless, she became indignant, saying, "Doctor, don't say that to me." At least Israelis find this incident hilarious.

When we first moved to Tel Aviv, we considered the patriotic gesture of doing street-patrol duty with the civil guard. We would be taught how to use a rifle, standard equipment while on duty. All I could think of was Mickey Marcus, a West Pointer who, as a volunteer in 1947, wrote Israel's first army manual. (He was portrayed by Kirk Douglas in the movie, *Cast a Giant Shadow.*) Mickey was killed by a camp guard, just off the boat, because Mickey didn't use the Hebrew password, the only word that the guard knew. I was certain that on duty something similar would befall me, or worse, I would kill someone.

Who can say what fostered this terrible battle with Hebrew? Was I trying too hard? Certainly I was determined to live in the Hebrew-speaking world of Israel. Was it from an inflated sense of my intelligence thereby setting too high a standard for myself? But, after all, I did graduate from Harvard Medical School. And did I not succeed at every new undertaking in my medical practice? With that track record, learning Hebrew should have been a cinch.

Was it my age? I was fifty-nine years old, nearly the oldest student in my first *ulpan*. I observed my grandchildren becoming bilingual as infants. So often I was impressed with the speed with which teenagers were learning the language even without the motivation that drove me. Marcia tried to console me by reminding me that the young students in my class had the advantage of sleeping with Israelis.

If age were a factor, why at age sixty-seven did I learn the advanced technology of Nuclear Medicine and why at seventy-one did I learn to type and to use a word processor?

Actually the answer, at least in part, may be quite simple. Awakening from general anesthesia once in 1998 and again in 1999, I spoke fluent Hebrew; Danny and Raina, who were with me in the recovery rooms, attest to that. That being the case, I can only conclude that fear of making mistakes and of sounding foolish has inhibited me from succeeding.

I have heretofore avoided the element of competition with Marcia. I have always marveled at her competence with languages as she guided me on walking tours in France, Italy, and even Russia. Without jealousy I boasted of her many talents. Yet, didn't I see her pulling away from me in *ulpan* as she moved to more and more advanced classes? I worried, "Will I be excluded from her new circle of Hebrew-speaking friends? How will I handle this separation?" Lastly, "Won't this cause our *aliyah* or, God forbid, our marriage to fail?" More than once I lay in a sweat at night contemplating these ominous possibilities. It's pointless to speculate, but what if Marcia had been less capable than I? As her teacher, would I have been less blocked? I doubt it.

Now, more than fifteen years in Israel and early into semi-retirement, I am content with what skill I have – I can get by when Hebrew is required. Despite my anxieties, I have a viable marriage and I haven't flunked out of Israel.

THE FAMILY TREE SPROUTS

During the years that I worked at Wolfson Hospital I took the bus whenever Marcia needed the car. This happened more often in the early years, since, in addition to attending Hadassah meetings, she baby-sat with our granddaughters in Jerusalem.

From time to time in the early morning hours a bald, pudgy, little man with a blind man's white-and-red walking stick would board my bus in the Florentine district of Tel Aviv. The area housed light industry and dilapidated apartment buildings. Passengers near the driver vacated a seat for him or he elected to stand. He would ride three or four blocks and get off unassisted. Obviously despite minimal vision he could function independently. Not once did he sit near me nor did we ever exchange greetings. Between the years 1985 and 1990 I saw him eight to ten times.

It was 1991. Our phone rang. A young woman asked when Elise's funeral would take place. (Elise was cousin Bernard Haimovitz's widow for whom Marcia had accepted much responsibility.) Marcia replied, "We buried her this morning in Jerusalem next to Bernard. Who are you?"

"I'm her niece Chana."

"How did you find out about Elise?"

"We visited her frequently in the nursing home. A nurse called us this morning to tell us that she had died."

It is true that we vaguely knew that Bernie had other family in Israel, but by design he chose to avoid our meeting them presumably so that our attentiveness would not be diverted. But neither did we take any initiative to make contact. Bernard's father, Zaida Meir Chaimovitz, was my father's older half-brother. At the end of their brief conversation, Marcia invited Chana and her widowed father to visit us the following evening. Their family name was Lazerovich.

At the appointed hour they arrived. I opened the door. There stood a plump girl about nineteen years old with dental braces and a warm smile. And behind her, initially hidden from view, was her father, a bald, pudgy, little man with a blind man's white-and-red walking stick, my fellow bus passenger.

His name was Eliyahu Chaim. His mother Tzipora was a sister to Bernard and therefore my first cousin. Eliyahu's great-grandfather for whom he was named, was my father's father. Also named for this original Eliyahu Chaim was my brother Allen and, in turn for Allen, brother Irv's son. I would hear the name in Hebrew when Dad would be called to the Torah, "Moshe Yonah ben Eliyahu Chaim." Thus, this new acquaintance was my first cousin once removed.

Eliyahu, a widower and an observant Jew, lived with Chana in a deteriorated section of Tel Aviv where I saw him enter the bus. We spoke English to Chana; she in turn, spoke with Eliyahu in Hebrew and Yiddish. He was retired; she was preparing to enter university.

Communication was not easy; I am ashamed to admit that we did not immediately bond. For the next three years we did invite them to the annual open house *Succah* parties on our roof but due to the distraction of the large number of guests, we conversed very little. Attempts to connect them with our friends also failed.

Finally, in March '99 we invited them for dinner. This time Eliyahu (nicknamed Eli) was more loquacious, speaking about himself, and about our family. He is the *chazan* (cantor) for *Shabbat* mornings in his synagogue and chants on a religious radio station on Saturday nights. His vision problem, retinitis pigmentosa, began at birth and has worsened over the years; Chana is mildly afflicted. For two hours after dinner he added name after name to our family tree, telling me about his mother's three sisters and two brothers, one of whom was Bernard. Sister Clara along with her husband Mordechai and two children Serena and Harry died in 1942 in the Holocaust; the other sisters survived the Holocaust and came to Israel between 1947 and 1950. Bernard had immigrated to New York in 1939 and to Israel many years later.

Family of Clara Chaimovtz Herskovitz, 1940, murdered by the Nazis in 1942.

The following *Shabbat* I went to Eliyahu's *shul* to hear him *daven.* He treated me like an honored guest by seating me close to the Torah Ark and giving me the third *aliyah* (call to the Torah), the most important of the seven *aliyot.* I found his chanting praiseworthy and repeatedly told him. It was evident that much of his recitation of the prayers was from memory.

With the impetus of Eliyahu's data, I subsequently added forty-six descendents from our common progenitor, Eliyahu Chaim, with his first wife, Eli's great grandmother, to the thirty-nine with his second wife, my grandmother. The pleasurable work of getting acquainted with these relatives has already started.

I sometimes wonder which other relatives I may have passed on the street, encountered at concerts, or ogled at the beach.

OUR VERY OWN WAR

Long before moving to Israel I had contemplated doing so. Certainly, I felt, I had a contribution to make to this young, struggling country. Yet, the realities of family ties and obligations, unachieved financial goals, and countless child-rearing problems outweighed my Zionist zeal. If only, I fantasized, Ben Gurion or Golda Meir would make a person-to-person call and say, "We need you," I would have surmounted all obstacles and just gone.

The call never came. By contrast many acquaintances didn't wait, whether it was the 1948 War of Independence or during other later crises. With or without spouses, they "caught the next boat." My hopes for being pulled to Israel were raised when in the early sixties, American Jewish doctors were asked to register their availability to serve in Israel in the event of war. I signed on a fairly short list. "It won't be long now," I thought.

Came the Six-Day war in 1967 and the Yom Kippur war in 1973. And which of us from the Pittsburgh area was called and went? Stanley Hirsch, vascular surgeon. Stan Bushkoff, thoracic surgeon. Gerald Wiener, orthopedic surgeon. My phone never rang. Skills in internal medicine, cardiology, and nuclear medicine hardly answered priority needs of the battlefield. I reasoned, "But can I not release a reserve army physician from civilian responsibilities?" Apparently not.

On our thirteen trips to Israel before finally making *aliyah,* numerous acquaintances tried to convince us to come. One friend (from my residency days at the Beth Israel Hospital), Professor Nathan Rabinowitz, requested, more accurately, demanded, that American Jews replace his battle-weary sons on the firing line; one had been seriously wounded in 1967.

After a peace treaty was signed with Egypt in 1979, it looked as though Israel would no longer have to settle differences with its Arab neighbors with cannons. My romantic, epic-making war stories were never to be written. Over the years it became clear that I needed Israel more than she would need me.

It's not as though I didn't make a contribution to Israel after our *aliyah*. I did develop the nuclear medicine department at Wolfson Hospital. I served in various capacities in the Israel Nuclear Medicine Society: as a longtime member of its board of directors, as nominating committee chairman, as treasurer, and as a representative of our society to the forerunner of the European Association of Nuclear Medicine at Goslar, Germany in 1987. I served on a committee for the oral examination of numerous applicants for nuclear medicine specialty certification. This carried an onerous responsibility; failing an applicant inflicted great pain, but to pass incompetence was a disservice to the public. (I did have the reputation of being easy.) And maybe just buying a newspaper or riding a bus helped create jobs.

Then in 1990 sabers started rattling. Iraq brashly and successfully invaded Kuwait. Saddam Hussein, the Iraqi dictator, defied the United Nations when ordered to desist and withdraw his troops. Under the leadership of the United States many Arab countries fell into line, voting for military action by the UN. A precondition for Arab cooperation was that Israel would not participate in the conflict. President George Bush, needing air bases in countries such as Saudi Arabia, prevailed upon Prime Minister Yitzhak Shamir to comply. Under the designation of Desert Storm, an arsenal of fighting equipment, ships, planes, and personnel descended into the Gulf region. Though our Israeli troops and air force were on alert, they never went into action. Israel geared itself for missile attacks and the possibility of poison gas and bacteriologic warfare.

Instructions were quickly publicized. Each person and household were to prepare for Hussein's aggression. Centers were opened throughout the country for distribution of gas masks; instructions were given on the spot. A single medication, self-administered atropine used against poison gas, was included in the kit.

The next priority was to ready the air-raid shelter located in most apartment buildings and homes, at least those built within the last thirty years. These shelters which had not been needed since the 1973 war, had become storage rooms. Ours was no exception, only that it was dank, foul-smelling and filthy. Marcia and I took it upon ourselves to do the dirty work for the four other families living in the building. We scoured every inch that wasn't rusted beyond touching, including the floor-level toilet. We checked the water pipes, the electrical outlets, and the emergency exit. We felt relieved and secure knowing we had this fallback; as it turned out, we never needed to resort to it.

Sealing a room in our apartment against poisonous gases and flying glass was the next order of business. We initially chose our main bathroom but after the first night switched to our bedroom. We scurried about purchasing scarce masking tape to reinforce glass windows throughout the apartment. For the sealed room we taped plastic sheeting over every opening to the outside, doors, windows, and air conditioner. We collected batteries for portable radios and flashlights, candles and matches, bottled water, juices, boxed milk, canned food, and first-aid supplies. The portable phone would play a key role.

At Wolfson Hospital we were trained to treat whatever Iraq might throw our way; we carried out disaster drills. Being a nuclear medicine physician (of little value except to cleanup after an atomic explosion), I was assigned to a team that would deal with minimal physical injuries and the psychiatric problems of casualties and their families. Initially we were to be on duty two hours, and to rest four hours.

At last I had my war! The first Scud attack was signaled by the ominous sound of a wailing siren, akin to the revving up of a motorcycle. Marcia was home alone. On hearing the siren she immediately donned her gas mask and sealed herself in our bathroom. She took with her the cache of supplies plus the portable telephone. She turned on the radio, which gave news and instructions, in Hebrew, of course. (After a few days, instructions in English, Russian, and French were interspersed.) How quickly we fell in love with the calming voice of Nachman Shai, the military broadcaster who kept us updated in a cheerful manner. The children called frequently during that first long night to see if Marcia was okay and to check her comprehension of the Hebrew announcements. Brother Jerry called from Pittsburgh because he had heard on CNN TV news that a Scud had fallen on Wolfson Hospital. Marcia immediately called Wolfson and learned that no Scud had fallen on us and that all was well. She immediately returned Jerry's call to reassure him that I was safe.

Shortly after, she received a call from a correspondent of our hometown newspaper who asked Marcia how she was managing. "Well, I'm sitting in the bathtub in a sealed room wearing a gas mask and reading a book." And that is how the article about her was headlined, "Former Aliquippa resident curls up with a good book during Scud attack."

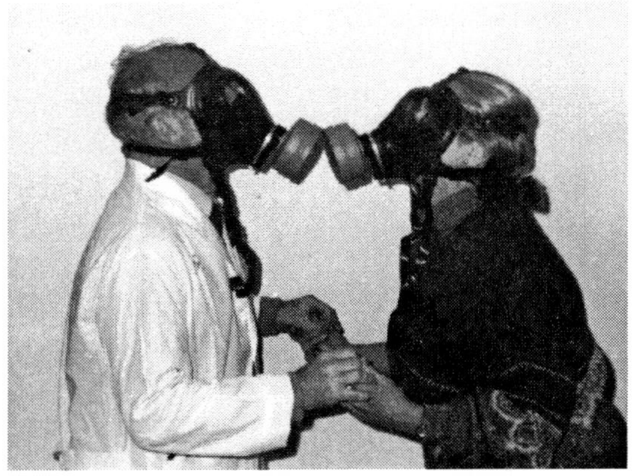

Marcia and I kiss in the bomb shelter.

"And tell me, what's going on outside?"

Marcia retorted, "I'm in my sealed room. You're watching CNN. You tell me." It took another four hours before the siren announced "All clear," and Marcia could remove her mask and go to bed.

And how did I serve my country that night? It was being holed up in the auditorium, deemed to be the safest place in my section of Wolfson Hospital. It was never made clear that the other physicians closeted with me and I were to be at other assigned places. My apprehension during the whole Gulf War was never greater than that night as I sat helpless and frustrated that none of those with me knew more. Fortunately only cuts from flying glass were treated in our emergency room that night; our absence wasn't noticed. Indeed a Scud had fallen into a field about a kilometer from the hospital but no harm was done.

After the first night, Marcia and I secured our bedroom which included a minibathroom. I supplemented precautions by putting pillows over our heads during the time spent in the sealed room; this seemed wise since most of the injuries were from flying glass. This revised setup proved much more comfortable than the initial one and was especially utilitarian when one *Shabbat* we had guests for dinner. One couple was at our front door when the siren went off. Another scampered in at thirty feet from our building, while two young women scurried back to their own apartment until the all-clear sounded. Visualize six of us sitting on the floor having muffled conversations through our masks. This attack, like most of the more than thirty others, lasted forty-five minutes. The piercing single-note siren indicating "all clear" was received like a symphonic tone poem.

Chana Adar, Trudy & Joe Katzenberg, Marcia & me, Chaim Adar, 1989, the guys' 64th birthday.

Our phone rang constantly with scores of calls from family, friends, and even former Aliquippa patients, offering moral support and praising us for our bravery. David Yachnovich, nephew of my Uncle Harry, who had just emigrated from Simferopol in the Crimea, offered lodging in Beersheva in his three-room apartment already housing five; "We have lots of room." Marcia's brother and sister-in-law in Long Island, New York called to offer care for our granddaughters, Maia and Tamar.

We didn't travel many places when off duty, but wherever we went, we carried boxed gas masks suspended from our shoulders like a large purse. With Joe and Trudi Katzenberg we once drove north an hour away to Kibbutz Givat Chaim where we picked oranges, replacing *kibbutzniks* on active army service. We felt like *chalutzim* (pioneers). Yes, we had our masks with us in the orchard.

As the war wound down we ventured a visit to the Yachnoviches in Beersheva. It wasn't that we were brave or foolhardy; rather, by that time we were confident that Saddam didn't have either the capability or the intention to use poison gas. We also knew that Saddam, in an attempt to conceal his Scud launchers, attacked almost exclusively at night. We did become apprehensive as night fell twenty minutes before our arrival home. Safe at last, but within another fifteen minutes, an alarm sounded, the last of the war. If it had happened when we were traveling, we would have sought refuge in any nearby building or just remained in our car.

From the second night of the war until it ended, Marcia and I were constantly together. The modus operandi at the hospital was changed. After the first night the staff worked twenty-four hours on-call in the hospital, alternating with twenty-four hours at home, but on-call back at the hospital if the need arose. During our first night together in the hospital Marcia and I slept on examining tables; after that we sealed my office and slept on chairs. During alarms my technician Shula and her husband Livio would scurry into our room, after which, as we did also at home, we sealed the space under the door with a wet towel and placed masking tape around the door frame. As soon as the all clear was sounded, I hurried to my station, never knowing what I might be asked to treat or what tragedies might have resulted from the Scuds that we heard exploding.

The most serious problem that I treated was that of a very agitated young man whose pulse was racing. (Probably so was mine but his for a different reason.) Thinking that he smelled gas, the patient took the atropine vial and injected his thigh through his trousers as instructed. The only mistake was that he inverted the syringe and instead of injecting the thigh, he injected his thumb. Since the thumb is so vascular, it was almost like an intravenous injection; the patient got the result we strive for in treating very slow hearts except that his dose was ten times the amount used for that purpose. I gave him ten milligrams of Valium and a ton of reassurance.

Israel experienced so many miracles during the Gulf War. With over thirty Scuds falling on Israel there was only one death as a result of an explosion. Uninhabited buildings that were severely damaged were situated next to inhabited ones. Apartment houses that had shattered walls had been vacated by chance; one, only hours before. Many old people and families with young children fled north or even to Jerusalem where no Scuds had fallen, presumably from Saddam's reluctance to harm Arabs living there. There were other deaths; at least one from a heart attack when a cardiac patient was startled from his sleep by the alarm signaling the first Scud attack, and another from suffocation due to improper use of his gas mask.

It was fortunate that our infant granddaughter Tamar enjoyed lying inside her *mamat* (a clear plastic crib-tent designed for those too small to wear a gas mask). A joke circulating during the Gulf War had Prime Minister Yitzhak Shamir, less than five feet tall, late for a meeting because he was stuck in his *mamat*.

Tel Aviv Mayor Shlomo Lahat disappointed us on two counts. First, he boasted about being on the roof of City Hall during an alarm, watching Scuds fly over into the sea, not an exemplary role model for the public who were ordered into their sealed rooms. Second, Lahat disparaged those who fled Tel Aviv during the war. Bumper stickers boasting, "I Remained in Tel Aviv," heaped insult upon injury. Actually leaving Tel Aviv was a rational reaction. Obviously, if Saddam had any plan, he was aiming at population centers, or in Tel Aviv in particular, at the army intelligence headquarters one mile from our apartment. If we had had small children, we too might have vacated the city.

We were ambivalent about the restrictions placed on our armed forces especially when we were bearing the brunt of Saddam's Scud attacks. On one hand we wanted to even the score with him rather than having others do it for us. On the other hand it was gratifying not to jeopardize either our ground forces or our pilots.

The response of Israelis to American troops that came to man the Patriot batteries (anti-Scud missile launchers) was heartwarming. Unlike "Yankee, Go Home" signs that heap scorn on US soldiers in other parts of the world, gratitude was universally expressed at every opportunity. In restaurants Israelis picked up the tab for G.I.s or at a minimum rendered handshakes and pats on the back. We were comforted by their professionalism and genuinely grateful even as doubts arose as to the effectiveness of the anti-Scud missiles.

One example of language problems surfaced one morning as Marcia and I approached Wolfson Hospital. We saw a huge billboard with the message, "We are all Patriots," a pun on the name of the American missile launchers. However, the sign was in Hebrew. Marcia translated, "We are all mushrooms?" A moment later she recognized her mistake. Mushrooms in Hebrew is pronounced "pitriot."

A cease-fire was declared on Purim, a celebration of the defeat of an earlier Hussein, Haman. We experienced great merriment out on the streets without our gas masks for the first time in six weeks! There seemed to be more costumed revelers than was usual for Purim.

Being in Israel at that time certainly beat the feelings of frustration and of impotency, and the frantic, frenetic scurrying about soliciting emergency United Jewish Appeal funds, that would have been my lot in the United States.

Come what may, we are here to do whatever is required should our very own war recur.

POLITICAL RABBINICS

A beautiful religious happening prompted me to tackle this most sensitive of issues. Marcia and I were walking one block from our apartment in Tel Aviv when we heard synagogue melodies coming from an apartment one flight up. A new Torah scroll was being dedicated. It was resplendent with a white velvet mantle and silver adornments. The men were dressed in *Shabbat* clothing; black suits or open white shirts and knitted skullcaps; the women wore *sheitels* (wigs). Within moments the throng descended to the street carrying the Torah under a *chupah* (a wedding canopy). As the crowd marched away, they sang spirited Hassidic music. The street was barricaded out of respect for the Torah as the procession weaved its way toward a nearby synagogue. We were proud of such a joyful demonstration of respect for the Torah. And yet, sad to say, not all our religious encounters here have been so pleasant.

There was a time that I looked upon Orthodox Jewry as the foundation of Judaism, as the storehouse of Jewish learning, and as role models for ethical living. It was their rabbis who frequently filled the pulpits of Conservative and Reform congregations who themselves were producing too few rabbis and teachers. I attributed to Orthodox rabbinic students a higher level of scholarship and a stricter commitment to tradition than to those in non-Orthodox *yeshivot* and seminaries.

Such an estimate was debated at the Pesach dinner table of Rabbi Joseph Heckelman in Safed in 1996. Joe, a graduate of the Jewish Theological Seminary, was host to two first-year seminary students. One, a young woman, accepting my estimate of a bygone age of Orthodox students' scholarship, admitted anxiety over her inadequate background, of never being able to catch up with Orthodox students who started intensive studies in childhood. "What will I do if asked . . . ?" While Rabbi Heckelman was deliberating his response, I quoted myself when faced with a colleague's medical question I couldn't answer, "If you'll come back in two hours, I'll be an expert." Joe added that the trade-off against the life-long training of the Orthodox rabbinic student is the acquisition of methodology of enlightened inquiry supplemented by non-rabbinic sources.

It grieves me to say that I am presently at odds with my ultra-Orthodox brethren. And not just at odds; I am on the ramparts against them. My discomfort began in a small way with my involvement on an organizational level with Orthodox rabbis in Pittsburgh. At Synagogue-Federation committee meetings they sneered at the inclusion of an agenda item dealing with assimilation. "We don't have that problem in our community," which, as with the evil son in the *Haggadah*, separated them from the Jewish community as a whole. Nor did they deem it their responsibility to join the effort to raise the level of Jewish education in Pittsburgh. Would not the Solomon Schechter Conservative Day School experience we were promoting have been more desirable than the public or non-Jewish private schools our children were attending? For them, it was "the Orthodox way or we're not interested." (It was irrelevant to them that Conservative and Reform Jews had been supporting their institutions for years.)

Many children from conservative affiliated homes attended the Orthodox Hillel Academy which offered an excellent college-preparatory program. And yet, when students elected to have *bar* or *bat mitzvah* ceremonies in their parents' Conservative synagogues, their Hillel Academy teachers refused to participate or even attend. "Men only" seating would have been arranged for them, if that was the issue. I remember receiving a telephone request for a donation to the Pittsburgh Kollel, an Orthodox study institute. The Rabbi-Director who was calling "pulled out all the stops." "You've been generous in the past . . . and your brothers contribute."

"I really would very much like to support you, but until your rabbis will honor our Conservative synagogues by *davening* with us, I will no longer contribute to any Orthodox organization." Years later, from Israel I was to urge my friends to cease contributing to the Orthodox and to contribute directly to Conservative and Reform movements in Israel, and not through United Jewish Appeal (UJA) either. It is only in recent years that any UJA funds were apportioned to non-Orthodox religious institutions in Israel; the government was equally negligent of them, and at times even hostile.

The opening round of my conflict with the ultra-Orthodox in Israel occurred in January 1983. I was volunteering at Hadassah Hospital while Marcia was helping Raina plan her wedding. Days before we arrived, Emil Grunzweig had been murdered in Jerusalem by a *kippa*-wearing fanatic who threw a grenade into a crowd of Peace Now demonstrators against the war in Lebanon. The act was vile enough, but more vile was the absence of outrage by the Orthodox community. But why should they express indignation? They had been condoning, yes, even encouraging, rock throwing at automobiles driven on *Shabbat*. The fact that the government was almost equally silent was also reprehensible. But would one not expect the rabbis to lead the way to virtuous behavior? Yet their interpretation of our Torah sanctioned this behavior. My disillusionment was ripening.

Once we moved to Israel our eyes were opened to the increasing involvement of the ultra-Orthodox – the black hatters – in the political arena. Movements with rabbinic leadership became pivotal power mongers, trading support with either of the two major parties in exchange for portfolios and funds of key ministries; often enough the funds leaked into private hands. Funding of institutions that existed only on paper, and school subsidies that were calculated according to falsely inflated numbers of students, were recently exposed; indictments were slow in coming. Rabbi after rabbi, and members of the Knesset, used parliamentary immunity to escape prosecution from indictments for flagrantly unlawful behavior involving public monies and power wielding. One long-standing member of the Knesset, a rabbi, was preparing to flee the country as his indictment appeared imminent.

The latest travesty is the case of Arieh Deri minister in the government and leader of the largest ultra-religious party, Shas. He was sentenced to four years of imprisonment after nine years of dragging out his indictment for fraudulent use of public money and for obstructing justice. He compared himself to Dreyfus while his spiritual mentors, castigating the courts, declared Deri innocent. His spiritual leader, Ovadia Yosef later vilified Supreme Court judges, who, while reducing the jail senrence to three years, reaffirmed Deri's guilt. Meanwhile the government, fearing political retribution prior to elections, postponed throwing him out of the Knesset. What is terrifying is a black-hatted culture which promulgates, "So what, if he used the money for his brother-in-law's new house? Are we not commanded to help our brothers?"

"Yes, but not with my taxes," I say.

It is not that secular Jews haven't been indicted for manipulation of state funds. But rabbis? They tarnish the very meaning of the word. What a Garden of Eden Israel would be if their peers would unfrock these rabbinic hoodlums! While I'm beseeching the Almighty, I will request that politicians stop seeking the blessings of aged "holy men" and that the rule forbidding the dispensing of blessings and talismans for voting "my way" be enforced.

When we were living in Kfar Saba in June 1985, seventeen schoolchildren and four adults from Petach Tikva were killed when a train hit a school bus. A rabbi, a govenment minister, pronounced that these children died because their parents had not resisted *Shabbat* screening of movies. He himself was not chastised, nor did any aggrieved father challenge him to a duel.

And there was Chief Ashkenazi Rabbi Lau, the youngest Auschwitz survivor, who spoke at a demonstration against the commonplace murder of women by their husbands. His solution for the phenomenon was banning violence on TV. A good start. But how about keeping guns out of the hands of violence-prone individuals or early warning systems that involve the police with wife abusers? Or divorce courts that are more user-friendly for female supplicants? Maybe even putting women like the Orthodox writer Naomi Ragen on the divorce court?

How can I relate our enormous sorrow at the murder of Yitzhak Rabin? His absence from the political scene dashed the already shaky hope of a durable peace with our Arab neighbors. Public outcry for unification of all citizens, left and right, toward a just society flickered briefly. The few who were crass enough to openly rejoice at Rabin's assassination were soon to find rabbinic justification in the concept of the *rodef,* the pursuer. Jewish law permits one to kill someone who in turn is poised to commit murder. This is legal self-protection, not murder. In cases of permissible abortion, the fetus is deemed to be a *rodef.* Twisted rabbinic logic concluded that Rabin's trading away parts of the Land of Israel was akin to being a *rodef.* "Rabin wasn't murdered; he was killed in self-defense." The threat of copycat murders looms heavily upon us.

We've been to more than one demonstration against the policy of excusing *yeshiva* students from national compulsory military duty. Ben Gurion never knew what a Pandora's box he was opening when his government offered 1,000 deferments in return for support of ultra-religious parties. It was also a noble attempt to replenish the loss of scholars during the Holocaust. The number has now grown to over 30,000. This isn't the six-year deferment that is offered to gifted medical students; this is a deferment for life. As religious students, most never earn a living themselves (or at least any declared income). They receive significant stipends and highly subsidized apartment mortgages from the government.

It is not to be forgotten that there are many Orthodox young men who serve a regular tour of army duty and many others who serve in the *Hesder Yeshiva* program which allows intermittent interruption of their Talmudic studies.

As I gaze upon some of the black-hatted young men on the street with their other-world expressions, I'm not unhappy that they aren't on the front lines defending me against invading Arab armies. I doubt that many are either physically or psychologically fit for military duty. It is equally true that because their studies are limited to acquiring religious knowledge, they are also unfit to enter the job market.

As a sop to the ultra-Orthodox, Ben Gurion's government also gave the Orthodox control of marriages, divorces, conversions, and cemeteries. Matters such as who is a Jew and, equally important, who is an acceptable rabbi, were left in their hands. Conservative and Reform marriages and conversions are not valid and there is no civil marriage. Young couples who wish to fight the system go out of the country, frequently to Cyprus, to marry; once Palestine becomes a state, Israelis will have shorter distances to travel. What a *shundah* (public shame) that will be!

By chance Rabbi Abraham Ravitz, later to be head of United Torah Judaism party in the Knesset, agreed at the last minute to officiate at Raina's wedding in 1983 when the rabbi of her choice took ill. While sitting with Rabbi Ravitz and my new son-in-law Zvika for the *ketuba* (marriage contract) signing, I mentioned that "there are three Conservative rabbis in attendance, one, Pesach Schindler, head of the World Council of Conservative Synagogues, another, the revered Joseph Heckelman from Safed, and the third, Jonathon Perlman from Beersheva. Each is dear to Raina. I would like at least one to participate under the *chupah.*"

Ravitz's immediate response was curt. "Our weddings in Israel are short."

I countered, "There's time. We're not going anywhere."

"In that case you can have your rabbi talk after Zvika breaks the glass."

"Rabbi," I wasn't watching my words, "isn't that ridiculous? You know the shouting, the hugging and kissing, and the music begin at that point."

"Well, then another option," he offered without conceding one iota of respect for my Conservative rabbis, "is to have your rabbi speak before the ceremony and then invite me to the *chupah.*" My anger was obvious, but not my rage. In retrospect, I should have accepted the latter option but at the time – it was before our aliyah and loss of naiveté – my goal was to get Raina married, not to wage a political battle. I therefore retreated, settling for an unspoken curse.

Whenever I contemplate rapprochement between Conservative and Orthodox Jews, I recall a conversation between my friend Rabbi Pesach Schindler and the wife of this same Rabbi Ravitz as was later related to me by Pesach. Pesach, one of the guest rabbis at Raina's wedding, and I have been friends for over thirty years. He composed and conducted a *Simchat Bat* (a religious baby naming) ceremony for my two granddaughters. He has raised his four children here, sweating out their years of service in the Israel Defense Forces as well as his own. Annoyed by a radio comment by Rabbi Ravitz's wife, whom he knew from their B'nai Akiva youth group in Brooklyn, Pesach telephoned her. After a few pleasantries he gave his point of view regarding universal military service, emphasizing parental anxiety during their children's tour of duty. "Don't you know," countered Mrs. Ravitz, "that an Orthodox woman experiences the same anxiety every day as she sends her sons off to the yeshiva." Pesach was nonplussed. There was no bridging that gap. He wished her well and hung up.

The problems of the *aguna* are universal throughout the Jewish world. This term refers to a woman whose husband has been missing for years as in a shipwreck and, even though presumed to be dead, this can not be proven. *Aguna* also refers to the woman whose husband refuses to grant her a *get* (a bill of divorcement) under any circumstances or without exorbitant demands of money and/or control of the children. The Conservative establishment has found *Halachic* (Jewish laws) solutions for both situations; the Reform movement has developed its own. With control of divorce in the hands of the Orthodox, these women have no recourse but to petition the religious courts year after year, most often to no avail.

Conversion policies rankle the whole non-Orthodox world. It is a highly charged, and indeed, a complicated subject. The Orthodox claim that their conversions are the only legitimate ones, requiring rigorous study and preparation by the candidate. However there are rabbis in Israel, who for a ransom, will do a "quickie" perhaps for an American basketball star who needs to be declared Jewish. (The Basketball Association's rules allow only three non-Israelis on a team.)

I'm not contesting the traditional requirement that one have a Jewish mother for acceptance as a Jew. The Reform movement does permit patrilineal Jewishness. On the other hand, Israel grants citizenship under "the right to return" to Russians who have at least one Jewish grandparent; certainly there are many recent immigrants without even this minimal requirement. It is estimated that there are 250,000 Russians, who according to Jewish law, are in need of conversions; the Orthodox rabbinate carries out 10,000 per year. It is only in the last few years that those who do undergo conversion are required to join the Orthodox community, to live Orthodox lives, and to send their children to Orthodox schools. Conservative and Reform rabbis are ready to fill the conversion void and within *Halachic* guidelines but are forbidden to do so. Meanwhile open hostility by Russian immigrants toward their adopted country festers as they are treated like second-class citizens despite serving in the army. And when they die, they are buried in Gentile cemeteries, or outside the Jewish cemetery walls, as was at least one Russian soldier. Of late, kibbutzim have provided burial sites for this group.

The problem of Orthodox exclusivity in burial practices is less burning. The sight of the disheveled burial attendants is appalling enough, but they do perform their job. With a little pushing, the family can control the graveside ceremony. Of course, no one can stop a woman from saying *kaddish* but she won't be counted in the *minyan* of ten required for its recitation. And at the close of the proceedings, when two lines are formed to comfort the exiting mourners, female mourners are excluded. At this moment there is only one cemetery under the control of the Conservative movement.

I've been skirting the issue that rends the Jewish world. "Who is a Jew?" has been on the Knesset agenda time and time again. The more that non-Orthodox Jews claim parity as legitimate Jews, the more the Orthodox establishment reads us out of the Jewish faith. Jonathon Sachs, chief rabbi of England, asserts that non-Orthodox Jews are not legitimate Jews. When the revered Reform Rabbi Hugo Gryn died in London, while even the Queen sent a representative, Rabbi Sachs absented himself from the funeral. He did speak at the memorial thirty days later without mentioning that Hugo Gryn was a rabbi. He thereupon did an about-face by offering an apology in the Jewish press for attending. (Hugo was a Holocaust survivor who lived with a family in my hometown while attending the University of Pittsburgh.) It is obvious that it is the Orthodox who have drawn the battle lines.

It was at dinner at the Rimon Inn in Safed at the close of Pesach in 1998 when Rabbi Joe Heckelman posited the question: "How would you feel if you awoke one morning and learned that the Conservative movement had declared itself a separate sect of Judaism?"

"You mean akin to divisions within the Protestant religion?"

"Exactly."

My first reaction was, "What a sad day that would be!" My second reaction was, "Great! The political black-hatted rabbis have already read me out of their faith. The strong kinship I felt for them decades ago no longer exists. They have ceased to be my brethren. They are outcast cousins, maybe." And finally, "Where do I sign?" The conversation gave me cause to wonder if my pious Zeyda, buried only half a kilometer from where Joe and I sat, would have been ashamed of me.

A year later at Pesach, I turned the question back to Rabbi Heckelman. "Where does the issue stand?"

"It hasn't gone much beyond a few private discussions. It's just too hot a potato."

A number of years ago the religious establishment issued an edict in the press, in Hebrew and English, to the effect that "anyone who thought he was fulfilling the commandment to hear the blowing of the *shofar* when he attended a Conservative synagogue on Rosh Hashanah, was in error." The following year, weeks before the High Holidays, Rabbi Tuvia Freedman, an eminent scholar of the Conservative movement wrote letters to the press challenging the Orthodox rabbis to again publish their banning edict. "Last year we had the largest High Holiday attendance in our history."

Profoundly pessimistic, I pray that the Messiah will come and recreate a feeling of brotherhood among our religious factions. May that day come speedily and in our time.

HADASSAH, MY OTHER FAMILY

Hadassah is a highly charged word for me. As I read it or hear it, immediately countless thoughts flood my psyche, personal and historical, beautiful moments, astonishing triumphs, and bitter losses. Though I've already chronicled my volunteer stays at Hadassah Hospital in the chapter, "Going up in the world," there is much more to add to Hadassah's impact on my life and that of my family.

Hadassah, the Women's Zionist Organization of America, became a household word in our family in 1944, after a chapter was founded in Aliquippa, Pennsylvania. Meetings were held in our living room with Mom and Aunt Rose Jackson as founding members. Initial-fund raising was on behalf of mother-and-child stations all over Palestine and for a network of hospitals. In 1912 the "Drop of Milk" program sent a donkey carrying cans of milk for children in Jerusalem. Then over the years came the annual ad book for which Mom and others solicited, and at times cajoled, businessman and professionals to buy as large an ad as possible. The annual banquets were enlightening, emotional, and entertaining. We learned about Hadassah's many projects in Israel: the Alice Seligsberg Vocational High School for Girls, the Brandeis Vocational School for Boys, and, later, the Hadassah Community College, School of Nursing, and, of course, the dental and medical schools.

There were inspirational speakers from National Hadassah. And how delightful were the plagiarized Broadway shows written by Marcia and directed by cousin Evie Sherman. Marcia enticed new members for Hadassah by recruiting their children for the cast. Even I got to bellow the song, "Sit Down, You're Rockin' the Boat."

Marcia and me at a Hadassah banquet in 1976.

The concept of Life Membership took root early in Aliquippa. Mom was among the first, being pinned at a party for her seventy-first birthday in 1958. In 1960 I gave Marcia a life-membership pin privately and tearfully at the hospital after she miscarried twins. Eight years later at an annual banquet Mom and Marcia's mother were surprised to receive three-generation pins after they had given life membership pins to our daughters. These public performances served to encourage others to follow suit. Hadassah concocted another ploy, "Hadassah Associate" for men. Thus, for $125, I too was pinned.

Stories of Youth Aliyah moistened many an eye. How rewarding to be identified with an organization that rescued thousands of Europe's young Jews in the thirties, continuing to do so throughout the rest of the century. It was Henrietta Szold, founder of Hadassah, who in 1934 established Youth Aliyah based on the plan of Recha Freier, a rabbi's wife in Germany. Marcia and I saw a film of Szold frantically attempting to persuade German parents to let their children go to Palestine, while in the background stood two Nazi storm troopers. Imagine Szold's gratification as she greeted her youngsters at the dock in Haifa or saw them subsequently issuing forth from Youth Aliyah Villages as healthy, highly motivated citizens of the future state.

In 1948 came the isolation of the magnificent Hadassah Hospital on Mt. Scopus in Jerusalem. World Jewry grieved for the seventy doctors and nurses murdered by Arabs under the indifferent eyes of the ruling British army during the daily morning medical convoy between West Jerusalem and Mt. Scopus. The convoy was pinned down with people dying in their vehicles. Only after many hours did the British Army disperse the Arab attackers. Contempt for the British will remain with me always. As Dad used to say, "I can forgive but I won't forget."

After the evacuation of Mt. Scopus, Hadassah Hospital resumed functioning in several old buildings, including a former harem, in Jerusalem. Hadassah proceeded to plan and build a new hospital on the western side of the city, in Ein Kerem, amidst warnings that it would be too far from the city's population centers. Are the myopic naysayers able to praise Hadassah's leadership as they now can see how the city has spread westward to the hospital? In December 1967, six months after the Six-Day War, Mom, Marcia, and I gazed on the vandalized structure of the once beautiful Mt. Scopus Hospital left deserted and unprotected by the Jordanians. How resplendent it was again when it reopened in 1975.

One might well connect the conception by New Yorkers of America as revealed by the famed cover of *The New Yorker* magazine with my conception of Israel's map. For New Yorkers, two-thirds of the United States is situated east of the Hudson River; on my map Hadassah's installations comprise two-thirds of Israel.

Hadassah, so important in my mother's life, dominated our home in Aliquippa. Within a year of settling in, Marcia became president of the Aliquippa chapter. After filling many of the regional chairs, she was elected president of Western Pennsylvania Region which included Pittsburgh. To meet the challenge she acquired a wealth of knowledge of

Jewish history and religion by reading old and contemporary literature, attending workshops locally, in New York, and at national conventions. When she was a panelist, she'd cram to be at least one step ahead.

Hadassah mailings were ubiquitous in the house. We read the monthly Hadassah Magazine from cover to cover. And our trips to Israel? Over half were Hadassah-sponsored or related. On a presidents' tour I was one of seven husbands with twenty-three regional presidents. I was later to report, "How would you like being on a trip with twenty-three Marcias?"

Young Judaea, Hadassah's youth organization, became one of Marcia's loves. She served on the advisory committee for years, helping to choose its directors so vital to the management and personality of the club. Though Raina and Amy were involved with B'nai Brith Youth Organization and spent summers at Camp Ramah (under the sponsorship of the Jewish Theological Seminary of America), Marcia was able early to direct Danny to Young Judaea. From the very outset Danny was fired with a spirit of camaraderie and commitment to Jewish values and to Israel. Over the years Danny's weekend activities were dominated by local and Pittsburgh Young Judaea meetings and activities and summers, by camping at Hendersonville, North Carolina (at which Raina was a counselor,) and, ultimately, Tel Yehudah in the Catskills. With Young Judaea he spent six weeks in Israel (his second visit). With youth leaders of Zionist movements from all over the world he spent a pivotal year in Israel before starting college. To this day, Young Judaeans and year-course participants are among Danny's closest friends here in Israel and in the States.

In so many other ways our family is linked with Hadassah. Marcia's sister Elaine was a frequent contributor of book reviews for chapter meetings in New York and Connecticut. Marcia's mother Madge was a Life Member. One Hadassah promotional film by chance shows Madge with her gorgeous white hair walking out of a Hadassah building in Jerusalem.

What else did we receive for all of our family's efforts?

1. Our daughter-in-law Shira's Uncle Eli was transported to Haifa from Cairo via France in 1949 by Youth Aliyah.

2. Zvika, our son-in-law, graduated from Hadassah Community College in Jerusalem in 1980.

3. Raina graduated from Hadassah Medical School in 1988, perhaps the first Life Member to do so.

4. Shira graduated from Hadassah's School of Occupational Therapy in 1988. In 1993 she was the first recipient of a master's degree in occupational therapy given by the Hebrew University.

5. Maia and Tamar, Raina and Zvika's daughters, were born at the Mt. Scopus unit of Hadassah Hospital, delivered by a midwife trained at Hadassah Hospital.

6. While at Hebrew University, Danny lived in *Hamagshimim Bayit* (a subsidized apartment for college age and older Young Judaeans) in Jerusalem. There he served as an adviser for resident-members of the movement.

7. My five months of volunteering at Hadassah Hospital between 1979 and 1983 completed the requirements for specialty certification in Nuclear Medicine.

Only Marcia, who worked to make all but the first event possible, is without an institutional certificate from Hadassah; a three-generation Life Membership pin hardly qualifies. How many youngsters and their families joined the Zionist ranks because of her organizing, inspiring, funding, and chauffeuring! How many visits to Israel she promoted! How many made *aliyah* because of her! As an example of her craftiness, she once argued in favor of giving a camp scholarship to a youngster from an affluent family feigning financial hardship. She chuckles, "The kid enjoyed the summer so much that the family was hooked into many subsequent summers, paying full fees. And Hadassah got the family too."

She is a past president of Tel Aviv Hadassah and even to this day is its driving force. She founded the Hebrew-speakers' chapter of Tel Aviv. She has served in many capacities on the National Board and continues to do so.

In December 1999 Marcia was voted "Volunteer of the Year" by

Hadassah Israel. Above and beyond that, I bestow upon her an Honorary Doctorate of Family Zionism at Hadassah University. And, of course, I, too, am one of the beneficiaries of all her labors.

THE CHAMOVITZ COLLECTION

It is doubtful that Sothebys would give more than a passing glance to the artwork that adorns our apartment walls. However, the word "adorn" says it all, for each item is a treasure to Marcia and me. I love being the docent for our many visitors as I describe each one and relate its unique story.

Working in the Nuclear Medicine Department at Wolfson Hospital I became acquainted with E. Modzelevich. During the course of his test, he gave me an announcement of an exhibition of his work at Kibbutz Bar-On in the Galilee. By chance soon after, during our annual visit to Safed in 1994, we detoured and arrived at the exhibit minutes before closing time. We purchased an impressionistic riverside lithograph of city buildings reflected in the water in blues and brown. Modzelevich died in 1999.

Hanging next to the Modzelevich is a brown, soft pencil drawing of the Western Wall by Steffa Reis made in 1970. In 1979 during my first stint of volunteering at Hadassah Hospital and living in Jerusalem, I arranged a forty-ninth birthday party for Marcia. One of the guests was Mura Zonis, a Jew converted to Christian Science, and cousin to our friend Mort Zonis from Boston. Mura was the manager of an art shop in the Intercontinental Hotel (now called Seven Arches) on Mt. Scopus and it was she who gave Marcia *The Western Wall.*

Under the category of Jewish geography is the following incident. Haifa friends Jack and Gila Abrahamson called – it was 1989 – to say that they would be spending a couple of days in Tel Aviv. Agreeing to come to dinner, they asked if they could bring a lady friend, an artist. During that dinner the friend asked Marcia if we were renters.

"Yes."

"The furniture is rented?"

"No."

"The paintings belong to the apartment?"

"No."

She thereupon turned in her chair, pointed to *The Western Wall*, and exclaimed, "That's my drawing! (We hadn't realized that our guest was Steffa Reis.) Where did you get it?"

Marcia told her its story, adding with a grin, "If you didn't get your fee from Miss Zonis, the dinner is your payment." Steffa accepted Marcia's terms.

Next on the wall is a gift from Dr. Narayan Shetty in Aliquippa in gratitude for my medical care of his father-in-law. It is a picture from India of two lovers, created in shades of wood inlays.

Many times a year we encounter photographs or movies of the Brooklyn Bridge, which Marcia with violin in hand walked across numerous times in her youth. When she visited an exhibition in New York of the work of Peter Zonis, son of friend Mort Zonis, Marcia spotted her bridge and purchased it. This lithograph, primarily in pastel blue, is lovingly hung above our TV.

In a corner wall next to large windows catching the morning sunlight is a gold and silver paper collage, called *Moon Sea* created by Laura Kaplan Popenoe, an established artist and friend of Marcia's from Music and Art High School in New York. It symbolizes a Japanese haiku poem:

Broken and broken
Again on the sea,
The moon so easily mends.

The massive immigration of Russians to Israel in the early nineties brought numerous artists and musicians. Superb musicians would initially support themselves by playing solo on street corners or in quartets along the beach. It wasn't long before they were filling the chairs of three new symphony orchestras. Thus it was also with artists whose wares were exhibited in street markets until they found placement as teachers and resident artists at universities.

One Russian, Kabischer, displayed his work in 1995 near the Shuk HaCarmel in Tel Aviv. Marcia and I, having initially decided to buy a painting just to support this artist, independently selected the same watercolor, a bleak winter view of gabled Russians houses. Kabischer now teaches in Haifa.

Next to the Kabischer work is that of my cousin Joseph Young given to us for arranging the funeral of his father, my Uncle Lou. It is a bold, black, brush painting of a Chassid with arms enfolding a Torah. In the background are a candelabrum and a Star of David. The pious Jew portrayed could have been, not his father, but his grandfather. Joe is a famous muralist and mosaic artist. We once sent it to him for a show in California. Anyone visiting in the Pittsburgh area must take a ride to Midland to the Catholic Church to see Joe's *The Presentation of the Blessed Virgin*, a mosaic of Italian ceramic tiles. Look closely and you will see Joe and his wife as Mary's parents and daughters as Mary and an angel. Joe also completed a mosaic in a chapel of the National Cathedral in Washington, D.C. in time for the marriage of Lucy, daughter of President Lyndon and Ladybird Johnson. Joe's latest accomplishment as an architectural artist is a Holocaust Memorial in Los Angeles.

Three floral works are grouped together. The first is a watercolor of pansies by Nora Frenkel. Nora, an Israeli for thirty-five years, was a classmate of Marcia's at Music and Art High School. In an exhibition here (she had also exhibited in the States) we saw large canvases of whirling snow scenes in New York City and impressionistic characterizations of kitchenware. Our painting is one of a group of exercises Nora executed in 1991 during the Gulf War. Anxious to avoid the numerous Scuds falling on Tel Aviv, she fled with her daughter and grandchildren north to Mikhmoret Beach. She took with her, a pad of drawing paper, watercolors, and brushes. Each day she went to a nursery to purchase the healthiest of flowers. Nora succumbed, in 1995, after an arduous struggle with cancer. Occasional visits for Scrabble with Marcia and medical support from me weren't much to offer. Her last work, a series of self-portraits, exhibited at the Tel Aviv Museum of Art, chronicled the ravages of chemotherapy and her disease, too realistic and pitiful to confront.

Below Nora's work is a watercolor of green foliage painted by our close friend Trudy Katzenberg. Trudy, a highly respected teacher of family therapy in New York, Chicago, and Israel, had studied art in New York. She is equally skilled in watercolor, charcoal, and oil.

We first met Trudy and her husband Joe when apartment hunting in Tel Aviv. We subsequently moved into their building for our first year in Tel Aviv, and became close friends. If Joe had been a Jewish scholar, I might now be a learned Jew. Alas, he was a tennis buff and so I, too, became one. Joe also introduced me to the world of Etzel, an acronym for Irgun Zvai Leumi, an organization founded in 1931 by Ze'ev Jabotinsky who broke away from Haganah in order to force the British out of Palestine more aggressively. Joe arrived from Czechoslovakia in 1938 at age thirteen, and by 1941, recruited by Etzel, he was blowing up bridges and railroad tracks. He traveled to the United States on an assignment in 1946, but did not return to Israel until asked to be part of the honor guard escorting the body of Ze'ev Jabotinsky. Joe and Trudy made *aliyah* in 1973.

The third floral piece is one of four needlepoint works in our living room. It was embroidered by a Pittsburgh friend, Ethel Comay. Ethel spends her winters in Tel Aviv. Her deceased husband Amos had been an outstanding philanthropist and a tireless worker for Israel and Jewish education. Their son, Shalom, also deceased, had been President of the American Jewish Committee.

Two embroidered items frame our front door. One is the Two Tablets of the Law – the ten commandments – by our friend Harriet Karp in Aliquippa. The background is blue, the writing, white. The second is Marcia's sister Elaine's *mezuzah* (an encased prayer placed on the doorpost of Jewish homes), embroidered over an oatmeal box. The wool box adheres to a gold velvet base with black stitched grillwork around it. Above the *mezuzah* is the Hebrew letter, *shin*, the initial of the name of God. A crown sits above the *shin.* Inside the box are the required Hebrew prayers as inscribed by Elaine's daughter Vicki.

Over the piano is the fourth needlepoint from a large French tapestry entitled, *Tree of Birds*. It is a magnificent work by Marcia's sister Elaine given to us for our fifteenth anniversary in 1969. Its orange and brown colors remain as vivid as on the day we received it.

One of the gifts from cousins Sidney and Rose Eger for taking care of their children in 1965, while they visited Israel, is a watercolor by a well-known Israeli artist, David Gilboa. It shows a sad, old, bearded Jew wearing a workman's cap.

Above the Gilboa is an oil portrait of Marcia painted in January 1949 by Harvey Dinnerstein while he was a student at the Tyler School of Fine Arts at Temple University. In addition to posing for her long-time friend Harvey, Marcia sat that one afternoon in Philadelphia for other soon-to-be prominent artists including Danny Schwartz, Burt Silverman, and Herb Steinberg. Marcia was eighteen at the time and a freshman at Sarah Lawrence College. Harvey, who became quite famous, must have been in his Modigliani period since Marcia's face has never been so elongated.

Continuing to the left is an oil, a scene of a narrow alley between old apartment buildings in Jerusalem with vague walking figures, at least one a Chassid. Danny bought it while spending the year after high school in Israel. Artist? "Sara C."

Behind our dining-room table is a numbered lithograph of a robust rooster by Reuven Rubin, Israel's most famous artist. My father-in-law bought it in Israel in 1959. Amy at age five years said, "Someone splashed the painting." Of course, that was Rubin's style, various-sized dots scattered over his paintings. Rubin's home, which was donated to the city by his widow, is now the Rubin Museum, located in our neighborhood. Marcia takes tourists there so often that she is treated like a docent.

My tour continues into our back rooms. There are two lithographs by an Argentinean, A. Goldstein purchased at the United Synagogue convention at the Concord about 1969 at a booth tended by Naomi

Meyer, wife of Rabbi Marshall Meyer of the Buenos Aires congregation. This has special meaning for us: Marshall was Marcia's childhood friend and the first Conservative rabbi in South America. One painting, dated 1966, in yellow- and-black is entitled *Simchat Torah* and shows two Jews dancing with Torahs. The second, dated 1967, in shades of blue, shows massive waves of water threatening three figures in black, one of whom is beseeching the heavens for respite. It is called *Jonah.*

Two others are painted by friend Saul Dorn who was a veterinarian in Aliquippa. One is a watercolor of our house in Aliquippa drawn after its completion in 1958. The other is an oil of Aliquippa's Jones and Laughlin Steel Mill along the Ohio River as seen from the hills of Plan 7, in 1966.

Another veterinarian, Dick Lasday, took up painting late in life. In 1997, he presented us with an oil, a quiet winter scene of a barn.

We acquired an oil painting by Hal Miller, married to my cousin, Bea Eger. Hal died in November 1997; Bea gave us the painting when we visited Memphis during *shiva.* It shows wheat fields in front of a water-cooling tower (associated with a nuclear reactor). Hal had been known as *Happy Hal*, the pivotal character of a children's TV program.

Our latest acquisition is a print of a watercolor illustration of two birds sitting on a flowering branch. Marcia bought it in Tel Aviv at an exhibit of the work of Walter (Bill) Ferguson. I first met Bill while taking a stroll in Beit Yanai, north of Netanya. My host introduced us and in the course of a brief conversation I learned that Bill's wife had gone to Music and Art High School. Relating this to Marcia at our host's home, Marcia exclaimed, "Is Ferguson's first name, Walter?" Marcia recalled that she had been in grammar school with him and then in another school in eighth grade where she last saw him. "Walter could draw anything." An hour later Marcia had a reunion with Walter. It was a delight to observe them reminiscing. Walter had made *aliyah* in 1965 and is an established illustrator of wildlife.

How can I omit our granddaughter Maia's first drawing? It's a butterfly in watercolor. At two and a half years she showed ease with brush and pencil.

Completing our collection are two sculpture pieces. One is a ten-inch iron cellist, a gift from Norman and Charlotte Thomashefsky when we departed for Israel. The other is an eight-inch bronze piece called *The Lovers*. The flow of a woman's arms around her lover's chest conveys gentle intimacy. The sculptor, Shoshana Shir, a Hadassah friend of Marcia's, has exhibited in Israel and in Europe.

I have saved our masterpiece for the last. It is a large gouache by Avraham Ofek (ofek means, "dawn"). Marcia's father bought it for us in Israel in 1967 despite my mother-in-law's having chided his impulsiveness, "Irving, what do you know about art?" Blues and greens predominate, revealing cacti in the foreground; a donkey, two faceless peasants behind on the left, and a blockhouse opposite them on the right. And now for its tale.

On one of our open-house *Succot* parties on our roof – it was 1991 – we invited a surgeon from Wolfson Hospital, Meir Crispin, and his wife Hani. Unlike most guests who brought wine or candy, they brought a book, a catalogue of the work of Avraham Ofek. It had been prepared for a posthumous exhibition. Marcia expressed delight, saying that we owned one of Ofek's paintings.

"That's not possible," Hani insisted. "We're familiar with every one of his paintings." We immediately took Meir and Hani down to our apartment to show them our Ofek. They were dismayed at never having seen this painting.

I said, "That's understandable since it had been in Aliquippa for seventeen years and then for an additional seven here in Israel."

Hani, asked, "Didn't you know that Avraham Ofek was Meir's brother?" Of course not. She explained, "There were three brothers. Their father had died before Avraham was born. Their mother died when he was seven months; Reuven was seven and Meir was eleven. Living in Bulgaria, each was adopted by a different family. Avraham had begun to paint in Sofia at twelve. His adoptive family made *aliyah* in 1949 – he was fourteen. He married at twenty-two and Hebraicized his name to Ofek.

"Meir had remained in touch with Reuven in Bulgaria and continued to do so after moving to Israel. In 1958 a hospital employee told him that she saw someone on TV 'who is the spitting image of you.' Meir called the TV station and that's how he was reunited with his baby brother."

Ofek died in 1990. In 1991 his work from 1956 to 1986 was exhibited in Ein Hod. I presumed that the exhibit organizers were also unaware of the existence of our painting. If it had been catalogued, it would have fallen into Ofek's Wadi Ara period in which he concentrated on Arab housing.

After this revelation, I photographed the painting and sent a print to Ofek's widow offering to lend it for future shows. (Originally purchased for $150, it was appraised at $3,000 in 1994. I mention the dollar amount only to credit my father-in-law with a keen eye for artistic value.) There was no reply until December 1997 when Marcia received a call from the Haifa Museum of Art, asking for permission to view our Ofek for possible inclusion in an exhibition, "Social Realism in the 50's – Political Art in the 90's." Eventually it was taken to Haifa. We visited our Ofek, amused and proud to see it prominently displayed – "Collection David and Marcia Chamovitz, Tel Aviv."

I remember well the advice given to us as we prepared our *aliyah:* "It helps ease culture shock if you take with you as many familiar objects as possible." We couldn't bring people, but the art work, we could. Seventeen of the twenty-five items listed here had been in our home in Aliquippa. We were acutely aware of the wisdom of this admonition when these seventeen "friends" joined us from America.

Can we be called Jewish chauvinists? Of course, since only the Indian wood inlay has no Jewish connection. Almost all the works are by Israeli artists, family, or significant American Jewish artists, friends of Marcia. Only the Ofek has a somber mood, the others, light and open. The colors blend from one painting to another and with the furnishings.

We enjoy our apartment. The art work is a crucial factor.

INTO THE FRAY ON BEHALF OF REFUSENIKS

Who could read Elie Wiesel's *Jews of Silence* and not hear the call to action? His description of *Simchat Torah* (a joyous holiday) on Archipova Street in Moscow was so powerful, his presence there so epochal in the struggle to liberate Jews from the Soviet Union, that we felt we had to replicate his journey. We had to follow in his footsteps, to contribute in whatever way the opportunity might present itself. And we did contribute.

Wiesel's visit took place in 1965; he wrote about it in 1966. Soon after reading his book in 1971, we began planning our visit for that autumn. It was fortuitous to have had an introduction to Moses Schoenfeld, dinner speaker for Western Pennsylvania Israel Bonds. Moses, a freelance United Nations correspondent, was from an illustrious British family. (His wife was involved with placing Russian-Jewish musicians in American symphony orchestras. At her request we hosted a Russian violinist who auditioned and received a position with the Pittsburgh Symphony Orchestra.)

Moses, himself an activist on behalf of Soviet Jews, deduced that our intentions were not capricious and gave us the name of Gabriel

Shapiro, a *refusenik* in Moscow. The word *refusenik* referred to a Russian Jew whose application for an exit visa was refused.

We also met with Jerry Goodman at the office for Soviet Jewry in New York. Jerry gave us hints as to appropriate behavior in the USSR, most particularly, to comport ourselves as inconspicuously as possible. He promised to supply us with reading materials for distribution to Jews we would encounter. On this same New York visit we contacted a travel agent who dealt with Intourist, the Soviet tour agency. We structured the tour so that we would be in Leningrad (the name was to become St. Petersburg again years later) for *Shmini Atzeret* (the last day of *Succot)* while permitting sufficient time to be in Moscow the following evening for *Simchat Torah*.

Why our focus on *Simchat Torah*? Wiesel described the evolution of the mass movement for *aliyah* especially among young Muscovites. It had become a custom to advertise on university campuses, "The operetta *Simchat Torah* will be performed the night of . . . on Archipova Street at the hour of . . ." News of the event spread as far as Tashkent, 2,000 miles from Moscow. On that night every year, beginning with a few hundred students in 1961, and increasing to thousands of young people raised in anti-religious homes, thronged the street at the Choral Synagogue of Moscow. They did not venture inside, of course, where mainly old Jews were praying. Stories abound of people meeting in disbelief, saying to one another, "I didn't know you were Jewish." Or the father in shock at the sight of his son, never realizing that the son had known that he was Jewish. We *had* to be a part of that throng.

Our first task was to gather as many religious items as possible. Harriet Karp, a friend, gave us her father's *tallit*; from Dad, we got another *tallit* and two sets of *tefillin*. But how were we to explain having two sets of *tefillin* to Russian customs inspectors? Only one is worn during morning prayers. This problem was solved when I learned from my rabbi of Rabbi Tam who wore two sets of *tefillin* simultaneously. We proceeded to collect *chai* pendants (whose two Hebrew letters mean life) and Star of David pins – we initially wore them to be more easily recognized as Jews.

We were chagrined at not receiving the books promised by Jerry

Goodman. Lo and behold, as we sat with seat-belts fastened at Kennedy Airport, an announcement came over the plane's loudspeaker, "Will Dr. Chamovitz please identify himself?" I complied sheepishly, certain that our cover was now blown. (We had been doing our best to keep a low profile.) A messenger handed us a large, brown paper bag filled with books – Russian-Hebrew dictionaries, Russian-English calendars with the Jewish holidays highlighted, and Leon Uris's historical novel *Exodus* in Russian. All of these were in short supply in Russia, available only via the underground press, *Samizdat*. We felt that all eyes were on us, including, we imagined, those of the KGB (the Russian secret police).

Our travel agent initially routed us via Munich but we vetoed that, still of a mindset that precluded setting foot in Germany. Instead we flew to Helsinki, Finland where we transferred to an Aeroflot (Soviet) plane.

It was still daytime as we landed in Leningrad. We approached two customs lines carrying our handbags and suitcases. We shied away from one inspector who was meticulously searching the bags of a returning young Russian, confiscating a copy of *Playboy*. Our choice was provident. The inspector, pointing to my carry-on bag, asked, "What's in here?" Not knowing the "correct" answer, I admitted, "religious and photographic equipment." Bingo! Without opening this or any of our suitcases, he cleared us. Was the customs officer a Jew? Certainly he could have profited on the black market from items he might have confiscated.

We were terrorized by the taxi ride into the city. We saw two huge billboards showing vile anti-Semitic cartoons. One I remember vividly showed a skullcap-wearing, hooked-nosed caricature of a vicious Jew holding a blood-dripping dagger poised over a cowering Arab woman and child. Our unspoken apprehension was now validated. We were in enemy territory – freedom riders entering Mississippi.

When we had our passports retained by the hotel reservation clerk, it added to our feeling of being in jeopardy. No one smiled or offered any greeting. Also having a hostile appearing woman on our floor, in custody of the key whenever we left our room, struck us as an infringement of our civil rights. We considered our primary mission, and accepted the situation. Mindful of the possibility of our room being bugged, we avoided saying anything controversial. I was concerned that the toilet flushed too slowly and too incompletely should the need arise to hastily dispose of incriminating documents. Our precautions were not without merit: this was the Soviet Union in the days of Brezhnev, the successor of Malenkov, Bulganin, and Khrushchev.

In preparation for our trip I obtained a letter of introduction from an old friend, Jesse Steinfeld, M.D., who at the time was Surgeon General under President Nixon. On arrival I submitted this letter to Intourist with a request to visit a hospital. Within days I was told that a visit was arranged for three weeks later, ten days after our planned departure. Again, cognizant of the primary purposes of our visit, I elected not to create a fuss. In the end I would get my wish – well, not exactly. Wandering through the Kiev airport prior to our departure, I came upon a medical clinic – or was it a museum? The attending doctor, who looked every bit like a washerwoman, showed me her stethoscope. It was a five-inch wooden, hollow tube, flared at each end, one end to be applied to the patient's chest, the other, to the doctor's ear. This was 1971; no, not 1871.

In each of the three cities we were to visit, we arranged half-day tours in order to give the semblance of ordinary tourists. That first morning in Leningrad we were taken to the Winter Palace, the Hermitage, and marveled at so many Rembrandts. The following morning we attended services at the Great Synagogue. Its *succah* was spacious but stark, obviously with no children to decorate it. We were told that the Synagogue remained in Jewish hands only because Jews maintained a constant presence there even during the siege of Leningrad in WW II.

In the balcony, the women's section, Marcia met eighteen-year old Anna Klabanyer. Anna was dressed shabbily with only her face and hands exposed, her countenance sad. From that initial meeting until we left Leningrad, Anna attached herself to Marcia, separating only at bedtime. She had graduated from high school but had not been accepted into a university. (The letter "E," meaning Hebrew in Russian, on her identity card had increasingly become an obstacle to acceptance into a university and to obtaining desirable jobs.) Still a member of *Komsomol*, the Communist Youth Organization, she volunteered as a cleaning woman at the Hermitage.

Anna's was the first name that we took for the purpose of helping to obtain invitations from "family" in Israel. This fiction would enable her to qualify under Soviet law for an exit visa to Israel. In addition, once satisfied with her authenticity, we referred Anna to Gabriel Shapiro in Moscow, the only contact we had with the *refusenik* community.

Through Anna we met a number of young people who also latched on to us. We were the pied pipers as the pack walking with us enlarged. We accumulated more names and more stories. To one, the *melamed* (a Hebrew teacher), who was in violation of the law which prohibited teaching Hebrew, we gave a *tallit* and *tefillin* and some of our reading material; he pointed out that fewer teaching aides were available in Leningrad than in Moscow. Two others I remember: Felix, an engineer, and Helen, a teacher. Each sought help with *aliyah*.

We arrived in Moscow in the early afternoon in time to make a trial run to the Choral Synagogue. The taxi driver appeared reluctant to help but after some cajoling, he said, "Oh, synagoga" and off we went to Archipova Street. A block or two from the *shul* there was a large red banner strung across the street. It presumably proclaimed commemorative celebrations of the Russian revolution. Jesting, I translated for Marcia, "Welcome, Religious Zionists of America."

To our delight, the synagogue, located halfway down a gentle slope, was only a twenty-five-minute walk from our hotel. Attached to the right side of the synagogue was an old two-story apartment house, to the left, a storage garage. There was a two-story hospital across the street. To the left of that structure was a large yard containing a totally enclosed green armored van. We were told that inside, the KGB watched with cameras and bugging devices. The street itself was approximately thirty feet wide with little traffic.

From the sidewalk several steps led up between four large white pillars to the *shul's* doors. This grand house of worship before the revolution in 1917 had once been crowded with men of all ages wearing shoulder-to-ankle *tallitot* who prayed along with eminent cantors. Now it was used only by a handful of old men. The many lighting fixtures contained naked bulbs. The pews were warped, cracked, and scarred. There was a shabby central reading table but at the far end, a magnificent *torah* ark made of marble with gold-leaf decorations.

We met no one but did accomplish our mission, which was to be certain of arriving on time for the performance of the "operetta." With a street map and self-taught Russian alphabet Marcia got us back to our hotel after a brief stop to view Red Square. We elected then and on numerous other trampings on the Square not to get in line to view Lenin's glass-encased sarcophagus. The whole idea of preserving Lenin for all to view was too repugnant and pagan. (For related, albeit different reasons, years later we chose not to be voyeurs in the red-light district in Amsterdam.)

We returned during the light of the early evening of *Simchat Torah* to find small clusters of Russians huddled in silence outside the Synagogue. Marcia and I entered; she climbed the stairs to the women's section. *Maariv* (evening) services had begun. I took a seat near the back on the aisle; no prayer books were available. Soon a once in a lifetime experience occurred. It happened during the *hakafot*, the parading with the Torahs. On the second or third go-round someone handed me a Torah, less than one-half the usual size, to carry in a complete circle within the *shul*. I was bursting with emotion as I clutched the Torah, parading in the crowded aisles, receiving the blessings of numerous old men and, I do believe, women too, as they kissed the fingers that had reached out to touch my Torah. Imagine *them* with their joyless lives blessing *me* who had everything. I was conscious that these were the people we had come to help. Did they all know, I wondered, that ten years before, Premier Khrushchev had announced that Russian Jews wishing to be united with family in Israel would be permitted to do so?

Outside was another story, as we were to discover after the *hakafot*. Now nighttime, the street was swarming with Jews moving from one group to another. The *New York Times* reported that there were 50,000 people on the street. It was a given that there were members of the

KGB in our midst. We have a photograph taken the following day of one man standing against the wall opposite the *shul* wearing glasses and what looked like a false nose. There was no question in my mind that he was one, that is, until I saw his picture years later during a lecture on newcomers to Tel Aviv.

It was obvious to all that Marcia and I were western visitors: my wide necktie, our jewelry, our cheerfulness. Like Rothschild stationed in a corner of the stock exchange with supplicants waiting in line for advice, we were approached by individuals and couples in patches of darkness. We communicated with broken English and body language. We were greeted with furtive smiles, they more aware than we that KGB cameras were doubtlessly rolling. The encounters were brief, almost always concluding with a handshake during which a scrap of paper was transferred to Marcia or to me. It took a leap of faith for them to put their lives on the line for we, too, could have been KGB.

We pocketed these scraps for later translation from Russian to Hebrew, but we already knew that these were requests for invitations from "family" in Israel, the first step in initiating the interminable, exasperating process leading to an exit visa. Most of the notes contained only names and addresses of those seeking to leave. Others suggested detailed ploys such as the following: "We had an aunt named 'Fanya,' a doctor. Fanya served in the army in Leningrad but was lost presumably in battle and never again heard from. Let a letter come from Fanya in Jerusalem whether living or dead." In all we pocketed over twenty-five requests. These, Marcia stitched into her coat lining, a ruse, we subsequently learned, well-known to the Russians.

It was inspiring to see, among the few other westerners in that crowd, a delightful young Argentinean couple combining Zionism with a honeymoon.

From several in the crowd we inquired as to the whereabouts of Gabriel Shapiro. We were told that he would arrive late. And so he did. A tall, thin, flaming redhead with piercing eyes approached with a broad smile. Here was our entree into the inner circle of the Russian *aliyah* movement. We warmed to one another instantly sharing comments about our mutual friend, Moses Schoenfeld. His English was functional but required great effort. Gabriel gave directions for meeting us the following evening. We parted, but not before he reinforced the necessity for keeping a low profile.

There were three instances involving people who failed to heed this admonition. One I read in the Jewish press, concerned a tourist from Chicago who blew a *shofar* in Red Square. He was immediately whisked out of the Square and evicted from the country. What did this idiot accomplish? If anything, he raised the surveillance level of Jewish visitors by the Soviets.

The second event involved my protégé, Eddie Perlow, a Pittsburgh lawyer. While we sat on the bus to a convention of the United Synagogue of America, I related tales of our recent trip to the Soviet Union. Eddie took the bait and on returning to Pittsburgh, began planning a trip with his wife and their three children. Within a month or two, well after *Simchat Torah*, he retraced our steps. All was going well until three days prior to their planned departure from Russia. Sitting in the Choral Synagogue in Moscow Eddie expressed dismay and anger, not in *sotto voce*, at the Soviet government for not allowing the printing of Jewish prayer books. A KGB agent in the audience heard Eddie and escorted him and his family back to their hotel and arranged for their immediate expulsion from Russia.

The third incident may not have been due to anyone's indiscretion. The KGB broke into the Moscow apartment of Professor Alexander Lerner who was hosting a clandestine meeting of *refuseniks* with New York Congressman James Scheuer. With the ruse that he didn't have his passport – how could he when his hotel had confiscated it – Scheuer was arrested, taken to the police station, and detained for forty-five minutes. How fortuitous, for now Scheuer could give personal testimony to the repressive nature of the Soviet regime.

On the morning of *Simchat Torah* we walked back to the Synagogue. On our way we fell in step with a forty-year-old scholarly looking, short, bearded man carrying a package wrapped in newspaper. Learning who we were, he opened the wrapping, revealing a prayer book. It was obvious that this book wasn't something he wanted to display to a passerby. That morning we also met mustached Zalman who had come from Tashkent to meet foreigners. Like our escorts in Leningrad, he followed us around satisfying himself that we would do what was necessary to help him get out.

Outside the synagogue the crowd was considerably smaller and older than on the previous night. Uniformed policemen were clearly visible, but not the KGB. A Georgian Jew was dancing. Slightly intoxicated, – on *Simchat Torah* a little *schnapps* is a *mitzvah* – in one hand he grasped an exit visa while in the other he held a plane ticket to Israel; he was leaving the next day.

That evening, as prearranged, we met Gabriel Shapiro in the subway. We rode together silently. Once we ascended to the open street he unfolded his personal tale of struggles to leave Russia. "They won't let you leave."

I commented that his "leave" sounded like "live."

"Both. They won't let you live or leave," again both words sounding different only to him.

David and Georgian Jew in front of Moscow Synagogue.

Eventually we arrived at the home of Israel Sivashensky, an eminent high-school mathematics teacher whose college preparatory books were classics. He lived on the threshold of poverty with his wife, son Gregory, and daughter Vicki. At this point in his life he was destitute. For having applied for an exit visa, he lost his job; his books were banned. We found him a withdrawn, depressed, emasculated human being. As we sat with the family, Gabriel worked feverishly to translate the rapid exchange of information. Gregory and Vicki described their expulsion from *Komsomol*. They gave us a red membership pin worn by Communist youth; to us it was a gift, but for them, a political statement.

A close friend of the Sivashenskys, Paul Goldstein, a philosopher and writer, sat unobtrusively in a corner of the living room.

As the evening progressed, Gabriel experienced increasing difficulty in translating. "My jaws hurt." Accordingly he phoned a friend to come help him and to meet us. Within minutes in walked Professor Lerner (in whose apartment Congressman Scheuer was later to be arrested), a short, chubby, cheerful man, resembling a businessman like so many of our uncles. Little did we know that it was as if Albert Einstein had entered the room. Lerner was a renowned professor of cybernetics; he had lectured all over the world. He was highly esteemed by the Russian academic community, acquiring perks of a luxurious apartment, a *dacha* (a summer home) in the Crimea, a car, and a grand piano. His daughter Sonya had appeared on the cover of a magazine, like *Time*, as the youngest woman ever to enter a Soviet medical school. When we met, she had started the first year. Son Vladimir, like his father, was a computer specialist. Lerner's English was competent. He was open and, despite his predicament, humorous. Of course, unlike Sivashensky, should he be fired from his job, he would have no immediate financial problem.

The following evening we were hosted by the Lerner family. Vladimir played the guitar and accompanied Sonya, who sang for us. They did not appear apprehensive over the coming upheaval in their lives. The family's earlier personal history explained Mrs. Lerner's depressed demeanor. They had two older daughters, who in 1939 were visiting their grandmother near the Polish border. Learning by short-wave radio that Hitler had invaded Russia only an hour or two before, Lerner sent a telegram to his mother-in-law telling her to immediately return to Moscow with his daughters. Tragedy struck. Stalin had issued orders cutting all communication with the western front. The telegram was never received. All three perished at the hands of the Germans.

Lerner gave us a typewritten essay he asked to have published in the *New York Times*. He also asked that we contact his American colleagues to have them publicize in the newspaper the dire predicament that was to follow his application for an exit visa and to appeal to the United States government to intercede on his behalf. We had been asked by Sivashensky to do likewise for him. We learned that the better the *refusenik* was known in America, the less likely that any harm would befall him.

It was ten days later in Athens that we read in the *International Herald Tribune* that Lerner had applied for an exit visa to Israel a few days after we met. His fairy-tale existence came to an abrupt halt. He was summarily fired from his university positions and booted out of the Party. Sonya was expelled from medical school. Vladimir, who had married a gentile who hated Jews, lost his job; his childless marriage ended in divorce when he too declared his intention to immigrate to Israel. His wife's anti-Semitism had initially posed no problem "since at the time we married, I was Jewish only by birth."

Lerner was also a marvelous artist. My snapshot of the family shows one of his paintings in the background; an old lady blessing *Shabbat* candles. As a present he gave us a charcoal drawing of a wooden village church. This we proudly displayed in our dining room in Aliquippa until years later when we passed it on to Sonya who was living in Rehovot long before her father was able to leave Moscow. We learned that Lerner's wife had died and that Sonya had been permitted to return for the funeral.

In the interest of chronology I will leave Lerner and Shapiro and continue on to Kiev, the third city of our tour. Initially our itinerary included Odessa where we were supposed to have met the family of Israel Yachnovich, Uncle Harry Jackson's oldest brother. Uncle Harry's two sisters were killed in the Holocaust by the Germans while Israel, the only brother who didn't immigrate to the United States, moved to safety in the Crimea.

Even though it was early October, a heavy snowfall in Moscow caused all planes to be grounded. We spent six hours at the airport waiting for a change in flying conditions. During that wait we were fortunate to commandeer chairs and to sit around a table, holding it by ordering tea from time to time. Sitting with us was an American couple, school teachers. As only happens to Marcia, the subject of the Rosenbergs came up because she had just read E. L. Doctorow's *The Book of Daniel.* This novel was really about the Rosenberg family. Our new companions, Jewish we learned, were on an American-Russian Friendship Society (Communist) tour. The husband asked, "Oh, you're interested in the Rosenberg sons? We took them in while Ethel and Julius were in jail awaiting trial, and ultimately until their execution as Russian spies in 1953." So much for a small world and Marcia's amazing ability for uncovering fascinating connections.

Finally Intourist rerouted us by overnight train to Kiev; as a result, we missed Odessa. We assumed that we would never again have the opportunity to meet Israel's son, David. Fate ordained otherwise; in 1990 we were in a position to expedite his absorption into Israel.

In lovely, old Kiev we encountered Indian-summer weather. However, considering the purpose of our trip, this particular visit was fruitless; we met no young people. At the *shul* in the Podel district we saw only old men sitting on splintered, wobbly pews. Managing with public transportation we crossed the Dnieper River twice to visit relatives of our Pittsburgh friend Doris Binstock. Her cousin Dina was married to a Lithuanian, Bumo, who was preparing their son for *bar mitzvah.* This family eventually got to Israel.

We were able to find the ruins of the Great Gates of Kiev. I posed for a photo, singing the theme from Moussorgsky's tone poem commemorating this massive structure. The imposing statue of Bogdan Chmielnicki on a rearing horse was not so pleasant. This tribal chieftain is revered by school children as leader of the uprising of Ukrainian peasants against Poland in 1648. There is probably no mention in the lesson plan of the massacre of 100,000 Jews by this "Chmiel the wicked."

Our last major visit was to Babi Yar. Previously, in Leningrad Marcia and I had met Mike, the editor of an anti-Bolshevik American Jewish journal published in New York. Mike and his wife had participated in a procession lasting many hours – it was Yom Kippur – from the Podel synagogue to Babi Yar to commemorate the thirtieth anniversary of the massacre of Jews by Germans and Ukranians. Jews came with wreaths and banners from all over Russia.

In contrast we arrived by cab and alone. We found the solitary marker, a three-foot-high stone on which was inscribed, "In memory of the 80,000 *Soviet citizens* murdered by the Nazis." No mention, of course, that almost all of the victims were Jews. Actually, we didn't see this inscription because of the flowers and banners remaining from the gathering two weeks before. "From the Jewish children of Kharkov," read one of the banners. We wandered around the wooded area where for years after the massacre, parts of skeletons made their way above ground, having been hastily and thinly covered over by their murderers. It was not difficult to imagine the cries, the shrieking, and the weeping amid the gunfire. In our hearts we blessed the writer, Yevtushenko, a gentile, for courageously memorializing Babi Yar with a poignant poem.

In a Moscow cab I sneezed. The driver said, "God bless you." I asked, "Did you hear what you said?" He made light of it by saying, "It's only an expression." In Kiev our guide said, "Thank God, we've had lovely weather." I questioned her as I had the Moscow taxi driver and she replied, "In the Ukraine we still have God."

Leaving Russia brought no respite from our anxiety, from constantly looking over our shoulders, until we left the Aeroflot plane at Athens Airport. The notes from the "handshakes" and the article by Lerner were potential reasons for incarceration had the KGB been inquisitive. Nor do I think that I was excessively dramatic in reminding myself of a Peter Lorre movie, when I entered a photography store in Athens. I had decided to make copies of all the notes and Lerner's letter. During the twenty minutes that the clerk took to return from the basement workshop, I imagined sirens blasting the air, police forcibly entering the shop grabbing me by the collar, handcuffing me, shoving me into a police van, and whisking me back to Lubyanka prison in Moscow. What a UJA talk that would have been when I was released in exchange for a Russian spy!

Moses Schoenfeld was awaiting our arrival at Kennedy Airport. It was only after transferring all our prized possessions that our mission was completed – or so we thought. For the next six months Marcia and I, either singly or together, were on the road speaking in synagogues, churches, schools, and meetings of fraternal organizations to publicize the plight of Soviet Jews. We raised a small amount of money, although this was less important than getting our audiences to sign petitions on behalf of Soviet Jews. We were interviewed by the press, both English and Jewish. We also made contacts with academia and congressmen to solicit aid for Lerner, Sivashensky, and Shapiro.

On one occasion after our trip we were successful in reaching Gabriel Shapiro on the phone. He told us he had been threatened by efforts to draft him into the army, a death sentence for a Jew known to be a *refusenik*.

What else could be done for Gabriel? A young American activist, Judy Silver, traveled to Moscow with her rabbi to arrange a marriage with Gabriel. From Gabriel we later learned that this marriage was merely a ploy, at least in his mind. When we hosted Judy in Aliquippa in her campaign to have Gabriel brought to America, it seemed that she was hoping that it would be more than a ploy. Maybe this too was part of the ploy. They divorced after Gabriel got to Israel.

What the trip to Russia meant to us certainly should be evident. We knew that we had seized an opportunity to participate in what was, and what continues to be, a historical chapter in the 4,000-year saga of the Jewish people. But I ask myself, "Did our trip accomplish anything?" Of course. "Did we not give solace and hope to all who met us in the three cities of our tour?" Certainly. "Did any of these Russians get out?" Yes, many. Though there probably were other Americans acting on behalf of those I am about to enumerate, we, at least, were among their earliest contacts.

We met Anna Klabanyer from Leningrad in Carmiel in 1974 (the year we met all the others listed below, excepting Professor Lerner). She was transformed from a timorous teenager to a vivacious young woman, appearing in shorts and a sleeveless blouse unabashedly disclosing considerable cleavage. She had married an Iranian but divorced him soon after a daughter was born. Marcia met Anna again after she moved to Haifa. In Carmiel, we also met the *melamed* and Helen, from Leningrad.

Zalman from Tashkent, whom we had seen in Moscow, met us in Jerusalem. He dated our daughter Raina once, driving his own car "like a madman."

We met Gabriel Shapiro in his mother's Jerusalem apartment near Hadassah Hospital. Subsequently we learned that he was teaching in a university in Chicago. We didn't fault him for his failed *aliyah* but obviously were disappointed.

Israel Sivashensky and his family came to see us in Jerusalem. Remember the severely depressed math teacher from Moscow? Well, you wouldn't have recognized him as he sat on the patio of the King David Hotel regaling us with stories and jokes. As with Anna, such a remarkable transformation! He had found employment as a teacher, while his children, Gregory and Vicki, were studing at the Hebrew University. Poor Ilan Chaim, our Hebrew-English translator, like Gabriel in Moscow, had a sore jaw trying to keep up with the rapid banter.

We had tea with Paul Goldstein in his apartment in the Baqa area of Jerusalem. He had remained the same contemplative, soulful writer.

Last, the Lerner family. Finally after the Soviet excuse of his having knowledge of state secrets grew increasingly untenable, Alex was released and immigrated to Israel in 1987 – after sixteen years in the status of a *refusenik*. He immediately received a professorship and a private laboratory at the Weizmann Institute in Rehovot where he has been working to develop an artificial heart. He lives with his son Vladimir. Since he was much in demand on the lecture circuit, spending at least three months in the USA, it took a year after his *aliyah* until we were successful in bringing him to our apartment for dinner. We showed him slides of our meetings in Moscow; we were disappointed that it took a while for him to recognize us. Though meeting him had been epochal to us, that he did not remember us was understandable. Although we were among the first foreigners to meet him at the time of his declaration to leave the Soviet Union – maybe the first – we were only two among thousands who subsequently made pilgrimages to his side. Add to this that I had grown a beard since our meeting. He did remember the drawing that he had given us.

In any event, this dinner closed the circle on our 1971 visit to Russia. Would we have had the adventure without having read Elie Wiesel's *Jews of Silence*? Doubtlessly not. Did the visit have an impact on our lives beyond the six months of intense involvement after the trip and the reunions in Israel in 1974? Probably, yes. Marcia's answer, in part, as to why we made *aliyah,* is that in Russia we encountered the struggle to move to Israel by Jews who could not, while we who could, didn't.

And maybe just in case there is life after death and an accounting, surely this *mitzvah* will guarantee us front-row seats, hopefully close to Elie Wiesel.

AFTERWORD

Bringing this autobiography to a close has required an arbitrary decision. Like spring waters finding their way to ground level, additional memories unceasingly arise from my subconscious, amending, and at times, correcting what I have written over the past four years. I'm saying to these memories, "Stop now. Wait for the second edition."

With the telling of our pivotal adventure in Russia, I take leave of the book still hoping to find an interest in life as fulfilling as that bestowed on me by Russia's refuseniks. Furthermore, retirement from an exciting medical career has forced me to find an activity that could fill the void that resulted. In this respect writing this memoir has served me well. Now, more than that, I have become challenged to appeal to a readership that includes my family and even beyond. Since there never is a dull day in Israel, there yet may be material for *By All Means, Resuscitate II.*

Each Yom Kippur Jews are required to take personal moral stock in order to arrive at a purer state of conduct. To help us, we recite a litany of common human indiscretions committed between the penitent and a fellow human being. The problem is that, like most of us, I never saw myself as having gossiped or maligned or cheated. Since the odds are that most of us, including me, have unwittingly gossiped, maligned, and cheated, prayers are recited collectively; "We have committed such and such." Another solution? Write an autobiography and wait for the readers' responses. As brother Jerry once said regarding medical practice, "Pile up your triumphs. With one mistake they all come tumbling down." Similarly any accolades for my memoir are swept away by one perceived slight.

The jury is out.

GLOSSARY

Aliyah: Moving to Israel.
Bar/Bat mitzvah: Boy/girl achieving religious maturity at age 13/12.
Chassid: Member of sect of Jewish mystics.
Cheder: Hebrew school.
Chupah: A wedding canopy.
Daven: Pray.
Haftarah: Special prophetic reading related to the weekly Torah passage.
Kaddish: A prayer for the dead.
Kashrut: Dietary laws.
Kiddush: Prayer over wine.
Kosher: According to Jewish dietary laws.
Maidel: A girl or a young unmarried woman.
Mazinik: The youngest child.
Melamed: A teacher of Jewish subjects.
Mezuzah: Prayers on parchment attached to doorposts.
Minyan: Quorum of ten required for reading the Torah and reciting certain prayers.
Mitzvah: A commandment, a good deed.
Olim: Immigrants to Israel.
Pesach: Holiday commemorating deliverance of the Jewish People from Egypt.
Purim: Holiday commemorating Queen Esther's triumph over Haman.

Seder: Ritual Pesach (Passover) meal.

Shabbat: Sabbath.

Shaliah: An emissary from Israel.

Shavuot: Holiday commemorating the receiving of the Torah at Mt. Sinai.

Shiva: Initial week of intense mourning.

Shochet: Ritual slaughterer.

Shofar: Ram's horn blown during the High Holidays.

Shul: Synagogue.

Simchat Torah: Holiday celebrating the completion of Torah reading cycle.

Succah: A booth put up for the harvest holiday of Succot.

Tallit: A prayer shawl.

Tefillin: Phylacteries.

Ulpan: Intensive Hebrew course for immigrants.

Veibel: A married woman.

Yahrzeit: Anniversary of a death.

Yeshiva: School for religious studies.

Yiddish: A European language written in Hebrew with German and Hebrew components.

Zeyda: Grandfather.

TIMELINE

David Chamovitz	Family	Events in Jewish History
	1887 Mother Mollie Eger born	
	1888 Father Morris Chaimovitz born	
	1889 Mother immigrates to USA	Anti-Jewish riots in Romania
	1903 Father immigrates to USA	
	Zeyda leaves Romania, to Palestine	
		1906 Dreyfus pardoned
	1910 Parents wed in Pittsburgh	Jews expelled from Kiev
	1912 Jerry born	Hadassah founded
	1921 Allen born	Haganah and Nazi party founded
	1922 Irvin born	League of Nations adopts Balfour Declaration
	1924 Bob born	
1925 Born in Pittsburgh, PA.		Hebrew U. opens Jabotinsky forms Revisionist Zionists
	1930 Marcia born in Brooklyn	
1938 Nov. 12, Bar Mitzvah		Nov. 9-10 Kristallnacht
1939-43 Aliquippa High School, PA.		
1943-44 Geneva College, Beaver Falls, PA.	1943 Allen killed, US Air Force	
1944-48 M.D. Harvard, Boston		1945 Allies defeat Germany/Japan
1948-49 Intern U. Pittsburgh	1948 Marcia Music/Art High School, New York City	State of Israel founded
1949-51 I131 Fellowship & Residency, Beth Israel, Boston		
1951-53 US Army Research Lab, Fort Knox, KY.	1952 Marcia B.A. Sarah Lawrence College, N.Y.	King of Jordan assassinated for negotiating with Israel
1953-54 Med. Resident V.A. Hosp. West Haven, CT.	1953 Nov. 13 met Marcia	
	1954 Mar. 14 wed Marcia	
1954-56 Fellow Lahey Clinic, Boston	1955 Mar. 15 Raina born	

1956-84 Practice Int. Med./Cardiol./Nuclear Med. Aliquippa	1956 Sept. 5 Amy born	Play *Diary of Anne Frank* premiers
1961 First trip to Israel		End of Eichmann trial
	1963 April 18 Daniel born	
1967 Dec. second trip to Israel		June, Six Day War
	1968-71 Marcia President W. PA. Hadassah	
1971 Trip to USSR		1st World Soviet Jewry Conference
1973-77 V. Pres. United Synagogue of America	1974 Mother and Father die	1973 Yom Kippur War
		1976 Entebbe rescue Jewish hostages
	1977 Marcia M.A. U. of Pittsburgh	
	1977 Raina makes aliyah	Sadat comes to Jerusalem
1979-83 5-mo. Volunteer Nuclear Medicine, Hadassah, Jerusalem	1979 April 19 Amy dies	
1980 Aliquippa Brotherhood Award		U.N. "Remove Jerusalem Embassies"
1984 Aug. 31 Aliyah, Absorption Ctr.	Dan makes aliyah	2,866 Americans & 7,000 Ethiopians make aliyah
1985 Nuclear Physician Tel Hashomer Hospital		Murderer of Peace Now's Emil Grunzweig in 1983 convicted
1985-97 Director Nuc. Med. Wolfson Hospital		1991 Iraqi Scuds fall on Tel Aviv
		1995 Prime Minister Rabin assassinated
	1996 Irv and Jerry die	
1997- Nuc. Card. Consultant Wolfson Hospital		